Primary Voices
Equality, Diversity and Childhood in Irish Primary Schools

Edited by

Jim Deegan, Dympna Devine and Anne Lodge

First published in 2004
by the Institute of Public Administration
57–61 Lansdowne Road
Dublin 4
Ireland

ISBN 1 904541 17 8

British Library cataloguing-in-publication data
A catalogue record for this book is available
from the British Library

Cover by Slick Fish Design, Dublin
Typeset in Garamond 10/11.5 by Carole Lynch, Sligo
Printed in Ireland by ColourBooks Ltd

We would like to dedicate this book to our children

Conor, Ciara, Patrick, Cian, Oisin and Harry

Contents

Notes on contributors ix
Acknowledgements x
Foreword xi
Michael Apple

Introduction

1 Equality, diversity and childhood in Irish primary schools 1
Anne Lodge, Dympna Devine and Jim Deegan

**SECTION 1:
Inclusion and the recognition of difference in the primary school**

2 Denial, tolerance or recognition of difference? The experiences of minority belief parents in the denominational primary system 17
Anne Lodge

3 'See no evil, speak no evil, hear no evil?' The experiences of lesbian and gay teachers in Irish schools 37
Sandra Gowran

4 Parents speaking of the educational experiences of their sons and daughters who have Down Syndrome 56
Mercedes Egan

5 A partnership of care: an evaluation of a Department of Education and Science initiative to combat early school leaving – the 8 to 15 Early School Leaver Initiative 75
Clare Ryan

6 Travellers and education: a personal perspective 92
Winnie McDonagh

SECTION 2: Prioritising the life-worlds of children

7 School matters: listening to what children have to say 109
Dympna Devine

8 Citizen child – the experience of a student council in a primary school 128
Owen McLoughlin

9 'Big Mad Words' – schools, social class and children's perceptions of language variation 144
Gerry MacRuairc

10 Interviewing the vampire slayers: active media consumption, imagination and gendered identity 164
Anne Lodge

11 Experiencing racism in the primary school – children's perspectives 183
Dympna Devine, Mairin Kenny with Eileen McNeela

12. Children's perceptions of other cultures 205
Hugh Gash and Elizabeth Murphy-Lejeune

SECTION 3: In conclusion

13 'Intentionally or otherwise': children and diversity in statutory and policy discourses in Ireland 225
Jim Deegan

14 Activating voices through practice: democracy, care and consultation in the primary school 245
Dympna Devine, Anne Lodge and Jim Deegan

Index 262

Notes on contributors

Jim Deegan is the Head of Education in Mary Immaculate College, Limerick.

Dympna Devine is a lecturer at the Education Dept UCD, where she also directs the M.Ed programme.

Mercedes Egan works with parents and children with Down Syndrome in the Kildare area.

Hugh Gash is a lecturer in St Patrick's College of Education, Drumcondra.

Sandra Gowran is a post-primary teacher who is currently working in the CDVEC Curriculum Development Unit, Sundrive Road, Dublin.

Mairin Kenny is a research consultant and former principal of a primary school for Traveller children.

Anne Lodge is a member of the Education Department, NUI Maynooth.

Eileen McNeela is a primary school teacher who has lectured in Business Studies in the Institute of Technology, Blanchardstown.

Gerard Mac Ruairc is a former primary school teacher and currently works for the Department of Education and Science.

Winnie McDonagh is an education development worker in the Barnardos Traveller education project in Finglas.

Owen McLoughlin is principal of a co-educational primary school in Dublin.

Elizabeth Murphy Le-Jeune is a lecturer in St Patrick's College of Education, Drumcondra.

Clare Ryan is principal of St. Leo's College, Carlow. She was National Co-ordinator of the Early School Leaver Initiative.

Acknowledgements

We are indebted to the contributors to this book. All of them found time amidst busy schedules to prepare and revise drafts based on studies they have carried out. We believe that these studies have important stories to tell about the primary school system from the perspectives of pupils, parents and teachers.

We wish to thank the following who read and commented on earlier drafts of the chapters: Angela Canny, Paul Conway, Brian Donovan, Ivor Goodson, Padraig Hogan, Cathal Kelly, Kathleen Lynch, Maire Nic Ghiolla Phadraig, Maeve O'Brien, Denis O'Sullivan, Norman Richardson and Michael Shevlin.

We are grateful to our colleagues in the Department of Education, Mary Immaculate College Limerick, and the Education Departments in University College Dublin and the National University of Ireland Maynooth for their interest and support. We would like to thank John Coolahan and Sheelagh Drudy in particular in this regard. Jim Deegan wishes to acknowledge the support of Mary Immaculate College Limerick which granted him a senior research fellowship. This enabled him to collaborate on this project with his co-editors.

We thank Declan McDonagh, Eileen Kelly and the IPA for their assistance in the publication of this volume. While the editors undertook the brunt of the work involved in preparing the manuscript for the publishers, we wish to thank Sheila Kent who assisted with some elements of this work.

We especially appreciate the patience and support of our families.

Foreword

Michael Apple

Education is too often thought of as simply the delivery of neutral knowledge to students. In this discourse, the fundamental role of schooling is to fill students with the knowledge that is necessary to compete nationally and internationally in today's rapidly changing world. To this is often added a caveat: do it as cost-effectively and as efficiently as possible. The ultimate arbiter of whether we have been successful at this is students' mean gains on achievement tests. A neutral curriculum is linked to a neutral system of accountability that in turn is linked to a system of school finance. Supposedly, when it works well, these linkages guarantee rewards for merit. 'Good' students will learn 'good' knowledge and will get 'good' jobs.

This construction of good schooling, good management, and good results suffers from more than a few defects. Its foundational claims about neutral knowledge are simply wrong. If we have learned anything from the intense and continuing conflicts over what and whose knowledge should be declared 'official' that have raged throughout the history of the curriculum in so many nations, it should have been one lesson. There is an intricate set of connections between knowledge and power. Questions of whose knowledge, who chooses, how this is justified – these are *constitutive* issues, not 'add-ons' that have the status of afterthoughts (Apple 2000, 2001, 2004). Further, it is unfortunate but true that most of our existing models of education tend to ratify or at least not actively interrupt many of the inequalities that so deeply characterise our societies. Much of this has to do with the relations between schooling and the economy, with gender, class, and race/ethnic divisions in the larger society, with the intricate politics of popular culture, and with the ways we finance and support (or don't) education. It is a critical dialogue about exactly these kinds of issues that we must stimulate in nations throughout the world and in the Ireland that is represented in this book. Along with the work of others (see for example Lynch 1999, Lynch and Lodge 2002), it shows that there are growing numbers of people in

Ireland who take seriously the need for such informed debate in ways that illuminate the possibility that things can be changed.

During one of the times I was working in Brazil, I remember Paulo Freire repeatedly saying to me that education must begin in critical dialogue. Both of these last two words were crucial to him. Education both must hold our dominant institutions in education and the larger society up to rigorous questioning and at the same time this questioning must deeply involve those who benefit least from the ways these institutions now function. Both conditions were necessary, since the first without the second was simply insufficient to the task of creating a critically democratic education.

Of course, many committed educators already know that the transformation of educational policies and practices – or the defense of democratic gains in our schools and communities – is inherently political. Indeed, this is constantly made visible by the fact that neo-liberal and neo-conservative movements have made teaching and curricula the targets of concerted attacks for years (Apple 2001). One of the claims of these rightist forces is that schools are 'out of touch' with parents and communities. While these criticisms are not totally wrong, we need to find ways of connecting our educational efforts to local communities, especially to those members of these communities with less power, that are more truly democratic than the ideas of 'thin' democracy envisioned by the right. If we do not do this, neo-liberal definitions of democracy – ones based on possessive individualism and where citizenship is reduced to simply consumption practices – will prevail (Apple 2001).

As this book demonstrates, similar issues are being struggled over in Ireland. Particular and identifiable groups of people have been and are being marginalised. Particular voices are and are not being heard. The role of critical educational research in understanding and countering all of this is crucial (Lynch 1999, Lynch and Lodge 2002).

Such research has three major tasks. First it must 'bear witness to the negativities that now exist.' That is, it needs to show how and why unequal relations of cultural, social, and economic capital are produced in schools. Second, it needs to defend the victories that have been made – through immense sacrifice by oppressed groups and their allies – in altering these relations. And third, it must analyse the current situation in a way that shows where there may be spaces to extend these victories. All of these tasks need to go on simultaneously (Apple et al 2003).

The book that Jim Deegan, Dympna Devine and Anne Lodge have produced helps all of us in taking these tasks seriously. It broadens the voices that are heard. It is more inclusive of the multiple groups and concerns that should be dealt with. And it exhibits a fine sensitivity to what is at stake for everyone if the schooling of young children is not increasingly committed to extending social justice inside and outside of educational institutions. Many more books of this type need to be written and published. They enable us to see more clearly what now exists and what needs to be done. Of course, doing what needs to be done requires political action inside and outside of education. But, then, the people of Ireland have a long history of challenging dominance. I hope that this history continues in the present and future as we all attempt to build an education that is worthy of its name.

Michael W. Apple
John Bascom Professor of Curriculum and Instruction
and
Educational Policy Studies
University of Wisconsin, Madison

Bibliography

Apple, M.W. (2000) *Official Knowledge*, 2nd ed., New York, Routledge.

Apple, M.W. (2001) *Educating the 'Right' Way: Markets, Standards, God, and Inequality*, New York, RoutledgeFalmer.

Apple, M.W., et al (2003) *The State and the Politics of Knowledge,* New York, RoutledgeFalmer.

Apple, M.W. (2004) *Ideology and Curriculum*, 25th Anniversary 3rd ed., New York, RoutledgeFalmer.

Lynch, K. (1999) *Equality in Education*, Dublin, Gill and Macmillan.

Lynch, K. and Lodge, A. (2002) *Equality and Power in Schools: Redistribution, Recognition and Representation*, London, RoutledgeFalmer.

Equality, diversity and childhood in Irish primary schools

Anne Lodge, Dympna Devine and Jim Deegan

Introduction

Irish society has changed enormously in the past forty years, moving from an economy centred around farming and a predominantly rural way of life to one that is increasingly urbanised and centred on industrial, service and post-industrial work patterns. Changing economic policy, coupled with membership of the broader European Community, has brought with it economic wealth as well as openness to influences from the 'outside'. Co-incident with such change has been the expansion and development of the education system at all levels. Economic expansion in the 1960s targeted education as a primary means through which Ireland could move toward modernisation and industrialisation. As is typical in post-colonial societies (Lynch 1989), parents saw education as providing the means through which their children could improve their life chances, gaining access to higher status employment than was available heretofore. The rhetoric of the period defined education as the great equalizer, an open competition, providing access to all (Devine 1999). Talent and ability, rather than status or privilege, were proposed as the new determinants of success or failure, with differences based on gender, social class, ethnicity or dis/ability ignored in this consensual and essentialist worldview (Drudy and Lynch 1993).

Curaclam na Bunscoile (*Primary School Curriculum*) (1971) embraced these ideals, with its emphasis on the maximisation of individual talent in an environment that was sensitive to and nurturing of children's developmental needs. Freed from the constraints of the Primary Certificate, which was abolished in 1967, the primary system was charged with the responsibility for the holistic formation of the young that took account of their emotional, intellectual, physical and spiritual 'needs'. However, the rhetoric belied practice, and with limited funding, an absence of sufficient in-service training for teachers, coupled with a reluctance on the part of teachers to fundamentally alter their practice, traditional didactic methods continued to predominate (Devine 1999, INTO 1985, O'Sullivan 1980). The 1990s witnessed a further period of development and change that has culminated in an Education Act, 1998 and the phased introduction of the *Primary School Curriculum* (1999). Forty years on, research into the functioning and operation of the Irish education system indicates that while positive advances have been made in terms of participation and achievement, inequalities based on gender, social class and ethnicity remain (Lynch and Lodge 2002, Devine et al 2002, Kenny 1997, MacRuairc 1997). Primary schooling, and early years education, is key to providing the foundations for children's learning in all respects, yet little material focusing directly on these changes within Irish primary schools has been published to date. This book redresses this absence by focusing on research that enhances our understanding of the experience of equality, childhood and diversity in primary schools.

In our consideration of change and development in primary education, a number of interlinked, key themes have emerged. Equality and diversity have been overshadowed in the debate about primary education in the past due to the predominance of a child-centred discourse with its emphasis on unproblematised nurturing, caring and sensitivity to children's needs. These emphases are encapsulated in two oft-quoted principles of the *Primary School Curriculum* (1971). These are the principles of the full and harmonious development of each child and recognition of and catering for individual differences. However, issues related to equality and diversity are central to the experience of primary education. As argued by Lynch and Lodge (2002) and Young (1990), equality is a complex phenomenon. Concepts related to recognition of difference and representation for all groups, including the marginalised and excluded, are equally as relevant as is the more traditional focus on redistribution of resources. While these have been studied in an Irish context in relation to second-level schooling (Lynch and Lodge 2002), they are also applicable in a primary context, as the various chapters in this book demonstrate.

This chapter begins that process by focusing on equality issues that are directly relevant to primary schools. Partnership and equality of respect and esteem for all involved in primary education are central to the arguments made. The analysis begins with an overview of the structure, ownership and control of the primary system, which has its roots in the nineteenth century. It then considers the impact that this has on the interpretation and enactment of partnership in schools up to the present day; in particular, how some voices came to be excluded and marginalised, while others continue to be prioritised.

Recognition and inclusion of difference

The present system of management and administration of Irish primary education remains rooted in the original structure established in 1831. After independence, the role of the Board of Commissioners of Education was taken on by the Department of Education, established in 1924. The central authority of the Department of Education exercised control over curriculum, text books, certification of teachers and inspection of schools. The school manager retained local control with responsibility for the hiring of teachers, who then had to be approved by the patron (generally, the bishop).

While National Schools were locally established, owned and managed, control was not vested in the local community; parents, teachers and children themselves were excluded from the management structure of their local National School. The Powis Commission proposed that Boards of Management of National Schools should be established in 1870 (National Education Convention Secretariat 1994); it was not until the mandatory establishment of Boards of Management in 1975 (OECD 1991) that teachers and parents were able to become actively involved in the management of their local schools. However, even after the establishment of Boards of Management in 1975, these effectively remained patron-controlled (Tussing 1978).

The Education Act, 1998 gives expression to a shift away from total patron-control of education, to a recognition of the importance of partnership with other (adult) participants in the education process. In certain respects, Irish education has become increasingly democratised in the last three decades at both local and national level. The Education Act, 1998 recognises a number of stakeholders in Irish education, including parents. Other recognised groups include the Teacher Unions (at primary level, the Irish National Teachers' Organisation), the Churches who own and manage the great majority of primary schools, the Department of Education and Science and the National Parents' Council. This latter group was established in 1985, and is the body that is intended to represent the interests of all parents of children in primary and post-primary schools. It is impossible, however, for one voluntary group to represent the diverse range of interests, needs and rights of all parents, and their children, in primary schools.[1]

Representative partnership is the model of democracy in Irish education employed at national level. Operating within this model, power is exercised among a small number of named, influential groups. In effect, at primary level, those with a professional interest (the INTO) or political interest (the Churches and the Department of Education and Science) are those who exercise the greatest control over education and who are entitled to engage with decision-making bodies such as policy committees, review bodies, and curriculum boards. There is no place in the current partnership model for the inclusion of groups representing the interests of minorities, including those from ethnic minority groups, those of minority beliefs, those who are differently abled and, of course, children. Implicit in the present partnership structure is the assumption that these interests are catered for by various representative groups. As we shall outline, throughout this book, this is not always the case.

Irish primary education is unusual by international standards in terms of the degree of private ownership of schools. However, the introduction of new legislation in recent years (i.e. The Education Act, 1998, the Education (Welfare) Act, 2000, the Equal Status Act, 2000) relating directly, or indirectly, to education has brought about a change in the relative levels of freedom that schools have to control all of their own internal practices. For example, if children are refused enrolment to, or are excluded from, a primary (or a post-primary) school, their parents or guardians have the right to appeal this decision to an independent appeals committee established under Section 29 of the Education Act. The school's decision to refuse enrolment, or to exclude, can be overturned by a decision of the Secretary General of the Department of Education and Science based on the recommendations made to him by the

---

1 The National Parents' Council represents the interests of all affiliated parent councils in primary schools. It is impossible to be certain about the make-up of the National Parents' Council (primary), but it is likely that the situation in the Irish context mirrors that documented internationally. Middle-class parents rather than working-class and minority parents are likely to dominate parents' groups at local level. Given that the onus for establishing parents' representative groups at local level falls to parents themselves, it is also likely that such groups will be established in schools serving middle-class communities. Studies conducted in Britain (Ball et al 1995) and the United States (McGrath and Kuriloff 1999) indicate that middle-class parents tend to engage more with schools, and to exercise significantly more influence over decisions by the school, than do their working-class counterparts.

appeals committee hearing the case. If children are discriminated against in terms of their access to, or participation in, education in a particular school, on any of the nine grounds[2] of any of the categories named in the equality legislation, parents or guardians may seek the assistance of the Equality Authority, and again, the decision of the school may be overturned by an outside body.

Such discrimination can derive from the traditional assumption of homogeneity in Irish primary schools. This is true of assumptions regarding belief, sexual orientation, ability or knowledge of, and conformity to, the system itself. Indeed, traditionally, schools have been organised formally and informally in order to segregate diversity whether it be belief, gender, ability, ethnicity, or indeed, social class. Since the mid-nineteenth century, Irish National Schools have been denominational in terms of their management and control as well as in their intake. The great majority (94%) of Irish National Schools are Roman Catholic, while most of the remaining six per cent are under Protestant management. The silence that surrounds issues of sexuality, and in particular, homosexuality, is closely connected to the religious ethos of schools. The strong tradition of single-sex schooling that has long characterised Irish education at both primary and post-primary levels can also be understood in the context of Roman Catholic beliefs in the past regarding the immorality of the mixing of the sexes (Akenson 1975, Drudy and Lynch 1993).

The existence of separate provision for those who are differently abled is by no means unique to the Irish education system, nor can it be particularly associated with the Christian churches, although many of the education and care institutions were founded and run by religious orders. Within education, all children were categorised as either 'handicapped' or 'normal' and separate educational provision was made for each group (Glendenning 1999, Egan 2000). While post-primary schools in Ireland are characterised by a notable degree of social class segregation (Lynch and Lodge 2002), the primary system is less differentiated in this regard. This is due to the close association between individual schools and their local parishes – in rural areas there is one Roman Catholic school to serve all the children of that parish, regardless of family wealth and status. However, in urban areas, given the segregated nature of housing developments and the parishes within which these neighbourhoods are located, there are much more obvious class

---

2 The nine categories listed in the Employment Equality Act 1998 and the Equal Status Act 2000 are: gender, marital status, family status, age, belief, sexual orientation, race, Traveller Community, disability.

differences between primary schools.[3] Furthermore, there is a wider variety of schools to choose from, including Gael Scoileanna, and Educate Together schools (multi-denominational in ethos).

Given this segregated tradition, there are difficulties in the equal recognition, inclusion and accommodation of difference at both systemic and local levels in Irish primary education. While many primary school children now inhabit increasingly diverse learning contexts, social supports from significant adults (including parents and teachers) are crucial in helping them to learn respect for difference. However, many adults – both those whose children now attend primary school, or those who teach within the primary system – have had little or no contact with people of minority beliefs, those who are differently abled, or people belonging to ethnic minorities. One must question their ability to equip children with the support and necessary skills to operate effectively and sensitively in an increasingly diverse school and social environment. While legislation gives rights to minorities to access and participate in education, it is much more difficult to challenge people's often unquestioned assumptions about the nature of society, the purpose of education and expectations regarding the status or rights of different groups.

Living and learning in a diverse Ireland

While Irish society has come through a period of rapid social change, structures and patterns of participation and representation have not necessarily moved in parallel with this change. There is a need to bring to the fore the realities of living and learning in an increasingly diverse Ireland and the role of primary schooling (as a key aspect of the education system where all young people are required to attend) in shaping and contributing to such change. It is also important to emphasise that our understanding and definition of diversity is one that embraces difference in all respects, to include gender, social class, ethnicity, dis/ability and sexual orientation. As has been shown, Irish education continues to operate on an assumption of heterogeneity in terms of ethnicity, religious belief and language. The integrated nature of the primary curricu-

3 The fact that the majority of schools that have been given disadvantaged status by the Department of Education and Science are located in urban areas bears out this point. While it is absolutely valid to argue that schools other than those with disadvantaged status also serve children who are themselves socio-economically disadvantaged (Haran and Tormey 2000, Walsh 2002), the fact remains that in large urban areas in particular, the cohort attending certain primary schools is almost entirely working class and disadvantaged while other schools in the same urban areas have a cohort that is largely middle class and relatively advantaged.

lum is particularly problematic for those who differ from the supposed norm of white, middle-class and Christian. Under the *United Nations Convention on the Rights of the Child* (1989), children also have the right to an education in their mother tongue. The area of linguistic diversity, other than provision for the Irish language, needs to be addressed also.

Historically, the Traveller community was under-represented in educational policy and practice in Ireland. Reports written during the last two decades have accepted at least nominally that the Traveller community has a distinct culture and they do not refer to their way of life as deviant or problematic. There is also a belief that the education system is insufficiently flexible to educate students who are nomadic rather than sedentary (Fanning 2000). Some Traveller young people have reported a sense of teachers 'giving up on them' because of their nomadic way of life and there is a general lack of recognition of the specific cultural values of Travellers. Traveller culture, values, traditions and history continue to have little visibility within school texts and other learning materials. This invisibility contributes to the sense of isolation and exclusion experienced by Travellers (Devine et al 2002, Fanning 2002).

Research on diversity in international contexts indicates that attempts to challenge the ideological and contextual bases of diversity in children's lives have not necessarily been successful in dispelling prejudice and discriminatory practices (Davies 1982, Deegan 1993, Troyna and Hatcher 1992, Shevlin and Rose 2003). Despite the glaring reality of diversity on our streets, in our workplaces, and on children's playgrounds, it remains a relatively 'unresearched' phenomenon in the social and political stakes of education in Ireland. Now more than ever, there is an imperative to raise the 'silenced voices' (Delpit 1988) of children and adults in diverse contexts. The question becomes how, and in what ways, do we think and act about diversity? We still know little about children's 'own' understandings of diversity, and how these meanings become embedded in their everyday judgments and lived experiences. Emergent indigenous research has begun to address the sociological themes of redistribution, recognition and representation of equality in older children's lives (Lynch and Lodge 2002), while a research base of work with younger children is also coming to the fore (Devine et al 2004, Kenny 2001, Cleary et al 2001, O'Keefe and O'Connor 2001).

For children, the broader social, cultural and economic developments have led to significant changes in their lives, some positive, some negative. Devine, Nic Ghiolla Phádraig and Deegan (2004) in their analysis of children's welfare in Ireland point to these contradictory patterns of development and change. There has, for example, been a gradual reduction in the number of Irish children in relative poverty, yet there is a greater risk of poverty for children in general than for adults in Irish society. This latter is particularly the case for children born into a minority ethnic group or to parents whose parents are unemployed (Sweeney 2002, Nolan 2001). Changing family forms ensure that the traditional nuclear family is less common than heretofore, while parent/child relations are increasingly characterised by autonomy and negotiation. Further, children are more and more targeted as consumers in a market driven economy, with status and inclusion in peer groups often marked by possession of 'in' games, toys, clothes and musical forms.

Developments within the sociology of childhood (Devine 2003, James, Jencks and Prout 1998, Mayall 2002, Qvortrup 1994) have highlighted the importance of listening to children's voice and of the minority status typically accorded to children in modern societies. These views of children and childhood question traditional approaches to the study of children, which have tended to be overly individualistic and developmentalist in focus. Such a challenge asserts children's active engagement with their social and cultural environment and their capacities to shape and contribute to the world around them. These studies emphasise the importance of documenting time and space in children's lived realities, affording the development of policy and praxis that best serves their interests, rights and needs. Such developments coincide with work in both the sociology and cultural psychology of education, which emphasises the importance of the cultural and social context in framing children's learning (Bruner 1996, Pollard and Triggs 2001, Vygotsky 1978). A focus on diversity then must also acknowledge the voices of children, as a distinct group from adults, taking account of their perspectives and views on the organisation of their school lives.

International and national developments in the political sphere have reflected this trend, setting the agenda for the promotion of children's rights and voice into the new millennium. The *United Nations Convention on the Rights of the Child* (1989), to which Ireland is a signatory, asserts children's right to express their views freely and to be consulted about matters affecting them.[4] The

[4] Article 12.1 'State parties shall assure to the child who is capable of forming his or her views the right to express those views freely in all matters affecting the child, the views of the child being given due weight in accordance with the age and maturity of the child.' Article 13.1 'The child shall have the right to freedom of expression, this right shall include freedom to seek, receive and impart information and ideas of all kinds, regardless of frontiers, either orally, in writing or in print, in the form of art, or through any other media of the child's choice.'

National Children's Strategy (2000) directly links into commitments under the UNCRC, providing for the first time an outline of government goals in relation to children and childhood into the new millennium. Inter-linked with such developments is the expanding notion of citizenship, to include conceptualisations of the child as an active citizen with the voice to be both heard and expressed (Devine 2003, Roche 1999, Wyness 2000). Curricular developments at primary level reflect this trend with the introduction of the *Primary School Curriculum* (1999). However, as Devine (2003) notes, education about citizenship does not necessarily imply education *for* citizenship. Educating children about democracy, justice and inclusiveness, about rights and responsibilities, will be most effective where children themselves are afforded greater responsibility through active involvement in school (Dewey 1938). However, as argued earlier in this chapter, it is questionable whether current partnership structures are open to this level of dialogue, either at local or national level.

Conclusion

Levels of interest in, and awareness of, key social justice issues in Irish society and Irish education have developed sharply in recent years. Irish society has become more visibly diverse and heterogeneous in the last decade, and debates around issues such as ethnic diversity and the rights of those with disabilities have gained prominence. The development and implementation of equality legislation (the Employment Equality Act, 1998; the Equal Status Act, 2000) has formed part of the backdrop to the increased prominence of social justice concerns. At the same time, there has been a growing awareness of the rights of young people not merely to be afforded greater respect in society, but also to be given the right to participate more actively in the naming of their own experiences and needs. *The National Children's Strategy*, launched in 2000, was concerned with giving voice to a wide range of young people, enabling them to define their own lived realities.

In giving voice to marginalised groups in the primary school, we have structured this book around two themes. In the first section, 'Recognition and Inclusion of Difference in the Primary School' the experiences of a number of groups of marginalised adults are documented. Chapter 2 focuses on minority belief parents, Chapter 4 details the experiences of parents of children with Down Syndrome while Chapter 6 provides the space for a parent in the Traveller Community to articulate her own schooling experiences and to consider current issues and concerns for her community regarding schooling. Chapter 5 outlines the experiences of socio-economically marginalised parents and children who participated in the Early School Leaving Initiative. Chapter 3 documents the perspectives of gay and lesbian teachers in the school system. Key issues relating to respect for and recognition of difference are teased through in these chapters. In the second section 'Prioritising the life-worlds of children' similar themes emerge but we have decided to separate these given their specific focus on the voices of children. Chapters 7 and 8 document children's perceptions of their rights and status in school and consider how their status can be improved through participation in a student council. Chapters 9, 10, 11 and 12 focus on the importance of culture in school (in its broadest sense) and how the non-recognition and mis-recognition of cultural difference can result in exclusion and denial of the life-worlds of children. The concluding section broadens the discussion, in Chapter 13, to a consideration of the denial in official discourses of children and diversity in recent policy frameworks. Core principles are outlined in Chapter 14 that articulate a vision for primary education that gives recognition, respect and voice to those currently excluded from full participation in the primary school sector. It raises awareness of the potential contributions that all voices can make to understanding life in the primary school.

Bibliography

Akenson, D. H. (1975) *A Mirror to Kathleen's Face: Education in Independent Ireland 1922-1960,* Montreal and London, McGill/Queen's University Press.

Ball, S. J., Bowe, R. and Gewirtz, S. (1995) 'Circuits of Schooling – a sociological exploration of parental choice of school in social-class contexts', *Sociological Review,* Vol 43, No 1, pp 52-78.

Bruner, J. (1990) *Acts of Meaning*, London, Harvard University Press.

Cleary, A., Nic Ghiolla Phadraig, M. and Quin, S. (2001) (eds) *Understanding Children*, Vols 1 and 2, Dublin: Oak Tree Press.

Davies, B. (1982) *Life in the Classroom and Playground – The Accounts of Primary School Children,* London, Routledge.

Deegan, J. (1993) 'Children's Friendships in Culturally Diverse Classrooms', *Journal of Research in Chilhood Education*, Vol 7, No 2, pp 91-101.

Delpit, L. (1988) 'The Silenced Dialogue: Power and Pedagogy in Educating Other Peoples's Children', *Harvard Educational Review*, Vol 58, pp 280-298.

Department of Education (1971) *Primary School Curriculum: Teacher's Handbook, part 1 and part 2*, Dublin: Stationery Office.

Devine, D. (1999) Children: Rights and Status in Education – a Socio-historical Perspective, *Irish Educational Studies,* Vol 18, pp 14-29.

Devine, D. (2003) *Children, Power and Schooling – How Childhood is Structured in the Primary School*, Stoke-On Trent, Trentham Books.

Devine, D., Kenny, M. with MacNeela, E. (2002) *Ethnicity and Schooling – A Study of Selected Primary and Post-Primary Schools,* Unpublished Report, Education Department, UCD.

Devine, D., Nic Ghiolla Phádraig, M. and Deegan, J. 'Time for Children – Time for Change?: Children's rights and welfare in a period of economic growth in Ireland', in Jensen, A., Arieh, A., Conti, C., Kutsar, D., Nic Ghiolla Phádraig, M., Neilsen, H. (eds) *Childhood in Ageing Societies: Country Studies on Children's Welfare and Everyday Life*, Vol 1 and 2, Trondheim, Norwegian Centre for Child Research and Tartu University Press.

Dewey, J. (1938) *Experience and Education,* Kappa Delta Pi.

Drudy, S. and Lynch, K. (1993) *Schools and Society in Ireland,* Dublin, Gill and Macmillan.

Egan, M. (2000) *Students who have Down Syndrome: a study of their school placements, educational supports and parental evaluation of their education,* Unpublished PhD thesis, Education Department, NUI Maynooth.

Fanning, B (2002) *Racism and Social Change in the Republic of Ireland*, Manchester: Manchester University Press.

Glendenning, D. (1999) *Education and the Law,* Dublin, Butterworths.

Government of Ireland (1998) *Education Act,* Dublin, Stationery Office.

Government of Ireland (1998) *Employment Equality Act,* Dublin, Stationery Office.

Government of Ireland (1999) *Primary School Curriculum*, Dublin, Stationery Office.

Government of Ireland (2000) *Education (Welfare) Act,* Dublin, Stationery Office.

Government of Ireland (2000) *Equal Status Act,* Dublin, Stationery Office.

Government of Ireland (2000) *The National Children's Strategy: Our Children – Their Lives,* Dublin, Stationery Office.

Haran, N. and Tormey, R. (2002) *Celebrating Difference, Promoting Equality: Towards a Framework for Intercultural Education in Irish Classrooms,* Limerick, Centre for Educational Disadvantage Research and Curriculum Development Unit, Mary Immaculate College.

INTO (1985) *Primary School Curriculum – Report and Discussion Papers*, Dublin, INTO.

James, C., Jenks, C. and Prout, A. (1998) *Theorising Childhood,* London, Polity.

Kenny, M. (1997) *The Routes of Resistance: Traveller and Second-level Schooling*, Aldershot, Ashgate.

Kenny, M. (2001) 'Traveller Childhood in Ireland', in Cleary, A., Nic Ghiolla Phádraig, M. and Quin, S. (eds) *Understanding Children – Vol 2*, Dublin, Oak Tree Press.

Lynch, K. (1989) *The Hidden Curriculum: Reproduction in Education: a Reappraisal,* Lewes, Falmer Press.

Lynch, K. and Lodge, A. (2002) *Equality and Power in Schools: Redistribution, Recognition and Representation,* London, Routledge Falmer.

Mac Ruairc (1997) *Big Mad Words – Perceptions on Language Variation in Schools: A Sociological Analysis*, Unpublished MEd thesis, Education Department, UCD.

Mayall, B. (2002) *Towards a Sociology for Childhood*, Buckingham, Open University Press.

McGrath, D. J. and Kuriloff, P. J. (1999) '"They're going to tear the doors off this place": upper-middle-class parent school involvement and the educational opportunities of other people's children', *Educational Policy*, Vol 13, No 5, pp 603-629.

National Education Convention Secretariat (1994) *Report on the National Education Convention,* Dublin, Stationery Office.

Nolan, B. (2001) *Child Poverty in Ireland,* UC, Vol 1, pp 245-260.

OECD (1991) *Review of National Policies for Education – Ireland,* Paris.

O'Keefe, B. and O'Connor, P. (2001) '"Out of the Mouths of Babes and Innocents ...." Children's Attitudes towards Travellers', in Cleary, A., Nic Ghiolla Phádraig, M. and Quin, S. (eds) *Understanding Children – Vol 2*, Dublin, Oak Tree Press.

O'Sullivan, D. (1980) 'Teacher Socialisation and Teaching Style in an Irish Cultural Context', *European Journal of Education,* Vol 15, No 4.

Pollard, A. and Triggs, P. (2000) *What Pupils Say: Changing Policy and Practice in Primary Education*, London, Continuum.

Qvortrup, J. (1994) 'Childhood Matters: an introduction', in Qvortrup, J., Bardy, M., Sgritta, G. and Wintersberger, H. (eds) *Childhood Matters: Social Theory, Practice and Politics,* Aldershot, Avebury.

Roche, J. (1999) 'Children: Rights, Participation and Citizenship', Childhood, Vol 6, No 4, pp 475-93.

Shevlin, M. and Rose, R. (2003) (eds) *Encouraging Voices*, Dublin, National Disability Authority.

Sweeney, J (2002) *Ending Child Poverty in Rich Countries: What Works?*, Dublin: Children's Rights Alliance.

Troyna, B. and Hatcher, R. (1992) *Racism in Children's Lives: A Study of Mainly White Primary Schools*, London, Routledge.

Tussing, A. D. (1978) *Irish Educational Expenditures – Past, Present and Future,* ESRI Paper No 92, Dublin, Economic and Social Research Institute.

United Nations (1989) Convention on the Rights of the Child, Geneva: United Nations.

Vygotsky, L. (1978) *Mind in Society – The Development of Higher Psychological Processes,* London, Harvard University Press.

Walsh, T. (2002) 'Educational Disadvantage: Policy and Practice in Ireland', paper presented to the Annual Conference of the Educational Studies Association of Ireland, Trinity College Dublin, 21-23 March.

Wyness, M. (2000) *Contesting Childhood,* London, Falmer Press.

Young, I. M. (1990) *Justice and the Politics of Difference,* Princeton, NJ.

SECTION 1

Inclusion and the recognition of difference in the primary school

Chapter 2

Denial, tolerance or recognition of difference? The experiences of minority belief[1] parents in the denominational primary system

Anne Lodge[2]

Introduction

Almost all primary schools in the Republic of Ireland are denominationally owned and controlled. Multi-denominational schools account for fewer than 1% of the total number of primary schools in the state. Approximately 94% of all primary schools are under Roman Catholic control, and the remainder are mainly, though not entirely, Protestant. This chapter is concerned with how minority belief parents and their children experience denominational schools. Cleary et al (2001) have highlighted the lack of research on children of minority beliefs in the Irish context. There is a similar absence of data on the experiences of parents of minority beliefs in an overwhelmingly denominational primary school system.

The majority of the Irish population remains at least nominally Roman Catholic (Inglis 1998, Tovey and Share 2002). However, Irish society has long included a minority holding other beliefs, including various Protestant denominations (White 1975, Bowen 1983, Caird 1985, Murphy and Adair 2003), a small Jewish

---

1 In this chapter, the term 'minority beliefs' encompasses those who are adherents of minority religious communities in Ireland as well as those whose beliefs could be described as secular, humanist or personal.

2 I would like to express my thanks to Dr Padraig Hogan, Education Department, NUI Maynooth, Professor Kathleen Lynch, Equality Studies Centre, UCD, and Dr Norman Richardson, Stranmillis College Belfast, for their insightful comments on an earlier draft of this chapter.

community (Keogh 1997), a growing Islamic community, people of the Bahá'í faith, Buddhists, Hindus, Sikhs, and adherents of the Greek and Russian Orthodox churches. There is also an increasing number of Irish people of humanist or secular beliefs. As demonstrated in Table 1 below, there has been a noticeable increase in the numbers of people professing minority and secular beliefs between 1991 and 2002.

This chapter reports on interviews conducted with people of minority belief including members of the Bahá'í and Buddhist communities, people of personal belief and one member of a minority Christian faith about their experiences as parents of the denominational system of primary education in Ireland. It is clear from these interviews that one of the key equality issues for those of minority beliefs is the right *not* to participate in aspects of the life of a denominational school that reflect a particular set of beliefs and practices. The problem for those of minority beliefs is that the religious dimension of a school's ethos is not necessarily confined to periods of religious instruction. Religious instruction in denominational schools is intended to be a daily event, and prayers and other religious events specific to one denomination occur regularly also. There is some evidence that schools are not aware of their legal obligations to minority belief children or their parents in this regard.[3]

In denominational schools the religious education that children receive has to be deemed appropriate by the Patron bodies. While Protestant schools cater for children of the various Protestant denominations and therefore do not provide religious instruction appropriate only to one group, religious education in Protestant schools is Christian in its outlook and has a scriptural focus. Many schools use religious events to mark the start and end of the school year – indeed, the Catholic Primary School Managers' Association (2000) recommends that religious values and practices should permeate the life of the school and advocates the fostering of close links between school and parish. The Jewish school closes early on a Friday in order to facilitate preparation for the Sabbath. In Roman Catholic schools, preparation for religious rites (First Confession, First Communion, Confirmation) are an intrinsic part of the school year. Regardless of the fact that ceremonies such as the First Communion have social and cultural meanings that may

[3] A case has been brought to the Equality Authority arising out of the failure by an individual school to provide alternative religious education requested by the parents of a minority belief child. Article 44(4) of the Constitution states that children of other beliefs are entitled to attend schools in receipt of public money without attending religious instruction in those schools.

well take precedence over their religious significance (Lodge 1999) they are fundamentally religious rituals that belong to one particular set of believers. Children of minority or secular beliefs cannot take full part in these events, yet they are often a core part of schoolwork for a particular class over a lengthy period (Lodge 1998).

Table 1: Population by religious grouping, 1991 and 2002

Religion	**Population (000s)**		**Percentage of total population**	
	1991	**2002**	**1991**	**2002**
Roman Catholic	3228.3	3462.6	91.6%	88.4%
Church of Ireland (incl. Protestant)	89.2	115.6	2.5%	3.0%
Christian (unspecified)	16.3	21.4	0.5%	0.5%
Presbyterian	13.2	20.6	0.4%	0.5%
Muslim (Islamic)	3.9	19.1	0.1%	0.5%
Orthodox	0.4	10.4	0.01%	0.3%
Methodist	5.0	10.0	0.1%	0.3%
Other stated religions[4]	19.8	40.0	0.6%	1.0%
No religion	66.3	138.3	1.9%	3.5%
Not stated	83.4	79.1	2.4%	2.0%
Total	3525.7	3917.2		

Source: Census 2003: Principal Demographic Results

The precise rights of those of minority beliefs in an overwhelmingly denominational education system are not entirely clear. As a number of commentators have outlined in recent years (Randles 1996, Report of the National Education Convention 1994, Glendenning 1999), the changing nature of Irish society has brought the difficulties arising out of the conflicting rights of denominational schools and minority belief parents and children into sharper focus. The 1937 Constitution protects the rights of

[4] A large number of minority belief communities are included in the 'other stated religions' category. These include the Bahá'í and Buddhist communities. There was a sizeable increase in the numbers of people describing themselves as Buddhist since 1991 – 986 (0.03% of the total population) said they were Buddhist in 1991 and 3,894 (0.1%) described themselves thus in 2002. The numbers saying that they were members of the Bahá'í community had remained stable – there were 430 (0.01% of total population) in 1991 and 490 (0.01% of total population) in 2002.

parents – Article 41(1) recognises them as the primary educators of their child(ren) and acknowledges their rights to provide for their religious and moral education, and Article 42(3) respects their rights not to send them to schools in violation of their consciences. In reality, however, parents of minority beliefs frequently have no alternative to their local denominational primary school (Glendenning 1999). There is implied support for denominational schools within both Articles 42 and 44 of the Constitution, and this is confirmed by subsequent judicial rulings (Glendenning 1999). Both the Education Act, 1998, and the Equal Status Act, 2000, recognise the rights of denominational schools to protect their (religious) ethos and to give preference in enrolment to their co-religionists. However, the right of schools to protect their religious ethos is not absolute.[5] Clarke (1998) argues that the Irish state is depriving minority belief parents and children of equal educational treatment as a result of its preferential support for particular (religious) beliefs.

The denominational nature of Irish primary schools

In 1831, the Irish Chief Secretary set up the Board of Commissioners for National Education, through which all government funding for, and control of, elementary education was to be channelled thereafter (Coolahan 1981). The approach taken by the Westminster government was a relatively laissez-faire one, in that the onus for the establishment of individual schools had to be borne at local level. The ownership and management of each new school was vested, not in the state, but in the person (generally a local notable or senior clerical figure) who sought to set up the school and found the necessary local financial contribution. This individual then became the new school's patron. Although Boards of Management involving lay people have been a feature of the Republic's primary schools since the mid-1970s, the system of management retains strong links with the denominational control structure that developed in the nineteenth century.

While it was the original intention of the Westminster government that the new elementary education system in Ireland would be an inter-denominational one educating children of different creeds together, there were objections to this from the outset from each of the three main Irish Christian churches (the Presbyterians, the Anglicans and the Roman Catholics). FitzGerald (2003) notes

5 The Equality Authority overruled the right of a Roman Catholic secondary school to set a quota on the number of pupils of a particular minority belief that it would enrol.

that the churches had effectively taken control of primary schools from the civil authorities by the middle of the nineteenth century. The relationship between the independent Irish state and the Roman Catholic Church was a close one for much of the twentieth century, and the Roman Catholic hierarchy exercised considerable influence over decisions taken by government, in relation to education, health, sexual and moral issues in particular (Cooney 1999). It would be a mistake, however, to believe that the various governments inevitably followed the advice of the Roman Catholic hierarchy on all policy issues. When the national interest (in particular, anything which might impact negatively on the possibility of future island unity) was in question, there is evidence put forward by Manning (1999) that these concerns took precedence over the desires of the Roman Catholic hierarchy.[6] In the main, however, a particular Roman Catholic outlook informed much of government and public thinking. The 1937 Constitution reflects Roman Catholic thinking of that time with its emphasis, for example, on non-interference by the state in the life of the family and the domestic role of women as mothers (Drudy and Lynch 1993, Cooney 1999).

The close relationship between (Roman Catholic) church and state was not at odds with the views of much of the Irish populace for the earlier decades of the twentieth century. As Akenson (1975) argues, the Irish population was generally content that Roman Catholic church personnel provided educational facilities and vindicated the constitutional rights and obligations of parents. Inglis (1998) has outlined the complex nature of the relationship between the Irish Catholic laity and clerics for much of the nineteenth and twentieth centuries. He explains how a particular form of morality and dependence on the clergy was woven into the fabric of family life, especially through the person of the mother.

[6] In 1955, there was a dispute between the Fine Gael/Labour coalition government and the Roman Catholic hierarchy in relation to the establishment of a third-level agricultural institute and the proposed representation of Trinity College on its board. The Roman Catholic bishops objected and also indicated that they had difficulties with the level of state subsidy already being allocated to Trinity as it was out of proportion with the numbers of Protestants in the state. In its rebuttal of the Catholic bishops' arguments, the government pointed out that Protestants accounted for almost one quarter of the total population of the island of Ireland and that in making decisions the government was obliged to take into account the 'broad conditions of national interest' (Manning 1999: 301).

Interviews with minority belief parents[7]

Semi-structured interviews were conducted with ten parents of minority beliefs and one Roman Catholic parent from various parts of the Republic of Ireland. The participants were selected strategically: three were members of the Bahá'í faith, three were Buddhists, three had beliefs that were personal to themselves and reflected their own spiritual and moral journey.[8] One interviewee belonged to a minority Christian denomination. The Bahá'í participants were contacted through the Bahá'í Information Office; the Buddhist parents were located through a contact in the Buddhist community.[9] Making contact with people of personal belief was more difficult. Two of the participants of personal belief were known to the researcher and agreed to participate in this research. The third such parent was contacted through Educate Together, the Patron body of multi-denominational primary schools in Ireland, as was the minority Christian parent and the Roman Catholic parent. The three interviewees contacted via Educate Together were involved in attempts to establish new multi-denominational schools.

All the interviewees had themselves attended denominational primary schools, all but one of them in Ireland. Each had at least one child attending a denominational primary school. The children of six of the minority belief participants were attending Roman Catholic schools and the children of the remaining four were attending Protestant schools at the time that the interviews took place. A couple of the participants had encountered two different school types – in one case, the child had initially been enrolled in a Roman Catholic school, but had been moved to a Protestant school. In the other case, the child had first been enrolled in a

---

7 When a draft version of this chapter was completed, the material was forwarded to those who took part in the interviews inviting their comments and asking whether their anonymity had been preserved to their satisfaction.

8 It is important that I make clear the fact that I regard the term 'non believer' as problematic and disrespectful. It implies an absence of belief or spirituality on the part of a person who chooses not to adhere to an institutionalised belief system. Each of the three participants whom I describe here as being of personal beliefs outlined to me during the course of their interview that they had their own private system of beliefs which permeated their life in moral and spiritual terms. They had all been brought up within a Christian church but had rejected it because it did not reflect their own moral and spiritual values.

9 There is no one Irish Buddhist community. Adherents of Buddhism can belong to many different traditions, including the Kagyu and Gelugpa traditions of Tibetan Buddhism, Rinzai and Soto Zen Buddhism and the many Theravadin traditions of South-east Asian origin. There is no one organisation that represents the interests or views of Buddhists in Ireland.

multi-denominational school and had then moved to a Protestant school as the family had re-located. Most (seven) of those interviewed were mothers, three other participants were fathers (see Table 2).

Table 2: Profile of Minority Belief Interview Participants

	Buddhists	**Bahá'ís**	**Personal beliefs**	**Minority Christian**
Roman Catholic schools (6)	Mother (2 children) Father (1 child)	Mother (3 children)	Mother (2 children) Mother (1 child)	Mother (1 child)
Protestant schools (4)	Father (1 child) *Multi-denom school also*	Father (3 children) Mother (1 child) *Catholic school also*	Mother (1 child)	

The interviews were informal and focused on a number of key themes, namely the parents' experiences to date of denominational schools for their children, their views on denominational education, their own beliefs and educational experiences. The interviews varied in length from about 15 minutes to approximately an hour depending on the issues that the participants wished to discuss.

Key findings

It was clear from the interviews that the educational choice facing most of the participating parents was a limited one between denominational (Roman Catholic or Protestant) schools. Only two of those interviewed (one Bahá'í parent and one parent of personal beliefs) could have chosen multi-denominational schools and opted not to, sending their children to a Protestant school in each case for personal reasons.

Education for the Catholic sacraments at school

A major difficulty facing minority belief parents concerned the centrality of particular religious events in the life of Roman Catholic primary schools and how non-participation in these events impacted on their children. This was stated by those parents who had opted for a Protestant school[10] as a key factor in that decision.

> I opted away from the Catholic school to avoid First Communion and Confirmation. There is a danger of them feeling left out. (Parent of personal beliefs with a child in a Protestant school)

> Initially she went to the local Catholic school but I foresaw difficulties with 2nd class – the first Communion year. (Bahá'í parent with a child who attended both a Catholic and a Protestant school)

For those parents whose only choice was the local Roman Catholic primary school, there were a number of difficulties arising out of the importance of sacramental preparation. For one parent, there was an awareness of the child's sense of discomfort about an event that was taking place without his engagement.

> He had no problem with the First Communion but he found Confirmation more difficult. He's older now … He sat in on the preparation at the Cathedral and he would have preferred to have been elsewhere. (Bahá'í parent with children in a Catholic school)

Others were concerned about teasing or bullying. One Buddhist parent described how his child was subjected to bullying by classmates that seemed to have started partly as a result of the child being singled out as different when he did not take part in the Communion preparation and ceremony. Another parent described how her child stopped wanting to go to school.

> The class began Communion training and [the child] started faking illnesses. I went into the school about it but the teacher insisted she was fine, there was nothing wrong. When I spoke to other parents they told me that some children were teasing her because she wasn't doing Communion. She didn't want to do Communion but she didn't want to be different. (Parent of personal beliefs with a child in a Catholic school)

One mother described her uncertainty about how best to handle the First Communion ceremony itself. Her child was not involved in the preparation and she 'felt badly that he was being separated from the others and different to them. The teacher has made him welcome to be part of the Communion but we are uncertain about it.' (Minority Christian denomination parent with a child in a Catholic school)

---

[10] Because Protestant schools cater for children of the various Protestant denominations, preparations for particular sacraments and other faith-specific activities or instruction are conducted at parish level.

A few of the interview participants were critical of the time given to religious ritual preparation in Roman Catholic primary schools.

> Communion [preparation] is a waste of time in school. (Buddhist parent with a child in a Catholic school)

> First Communion and Confirmation take up a lot of time. (Bahá'í parent with children in a Protestant school)

Religious instruction and ritual involvement

Parents' expectations differed with regards to whether their children should be involved in religious education and the religious ritual elements that are part of day-to-day life in a denominational school. Some had no difficulty with their daughter or son taking part in the religious aspect of school life and curriculum while others considered it inappropriate.

> We insist that our children attend religion classes and take part in services. Our children are involved in the religious life of the school. They are officially invited to school [religious] ceremonies. (Bahá'í parent with children in a Protestant school)

> The teacher was teaching the children to bless themselves in week one in Junior Infants. Despite knowing the family's religion there was an expectation that she would take full part. (Bahá'í parent talking about her child's initial experiences in a Catholic school)

For some of the parents, the key issue was how removal from daily religion class might impact on their children's experiences of school.

> We decided not to take the children out of religion classes, as it would not be fair to them. (Bahá'í parent with children in a Catholic school)

> There are difficulties for those [parents] who want to take their child out [of religious instruction]. The child is singled out, seen as different. There are social consequences for the child. (Parent of personal beliefs with a child in a Catholic school)

Ongoing participation in the school's religious instruction was problematic for some of the parents interviewed because it caused the child to be presented with contradictory messages about belief and spirituality. One parent explained this difficulty as follows:

> He is coming home with the school's religion. I can't pass on my own spirituality as it would confuse him. I don't want to contradict the teacher or to cause him to be different. The personalisation of God bothers me. He's getting two definitions of God – one at home and one at school. (Parent of personal beliefs with a child in a Protestant school)

Schools seemed to respond to parents of minority beliefs very differently with regards to how religious instruction and involvement in religious activities should be handled. Some gave choices to the parents while others made clear an expectation that all children should participate in every aspect of the life of the school regardless of belief.

> The school is open to his non-involvement in religion classes but I'm happy to have him involved. (Buddhist parent with a child in a Catholic school)

> When we enrolled the children the principal talked to me about [the school's] diverse intake and how Muslim and Hindu children participate fully in religion class. Then she asked me how I would like to handle the situation ... We are told that parents can say no but we haven't been informed about trips to the [Catholic] church. (Buddhist parent with children in a Catholic school)

One parent of personal beliefs did not want her child to participate in religious instruction in her Catholic school. She asked her daughter's teacher on a number of occasions to provide the child with alternative activities during religion time. However, 'the teacher wouldn't provide any alternative [activity] in spite of me asking'.

Parents commented on how schools and teachers reacted to them as people with different beliefs. In some instances, they were impressed with the openness of school personnel, their interest and willingness to learn about difference and their efforts to integrate children of other beliefs into the life of the school.

> The teachers are more and more open. The school is very understanding. (Bahá'í parent with children in a Catholic school)

> The principal and the teachers have always been aware of my beliefs and they are very welcoming. Their attitudes are very positive. There have never been any difficulties. (Buddhist parent with a child in a Catholic school)

> The teacher and the principal have been very supportive and sensitive and open. I'm very impressed with the school. (Minority Christian parent with children in a Catholic school)

However, for some parents, the situation was quite different and more fraught with difficulty. Sometimes these problems were implied rather than overtly stated. A Buddhist parent described how she had a sense when initially enrolling her children in a Roman Catholic school that access to the school might have been refused on religious grounds as a result of being told that the decision would be made by the Board of Management and that the local parish priest was involved with this Board. Other difficulties arose out of the assumption of homogeneity and practices arising out of that assumption. One parent discussed how meetings between the school and the community in the evenings always opened with a (Catholic) prayer and how this impacted on her partner:

> Any meetings at the school always open with a prayer and this alienates my partner. (Parent of personal beliefs with a child in a Catholic school)

Another parent felt that denominational schools take no account of the needs of those of minority beliefs.

> There should be allowances made for people who're different [in terms of belief]. (Parent of personal beliefs with a child in a Catholic school)

There was no evidence emerging in the interviews, however, that principals or teachers were deliberately attempting to exclude or alienate parents and children of minority beliefs. Rather, the difficulties appeared to have arisen as a result of individual or institutional uncertainty as to how to appropriately accommodate religious difference in a denominational school. For example, one Bahá'í parent moved her child from a Catholic to a Protestant school partly in order to avoid the difficulties to which the First Communion year would give rise. When the child was leaving the school, the principal sought reassurance, saying to this parent 'I hope it isn't the difference in beliefs'.

The denominational nature of Irish primary education

Many of the parents interviewed expressed clearly their preference for a wider choice of primary schools and stated that, had such schools been available to them, they would have sent their children to multi-denominational or non-denominational schools.

> I would prefer a non-denominational or a multi-denominational school as an option. (Bahá'í parent with children in a Roman Catholic school)

> If I had another child I might go for a multi-denomational school – I would have chosen it for [this child] if it was available at the time. I see it as a better environment. (Buddhist parent with a child in a Roman Catholic school)

Some of the parents had either lived abroad themselves and had taken note of the types of schools available in America, Britain and elsewhere, while others stated a general awareness that schools in other jurisdictions were usually not tied to specific beliefs.

> Denominational schools are an awful shame. In America you can choose a non-denominational school. (Parent of personal beliefs with a child in a Protestant school)

> I would prefer non-denominational schools. There was more religious diversity in America. But there was no religious education at school so nobody was left feeing different or odd. (Buddhist parent with children in a Roman Catholic school)

> Having denominational schools is a very single-minded approach. Personally speaking I believe there should be choices. There are choices in other countries. (Parent of personal beliefs with a child in a Roman Catholic school)

One of the parents noted that, even where there was an available multi-denominational school, the prevailing Christian culture of Irish society impacted on the ethos of these schools too:

> Christianity is the prevailing ethos even in multi-denominational schools due to the teachers' own cultural backgrounds. There is a certain way of looking at the world – it doesn't occur to people to ask questions. Things are taken for granted. (Buddhist parent with a child who attended both a Protestant and a multi-denominational school)

All of the parents who participated in these discussions had been brought up as Christians (mainly Roman Catholics) and all had been educated in schools associated with the various Christian denominations. One of the participating parents had been brought up in Britain. Most of these parents were people who had made a choice in adulthood to explore and express their individual spirituality and had either become involved with religious groups such as the Bahá'í or Buddhist communities in Ireland or had come to a personal understanding of their own beliefs and practices. One of those who had such personal beliefs explained:

> I grew up Catholic but I moved away from it. The teachings of Christ are a cultural part of me but I rejected the institution of the Church. (Parent of personal beliefs with a child in a Roman Catholic school).

The fact that all of these parents had experienced their own education in denominational (mainly Roman Catholic) schools meant that they had an insider's understanding and knowledge of the way in which belief had been transmitted there. The fact that they had made individual choices to move away from the religious institutions associated with these schools meant that some had quite a negative view of such activities and were very definite that they did not want their children exposed to this type of education if possible.

> I went to a Catholic school. I didn't want my child indoctrinated. (Parent of personal beliefs with a child in a Catholic school)

> I had a bellyful of Catholicism from my own educational experiences. The ritual issues took up a lot of school time – they were fed to children and I resented it deeply. (Parent of personal beliefs with a child in a Protestant school)

Not all parents interviewed shared these views however. One argued that it was important for a child belonging to a minority faith family to have an understanding of the majority culture.

> The denominational nature of Irish schools isn't a bad thing. It is to be expected culturally. There is no harm for a child to have an understanding of the majority culture but also to understand the deficiencies in it. (Buddhist parent with a child who attended both a Protestant and a multi-denominational school)

Parents who participated in these discussions differed as to their hopes for the religious education of their own children. Some stated that they wanted to pass on their own spirituality to their children but felt curtailed in doing this because their children were getting contradictory messages from the denominational school they were attending.

> I have come to a personal understanding of spirituality … I would like to pass this on to my children. (Parent of personal beliefs with a child in a Protestant school)

> I have an issue with denominational schools. People's private beliefs are a matter for the family. There shouldn't be preference given to one denomination over another, or to any denomination over none. It isn't the place of school to offer religious instruction. (Parent of personal beliefs with a child in a Roman Catholic school)

Some of the parents felt that it was important that their children were educated in an environment where spirituality made up a part of education but where, at the same time, the family's beliefs were respected.

> I would prefer a school where the religious element is part of the school but I also want some flexibility and I found this comfort-zone in the Protestant school. The school is okay with what the family and the child believe. (Bahá'í parent with a child who attended both a Catholic and a Protestant school)

> If I had other choices I would select the same [the Protestant school] because I prefer there to be a spiritual dimension to education and I feel that children wouldn't get it in a multi-denominational school. It is especially important at primary level. The spiritual is a significant part of education alongside the academic and social dimensions. While it is important that children are educated spiritually at home it isn't enough. They need to be part of a spiritual community and to experience another religious dimension outside the home. (Bahá'í parent with children in a Protestant school)

While a few might have preferred to have schools reflecting their own beliefs available to them others were not sure that this would be the most educationally appropriate option.

> I wanted a spiritual and moral dimension to education but couldn't hope for a Bahá'í school. (Bahá'í parent with a child in a Protestant school)

> In the UK some Buddhist schools have been set up. I'm not sure about these – they could be a narrowing down too. (Buddhist parent with a child who attended both a Protestant and a multi-denominational school)

A number of the parents noted the importance for the education of *all* children of being in religiously mixed environments. Three of those who participated in the interviews were involved with local committees interested in establishing a multi-denominational school.

> It is important for other children to learn some people are different. It is important for education. (Parent of personal beliefs with a child in a Catholic school who is involved in a committee to establish a multi-denominational school)

> I see mixing of beliefs as a key factor in wanting a multi-denominational school for my child. It is important to learn about each other's beliefs. (Minority Christian parent with a child in a Roman Catholic school who is involved in a committee to establish a multi-denominational school)

> You come out of a multi-denominational school better prepared at the end of it. Putting all children together in a school for mixed religions is more balanced and meets the needs of the new cultures. (Roman Catholic parent with children in a Roman Catholic school who is involved in a committee to establish a multi-denominational school)

These parents were not alone in expressing such sentiments. Another parent also prioritised the benefits of moving away from the traditional model of provision of education segregated on religious lines.

> I would prefer a more diverse mix of students of all beliefs. The wider the range of options for children the better, so that they can make up their own minds. (Buddhist parent with a child who attended both a Protestant and a multi-denominational school)

The first multi-denominational school was established in the Republic of Ireland in Dalkey in the early 1970s (Hyland 1989). The number of these schools remains very small and most are located in large urban areas. Because there are so few such schools, many people who would prefer a multi-denominational school but who do not have that choice opt instead for a Protestant school. Indeed, there is some evidence that Protestant schools have been utilised in this way in the past by those who did not wish their children to be educated in a Roman Catholic primary school (White 1975).[11] Two Bahá'í parents stated that they were very happy with the way in which their local Protestant schools made them feel welcome and had an inclusive ethos with a spiritual dimension. One of these parents noted how assembly in her child's school allowed for the visible celebration of different people's beliefs, prayers and culture. She said that this might have been a reflection of the multi-cultural nature of the area in which the school is located. However, another parent expressed disappointment about her experience of her local Protestant school – she had attended a Roman Catholic school herself and was surprised that religion was a similarly significant dimension of life in the Protestant school to which she sent her child.

> The [Roman Catholic] ritual issues took up a lot of school time – they were fed to children and I resented it deeply. Now I'm finding that it is the same in the Protestant school. (Parent of personal beliefs with a child in a Protestant school)

One of the Buddhist parents had experience of both a Protestant and a multi-denominational school due to the fact that the family had moved during the child's time in primary school. His understanding of the position of Protestant schools was that 'the Protestant schools can be more orthodox Christian than current Catholic schools due to the fact that it is a small community and they are conscious of preserving their ethos'.

---

[11] There is also some evidence that Protestant schools were favoured by some non-Protestant parents who regarded them as the more middle-class, exclusive option (Robinson 1998).

The subordinate status of minority beliefs in the Irish denominational primary system

The denominational and confessional nature of the Irish primary education system does not allow for equal recognition or respect for difference.[12] The values, practices and perspectives of the dominant group (in particular, the Roman Catholic church) are expressed as cultural and institutional norms in Irish primary education. This includes daily religious instruction and prayers and the celebration and marking of liturgical events throughout the year as well as the sacramental preparation and participation specific to Roman Catholic schools. The fact that the ceremonies of other religions or, for that matter, of individual family practices, are not highlighted in the same way at school as Catholic Communion or Confirmation confirms their subordinate status. Differences in belief are denied in the denominational primary system and those whose beliefs are different are rendered invisible and subordinate.

There are points during children's time in primary school when the dominance of the culture and practices of Roman Catholicism are particularly apparent. This is most true of the sacraments of Communion and Confirmation. The minority belief parents who participated in this research singled out the significance of these sacraments in Catholic primary schools as being of particular difficulty (or potential difficulty) for them and for their young children. The singling out of a child as different can result in that young person experiencing exclusion, teasing or bullying, discomfort and a sense of isolation. Parents' concerns for their child(ren)'s happiness and sense of inclusion in the school community were not limited to these sacraments. Some also expressed worries about how they should manage the issue of daily religious instruction. One parent explained how she felt that she had to subordinate her own spirituality to that of the school in order not to confuse her young child.

The small-scale research conducted for this study demonstrated that there were significant differences in the experiences of minority belief parents. The range of experiences outlined by the participants in this research reflects many of the findings of current research conducted with minority belief parents in Northern Ireland (Richardson 2003). Some parents were happy with the extent to which teachers, principals and schools were including

---

[12] Lack of respect for, or the unequal esteeming of difference by the majority or dominant culture has been described by Young (1990) as cultural imperialism. This type of injustice is experienced by subordinate groups as cultural domination or invisibility (Lynch and Lodge 2002).

and valuing difference while others felt that there was no real attempt made to understand or respect their family beliefs. The difficulty for families of minority belief within an overwhelmingly denominational education system is that there is no obligation on such schools to treat those of other beliefs with respect and recognition. Indeed, the rights of the patron of denominational schools to protect the ethos of their schools is recognised in law. Some of the parents and their children had very positive, inclusive educational experiences in schools that were keen to facilitate the majority belief children in learning more about different beliefs and that were pleased to recognise the prayers or celebrations of other beliefs.[13] In other schools, these parents felt that their beliefs would be tolerated so long as they were willing to conform to the expected behaviours and activities of the school and the class and not make demands for special treatment. As Baker et al (2004) argue, those who are powerful or who are the majority in a culture can tolerate their subordinates without equally esteeming or valuing them. Toleration does not allow for the possibility of the majority culture critically questioning itself, learning from the difference of the minority or allowing that subordinate group to be given equal recognition or respect. Echoing this argument, one of the parents in this research explained:

> I would prefer greater choice of schools that reflect diversity and people's rights to have their children in an environment that is respectful of their beliefs. There is a difference between being welcomed and nurtured and being tolerated. (Bahá'í parent with a child in a Protestant school who had previously been enrolled in a Catholic school)

Non-recognition of belief difference has been institutionalised in Irish primary education at a systemic level. The traditional choices for parents and children at primary level have been between schools controlled by a limited number of Christian denominations, reflecting the nineteenth-century realities outlined already and based on an assumption of a Christian population desiring universal segregated, denominational education. The provision of

---

[13] It emerged in this research that parents who were adherents of a recognised faith group were more likely to report respectful experiences in the denominational school where their children were enrolled. Those parents who reported having most difficulty and concern were people who had personal beliefs. Only one of these parents had specifically explained her beliefs to the school; the other two regarded their beliefs as private and did not discuss them with the school or their children's teachers. However, given the small-scale nature of this research it is not possible to draw any inferences from this finding.

primary schools continues to reflect a very limited notion of difference, in which Roman Catholicism is the culturally dominant norm in society and all those who are 'other' are assumed to be Protestant. This reflects a long-held notion of Irish identity as Catholic and Gaelic while those in Ireland who are 'other' are Protestant and unionist (Tanner 2003). The particular model of management of Irish primary schools with the necessity for local initiative, financial contribution and a local patron, has made it very difficult for other types of primary schools to be established.

The Irish primary education system is predicated on an assumption that all Irish citizens belong to one of a few Christian denominations. This is a consequence of the religious and political realities and tensions at the time the system was established in the mid-nineteenth century. While the belief profile of the Irish population has changed, the system of management and control of most primary schools still reflects nineteenth-century patterns. As the 2002 Census reveals clearly, the numbers of adherents to other beliefs and those of personal belief are growing. This is not only a consequence of increasing inward migration but is also a reflection of the changes within Irish society. An increasing number of Irish people are experiencing difficulties with aspects of the system because there is little or no recognition within it of their beliefs while at the same time a particular set of beliefs continues to be given preference. Until such time as there is a genuine willingness by vested interests to adapt the education system so that it recognises and respect the rights of those of minority belief rather than merely tolerating their presence, some children and their parents will not be equally esteemed in primary education. All children, regardless of belief, suffer as a consequence of this non-recognition of difference that characterises the Irish education system and fails to reflect the reality of an increasingly diverse Ireland. As Dewey (1963) has argued, in order to adequately educate young people for membership of a diverse society, it is essential that their school communities actively and respectfully reflect that diversity.

Bibliography

Akenson, D. H. (1975) *A Mirror to Kathleen's Face: Education in Independent Ireland, 1922-1960,* Montreal and London, McGill-Queen's University Press.

Baker, J., Lynch, K., Cantillon, S. and Walsh, J. (2004) *Equality: From Theory to Action,* London, Palgrave.

Bowen, K. (1983) *Protestants in a Catholic State: Ireland's Privileged Minority*, Dublin, Gill and Macmillan.

Caird, D. (1985) 'Protestantism and National Identity', in J. McLoone (ed.) *Being Protestant in Ireland: Papers presented at the 32nd Annual Summer School of the Social Study Conference*, Dublin, The Social Study Conference.

Catholic Primary School Manager's Association (2000) *Management Board Members' Handbook (Revised 2000)*, Dublin, CPSMA.

Central Statistics Office (2003) *Principal Demographic Results,* Dublin, Stationery Office.

Clarke, D. M. (1998) 'Education, the State and Sectarian Schools', in T. Murphy and P. Twomey (eds) *Ireland's Evolving Constitution 1937-1997: Collected Essays,* Oxford, Hart Publishing.

Cleary, A., Nic Ghiolla Phadraig, M. and Quin, S. (2001) 'Introduction', in A. Cleary, M. Nic Ghiolla Phadraig and S. Quin (eds) *Understanding Children Volume 1: State, Education and Economy*, Cork, Oak Tree Press.

Coolahan, J. (1980) *A History of Irish Education,* Dublin, Institute of Public Administration.

Cooney, J. (1999) *John Charles McQuaid: Ruler of Catholic Ireland,* Dublin, The O'Brien Press.

Dewey, J. (1963) *Experience and Education,* New York, Collier Books.

Drudy, S. and Lynch, K. (1993) *Schools and Society in Ireland,* Dublin, Gill and Macmillan.

FitzGerald, G. (2003) *Reflections on the Irish State*, Dublin, Irish Academic Press.

Glendenning, D. (1999) *Education and the Law,* Dublin, Butterworths.

Government of Ireland *Bunreacht na hEireann,* Dublin, Stationery Office.

Hyland, A. (1989) 'The Multi-denominational experience in the Irish national school system of education', *Irish Educational Studies*, 8, 1, pp 89-114.

Inglis, T. (1998) *Moral Monopoly: The Rise and Fall of the Catholic Church in Ireland,* Dublin, UCD Press.

Keogh, D. (1997) *Jews in Ireland*, Cork, Cork University Press.

Lodge, A. (1998) *Gender Identity and Schooling: a two-year ethnographic study of the expression, exploration and development of gender identity in seven to nine year old children in their school environment*, Unpublished PhD thesis, Education Department, National University of Ireland, Maynooth.

Lodge, A. (1999) 'First Communion in Carnduffy: a religious and secular rite of passage', *Irish Educational Studies*, 18, pp 210-222.

Lynch, K. and Lodge, A. (2002) *Equality and Power in Schools: Redistribution, Recognition and Representation,* London, Routledge Falmer.

Manning, M. (1999) *James Dillon: A Biography,* Dublin, Wolfhound Press.

Murphy, C. and Adair, L. (2003) *Untold Stories: Protestants in the Republic of Ireland, 1922-2002,* Dublin, Liffey Press.

National Education Convention Secretariat (1994) *Report,* Dublin, Stationery Office.

Randles, E. (1996) 'Relationship of Church to Schools: Its Nature and Value', in *Pluralism in Education: Conference Proceedings*, pp 209–218.

Richardson, N. (2003) 'Curricular, Faith and Pastoral Issues for Minority Faith Children in Northern Ireland Schools: The Views of their Parents', paper presented to the *Diversity, World Faiths and Education Conference*, Belfast, 19 November.

Robinson, H. (1998) *Protestants in the South of Ireland Since 1922: Stereotypes within Society and the Newspapers,* Unpublished Masters in Equality Studies thesis, Equality Studies Centre, UCD.

Tanner, M. (2003) *Ireland's Holy Wars: The Struggle for a Nation's Soul 1500-2000,* New Haven, Yale Nota Bene, Yale University Press.

Tovey, H. and Share, P. (2002) *A Sociology of Ireland: Second Edition,* Dublin, Gill and Macmillan.

White, J. (1975) *Minority Report: The Protestant Community in the Irish Republic*, Dublin, Gill and Macmillan.

Young, I. M. (1990) *Justice and the Politics of Difference*, Princeton, Princeton University Press.

Chapter 3

'See no evil, speak no evil, hear no evil?' The experiences of lesbian and gay teachers in Irish schools

Sandra Gowran

Introduction

Issues of sexuality rarely, if ever, receive attention within Irish educational discourse; issues of lesbian and gay sexuality are even more noticeable by their absence. This chapter documents some of the more pertinent issues encountered by lesbian and gay teachers in Ireland, in particular it identifies and explores the difficulties and issues experienced by these teachers in being open about their sexual orientation. The chapter reports on the key findings of interviews carried out with a small number of primary and post-primary lesbian and gay teachers. It also aims to counter common assertions that discourse on issues of sexuality and, more explicitly, lesbian and gay sexualities, are not appropriate within the context of primary schools. The paper will demonstrate how issues of sexuality are intimately linked with human identity and integrity and, therefore, are fundamentally relevant to ensuring the inclusion of all for whom this issue is relevant, that is not only lesbian and gay teachers but also students who may be beginning to identify as lesbian or gay, students with lesbian or gay parents, grandparents, aunts, uncles, sisters, brothers, in short a sizeable proportion of users and providers of education within Ireland.

The interviews reveal that the issues encountered by lesbian and gay teachers are primarily ones of inequality and have their roots in the dominant culture of heterosexism[1] that pervades society as a whole, and which results in the oppression and vilification of

[1] Heterosexism is the authoritative construction of norms that privilege heterosexuality (Fraser 1995).

lesbian and gay sexualities whilst simultaneously rendering them silent and invisible. Moreover, the research shows little variation whether the teacher works in the primary or post-primary sector, or within denominational or non-denominational settings. The relative dearth of research and writing in Irish education about issues relating to sexuality (Lynch and Lodge 2002), and in particular homosexuality, is an indication in itself of the silence and secrecy with which these issues are treated within our education system. Research carried out in Ireland and elsewhere indicates that the issues encountered are seriously destructive and debilitating for the social, emotional and intellectual development of young people who identify themselves as lesbian or gay (Collins et al 1995, Harbeck 1992, Mac An Ghaill 1991, Rofes 1989, Scott 1989). These findings, coupled with the research conducted for this paper, bring to the fore the need for sexual identity to be considered as an essential part of human identity, one which needs to be valued and nurtured as much as all other aspects of human identity.

Theorising silence

Any discussion of sexuality in relation to an institution such as that of Irish education would be incomplete without reference to the particular historical forces and factors that have shaped what is considered 'natural' or 'normal', in this case heterosexuality (Foucault 1981, Inglis 1998). Whilst the Christian Churches' influence on the discourse around sex and sexuality has undoubtedly lessened in recent years, its imprint will have lasting effects. From the late nineteenth century in Ireland the discourse on sexuality was dominated and controlled by the Roman Catholic Church and resulted in the indoctrination of the predominately Catholic populace with a (hetero)sexuality of chastity, modesty, temperance and self-control as its central defining features (Inglis 1998). Anything other than married sexual love was seen as a threat to the natural order of things. Homosexuality was reconstructed as deviant and inferior to the dominant sexual expression of heterosexuality (Young 1990). Within this context what resulted was the authoritative construction of norms that privilege one culture over another (Fraser 1995); in this instance (married) heterosexuality was privileged over all other expressions of sexuality and sexual orientation.

Teachers working within this context occupy an unusual situation when compared to other employees, in that they are partly a product of the system that they now work in, and are therefore subject to the institutional and cultural bias of that system. In the long history of its influence on Irish education the Roman Catholic Church has been quite successful in shaping young peoples' sexuality through its ability to control what is taught, said and done in the schools that are under its influence. Generations of teachers have grown up in this system and it is likely that they have embodied the silence that surrounds sex and sexuality, and its perceived sinfulness; this in turn is passed onto the generations of students that they teach (Inglis 1998). It is likely that lesbian and gay teachers have further embodied negative messages about 'deviant' sexualities from direct statements from the Christian Churches about the practice of homosexuality as being 'contrary to the laws of nature' and 'objectively disordered' (Agnew 2000 citing Pope John Paul II). In short, all teachers (regardless of their sexual orientation) educated within such an environment have learned the hidden rules and regulations whose transgression exacts severe punishment in their minds, if not in reality.

Non-recognition in the form of silence, and misrecognition and disrespect in the form of homophobia[2] and discrimination, are the quintessential inequalities surrounding the issues that lesbian and gay teachers face. They are a direct result of what Fraser (1995) describes as the cultural-valuational structure of a society that privileges heterosexuality and renders other forms of sexuality either invisible or deviant. Invisibility and silence around issues of sexual orientation are particularly common within the context of Irish education (Lynch and Lodge 2002, O'Carroll and Szalacha 2000) reflecting the prevalence of heterosexism. The net effect of such dominance is that those who do not fit into the dominant mould are effectively forced to displace their sexual identity from their public identity in such a manner as to render it invisible. Identity and the recognition of one's identity are fundamental defining characteristics in human beings (Taylor 1931). Sexual identity is central to developing a full interpretation of the self (Inglis 1998). Consequently, lack of recognition of one's identity, including sexual identity, is a form of oppression, in that it inhibits people from developing and exercising their capacities and expressing their needs, thoughts and feelings (Young 1990). In short, it prevents an individual from striving towards his or her ontological vocation to become fully human (Freire 1972).

Such oppression is a result of the everyday well-intentioned practices of liberal society, in which most people (heterosexual people in this case) do not understand themselves as agents of oppression. This lack of understanding causes minority groups to

---

2 Homophobia is used generally to refer to the manifestation of hatred directed at gay men, lesbians, bisexuals as well as other minority sexualities. It differs from other phobias in that hatred, as well as fear, are the emotional responses.

suffer deep injustices as a result of ordinary interactions, media and cultural stereotypes, as well as the structural features of bureaucratic hierarchies (Young 1990). Heterosexism effectively permeates the core of daily life and school activities. Frequently it is argued that one's sexuality has nothing to do with one's role as a teacher. This quite simplistic argument fails to take cognisance of the fact that ' ... heterosexism is a worldview for most people, it is probably not even conscious. It is a mind-set ... ... it is also a bias' (McNaught 1993: 47). Consequently, lesbian and gay teachers do not enjoy the same freedom that heterosexual teachers enjoy in the integration of their sexual and public identities. The majority of lesbian and gay teachers believe that a strict separation between their personal and professional lives is required if they are not to risk being subjected to prejudice, discrimination and accusations of hidden sinister agendas (Griffin 1992, Collins et al 1995). This false duality between the private and public spheres of life means that they are not free to be their full human selves in the work place. This is critically problematic for lesbian and gay teachers, but also symptomatic of the denial of the emotional and affectual dimension of life and our emotional selves as being a necessary part of our full human identity.

Although not within the scope of this paper to elaborate upon, it is nevertheless important to highlight that issues around sexuality and homosexuality are major threats to traditional cultural ideology associated with dominant masculinities and gender relations (Connell 1989, Harbeck 1992). Schools, both primary and secondary, are the mirrors of the values and attitudes of society in general, they serve to maintain and reproduce the social and (hetero)sexual hierarchies of the society in which they are placed (Connell 1989, Cooper 1989, Epstein and Johnson 1994, Mac An Ghaill 1991, Redman 1994). Although they do not operate in a vacuum, Connell (1989) sees schools as having a powerful and decisive influence in the formation of dominant masculinities, and their associated gender relations. This traditional, dominant ideology is exerted by instilling the norm of universal heterosexuality, and marking sexual difference as deviant and inferior (Young 1990).

As such, lesbian and gay teachers are not only oppressed by lack of recognition of their existence, they are further alienated by being '... regarded as the pathology of the healthy society' (Freire 1972: 48). This misrecognition results in a paradoxical oppression whereby the individual requires recognition as a human being from the dominant culture, but is in return judged by the same group to be different, marked or inferior (Young 1990). The paradox results in the individual forming a double consciousness, being defined by two cultures, the dominant and the subordinate, at the one time invisible but also marked out as different (Young 1990). The misrecognition that is inherent in this process often results in homophobia, and finds expression in disrespect and violence; another form of oppression (Young 1990). As a result of homophobia, non-dominant sexualities are 'disparaged, subject to shaming, harassment, discrimination, and violence, while being denied legal rights and equal protection' (Fraser 1995: 77).

Methodology

In order to explore whether the theoretical account of oppression outlined above is relevant within the context of Irish education it was necessary to hear what it is like for lesbian and gay teachers in Irish schools today. The seven teachers[3] who participated in the research were identified through personal contacts of the author. The participants in the interviews are mainly from the post-primary sector. As the author herself worked in the post-primary sector, it was easier to make contact with other second-level teachers. Difficulties in accessing respondents in this area have been noted in other research carried out in this field (O'Fathaigh 2003). Two primary teachers were also interviewed. Very similar issues concerned teachers in both sectors. It is important that people appreciate the degree of silence around sexuality, especially within caring professions such as teaching where people's concerns are compounded by the fact that many of them are employed in denominational schools and, as a consequence, their legal rights are not entirely clear. These issues are discussed in depth throughout this chapter.

All participants were assured of full anonymity both for themselves and their respective schools. Such an assurance was not only essential to guarantee the integrity of the research process but is of utmost importance to guarantee the safety and protection of lesbian and gay teachers working within a state in which employment equality legislation is perceived as leaving them vulnerable to discrimination by religious employers who may consider their sexual orientation, if discovered, undermines the religious ethos of the institution. The Employment Equality Act, 1998, permits such

---

[3] The participants in the research comprised of seven self-identified lesbian and gay teachers (five lesbians and two gay men). Five of the interviewees were from the post-primary sector. Two interviews with primary sector teachers were conducted later to compare similarities and differences in experience between the post-primary and primary sectors. All seven teachers were asked the same questions through the same interview process.

employers to take 'action which is reasonably necessary to prevent an employee or a prospective employee from undermining the religious ethos of the institution'. The threat of such 'reasonable action' was felt strongly by most of the teachers interviewed. For this reason pseudonyms are used in reporting the research findings and schools are described only as primary or post-primary and denominational or non-denominational, in order to further safeguard the participants anonymity.

The interviews conducted were built around questions drawn from research carried out in other cultural settings (Griffin 1992; Woods and Harbeck, 1992). Amongst other issues, the questions explored the general climate of schools in relation to lesbian and gay issues, the level of safety to be 'out'[4] in schools; how teachers manage their lesbian or gay identity in relation to their role as teacher; participants' own experiences as lesbian or gay educators. As outlined above, the research aimed to explore the issues and makes no claims to be representative of the entire teaching body of lesbian and gay teachers. However, the similarities of experience, despite school type or level, and their striking similarities with more extensive research (Collins et al 1995; Griffin 1992; Woods and Harbeck 1992) are worthy of note.

Key findings

This section illustrates key findings of the research and documents what it is like for lesbian and gay teachers in the Irish education system and in particular how non-recognition, misrecognition and disrespect are experienced by these teachers in their everyday working lives. Selected quotations are used to illustrate key findings.

For all the teachers who participated in the research the process of internalised oppression began in their own schooling where heterosexuality was implicitly if not explicity hegemonic. None of the respondents received any education about sexuality issues, including lesbian or gay issues, whilst at school. Essentially, sexuality had no name; the sexuality of people who were gay or lesbian was especially nameless. Whilst one may argue that this

---

4 The term 'out' refers to being explicitly open about one's sexual orientation within a heterosexual environment. The converse term 'closeted' denotes individuals who remain silent or secretive about their sexual identity. It should be noted however, that the issue of being 'out' is more complex than what is described here for ease of the uninitiated reader. For many lesbians and gay men there are many dimensions to simply being 'out' or 'closeted' and these vary depending on the context and company they find themselves in at any given time. Indeed this becomes apparent from the research findings within this paper.

may have had positive benefits insofar as sexuality was not always explicitly presented as heterosexual, it also had considerable limitations as students had no opportunity to explore their view on sexuality, or to understand their own sexuality in relation to dominant norms, as this female teacher recalls:

> ... when I look back now I kind of think that some things that I was experiencing and not able to name were part of my experiencing difference growing up lesbian. I was quite lonely during much of my adolescence and I know I was really feeling different at that time ... I knew somewhere that this was to be hidden and not ok socially, that people did not talk about this ... (Sheila, post-primary, denominational)

In light of the historical context of the discourse on sexuality in Ireland, it is not surprising that invisibility and silence around sexuality were recurrent themes in the participants' stories. The same teacher believed that there was, in fact, a positive aspect of this invisibility and silence for her in that she was saved from '... not having them [the teachers] mess around with my mind ...'. The belief held by this respondent, that she was saved in some manner from 'corruption' is quite untenable, in that she clearly received a covert message that there 'was something wrong' with homosexuality. This response clearly illustrates a (heterosexual) cultural imperialism whereby the dominant norms have rendered the minority (lesbian, in this instance) invisible at the same time as marking it out as an inferior reduced mode of being (Young 1990, Freire 1972). Further evidence of such stigma is apparent in how the same teacher describes her struggle to reconcile the stigmatised identity of lesbianism with her feelings and actions as she came to recognise her sexuality:

> ... I didn't know what lesbians were; I didn't know that what I was doing [falling in love with a woman] was lesbian. I thought lesbians were kind of old women who hung around toilets ... and I was not one of those. (Sheila, post-primary, denominational)

The climate of schools in relation to lesbian and gay issues

The climate of schools in relation to sex and sexuality is very important in shaping attitudes and values and in particular those relating to lesbian and gay sexuality. Indeed, how sex and sexuality are addressed in schools is an important gauge indicating the level of inclusiveness and equality present. Respondents were asked to describe their workplace in terms of how it deals with lesbian and gay issues. Responses demonstrated that the invisibility and silence that teachers experienced during their school years is still very much in evidence today. Although some did refer to the openness of some staff to difference, the domination of heterosexism was very apparent from the responses received:

> It [issues of sexual orientation] has never arisen, it doesn't arise. (Paul, primary, denominational)

> I have never heard anything mentioned [about sexual orientation] at all, not once, never. (Maeve, post-primary, denominational)

This complete denial of the existence of both lesbian and gay teachers, and students, is further evidence of the prevalence of heterosexism, displaying striking similarities with research conducted in different cultural contexts (Griffin 1992, Woods and Harbeck 1992).

Split identities

McNaught (1993) claims that all individuals have a public and a private sexual orientation identity. For heterosexuals these identities are nearly always the same, but where there may be severe penalties for honesty in relation to one's sexual identity, a lesbian or gay man must choose what they disclose in any given situation. 'When our behaviour and/or our identity are different than our orientation, it can take a terrible toll' (McNaught 1993: 33), as evidenced by this teacher's comments:

> ... I think the ability to be unable to become unconscious of who we are, all the time, is ... detrimental mentally because you are continuously aware of situations, you can see them coming a mile off, you spot them and you immediately go into a kind of an adrenaline rush in your head where you are working out how do I avoid this, how do I remove myself from this ... (Mary, post-primary, denominational)

A World Health Organisation report (WHO 1991, cited in Collins et al 1995: 4) concluded '... that people who hide their sexual orientation for fear of discrimination or alienation live less fulfilling lives, encounter additional stress and are placed in situations that are not conducive to safe sexual practices'. The toll that this exerts inhibits lesbian or gay individuals in their ability to develop and exercise their capacities and express their needs, thoughts and feelings, and as such is a form of oppression that has its roots in the '... unquestioned norms, habits and symbols, in the assumptions underlying institutional rules and collective consequences of those rules' (Young 1990: 40-41). The quotation that follows illustrates how these unquestioned norms, habits, and symbols can unintentionally lead to the exclusion of lesbian and gay teachers and their subsequent denial of certain benefits enjoyed by heterosexual teachers in recognised partnerships:

> I think people don't realise, they think your private life is your private life, and that nobody shares their private life really at work, and they don't realise how much they really do share. Like I know whether my colleagues are married or not, often although not always, whether they're going out with someone or not. If they are they usually feel free to have that partner, or lover, or whatever, come and collect them or drop them off. And they get all kinds of little approvals ... ... whip-rounds for somebody having a baby, somebody getting married or engaged, or recognition that their partners would be sick and this kind of thing. (Sheila, post-primary, denominational)

Managing split identities

Given that teachers are not encouraged to be 'out' in schools, the interview focused, in part, on asking participants questions regarding the management of their sexual identities whilst in school. Participants were asked initially if they saw a separation between their home (lesbian or gay) identity and their (teacher) public identity. Again responses were varied, some said that while they were 'out' to some colleagues they did 'deliberately hide it from others' (Sheila, post-primary, denominational). Others remarked that they 'don't make any claims ... in any direction [sexual identity]' (Mary, post-primary, denominational), or that '... in a teaching environment I become asexual. I don't really have a powerful lesbian logo stamped on my head ... ' (Orla, post-primary, non-denominational), or '... neither do I shout about who I am in my private life, or in school' (Maeve, post-primary, denominational). However when asked as to whether they ever censored conversations in school when speaking about their private lives the responses were somewhat in contradiction to the above:

> ... I've come out to two other teachers but I haven't come out to the rest of the staff and I don't mention things like ... oh, I was at the lesbian arts festival last weekend or something, I am aware of avoiding that ... (Ann, primary, denominational)

> ... if I was in a staff room context, I would use the word 'them' or 'they', as opposed to naming the person ... I suppose I would, I'd do the pronoun thing. (Orla, post-primary, non-denominational)

In light of these responses it seems that these teachers do, perhaps unconsciously, censor what they say in relation to their private (sexual) identity whilst in school. This indicates that there is a separation between their home (lesbian or gay) identity and their (teacher) public identity. With regard to other identity management strategies – all participants said that they regulated what they say in formal/informal interactions with students. Indeed some teachers expressed severe anxiety and fear of adverse reactions from students if they were to be 'out':

> ... it [homophobia] could get more sadistic, very more subtle maybe, but its quite intimidating. And, I suppose, I'm very conscious of the fact that I live very close to the school and that it could be a home attack ... (Orla, post-primary, non-denominational)

Participants were then asked quite an open question with regard to mechanisms against disclosure of sexual identity in situations that they did not choose. There was an overriding sense of privacy around most of the participant's sexual identity, to which they felt that others were being intrusive in asking questions of them:

> ... it depends on the question and the way it was asked, some people are just born nosey. (Orla, post-primary, non-denominational)

> ... if it's a stranger or someone that I felt is just being curious I certainly wouldn't give them the information just for the sake of it. (Tom, post-primary, denominational)

> ... if I was asked questions about certain things I would be vague and people would know that there are certain lines that they don't pursue. (Mary, post-primary, denominational)

Other strategies used to deflect attention from them included not focusing directly on the issue of sexuality, or by preparing for the situation before it arose:

> ... in recent years I haven't been as eager [to pursue lesbian or gay issues] because I felt there were repercussions to that ... And I tried in other ways to get across the ideas of tolerance, respect and understanding ... (Mary, post-primary, denominational)

It is clear from the above that lesbian and gay teachers utilise various strategies to ensure that their sexual identity is not disclosed in situations that have not been chosen by them. Those referred to above involved regulating topics that they covered to take the attention away from lesbian and gay issues, also careful preparation for situations that could be confrontational and their avoidance. There are perhaps other protective mechanisms that teachers employ that they become desensitised to as this teacher refers to:

> … protecting myself becomes so habit, so much of a habit I almost don't know when I'm doing it or not doing it … (Sheila, post-primary, denominational)

What is clear however is that being a lesbian or gay teacher in an environment that does not welcome diversity can make a big difference to them and their lives both in and outside of school, as encapsulated by this teacher:

> … I think that at various times over the last several years, I have felt this threat or sense of fear within me because of my lifestyle and my sexual identity … and I would be aware that it can, over a long period of time, affect my health in terms of stress, and not in an overt way … but deep inside me in the pit of my stomach … [I am] very aware of … … where I felt my soul was displaced, because my soul was the soul of a gay woman it had been displaced from myself in order for me to exist in this situation … (Mary, post-primary, denominational)

The separation of professional and personal lives that is depicted by this teacher encompasses the essence of the oppression felt by many lesbian and gay teachers – it strikes at the very core of human identity and dignity. The stress that this teacher refers to is not overt, nor is it apparent to the unobservant eye; however, it is real to the individual suffering it, as are the compromises they may make to avoid it in the future. Therefore being a lesbian or gay educator, within an institution that denies their existence and makes it impossible for them to integrate all the aspects of their lives, does make a very real difference – to the individual lesbian or gay teacher.

Misrecognition and disrespect

This, and other research, found that despite the fact that it seems unacceptable to positively include lesbian and gay issues and identities, it is, however, evidently acceptable to denigrate them, given the reports of homophobia and harassment that this section reveals (Mac An Ghaill 1991, Trenchard and Warren 1987, Woods and Harbeck 1992). All of the teachers interviewed had encountered homophobia in their workplaces, either personally or having witnessed it in relation to someone else. In all cases homophobia was expressed in comments and jokes:

> … It [homophobia] would take the form of banter, either sexual banter or slagging, at times among themselves [male staff] … there's always an underlying insult in it. (Mary, post-primary, denominational)

A number of the teachers interviewed had experienced homophobia directly from both students and teachers within their schools.

It should be pointed out that the issue of harassment by students due to sexual orientation was felt most strongly by those teachers working in the post-primary sector; it was less of an issue for the primary teachers. However, both primary teachers interviewed felt the fear of harassment from older students in the latter stages of primary level.

The following is a report of an incident in which one teacher tells of an attempt by someone to have him removed from his position due to knowledge of his sexual orientation:

> … an anonymous letter was sent to the principal … saying was she aware of the fact that I was a gay man living with another in [name of area] and did she consider me suitable to be teaching in junior infants … … It undermined my confidence personally and professionally and also too there was the idea well who the hell knew where I lived … … I found it nasty, scary that someone disliked me, hated me, so much that they wanted me to actually lose my job. (Paul, primary, denominational)

All incidents of homophobic harassment are damaging to those they are directed at, arguably more damaging are those of a violent nature.

Participants were also aware of homophobic actions and comments directed at students, both by teachers and students alike:

> I've seen a homophobic … expression with kids who they [male teachers] thought could be gay and some of it was their own sense of being uncomfortable around these students. Or I suppose in a very unconscious way, colluding in the bullying that was happening by not making a stand for these students, by letting it happen … bullying is a huge issue … a large proportion of the bullying is based on a suspicion that boys are gay. (Mary, post-primary, denominational)

The condoning of homophobia by schools evident from this research matches that which was found to be evident in other studies (Lynch and Lodge 2002, Mac An Ghaill 1991, Trenchard and Warren 1987). It also demonstrates how much of the homophobic actions and comments were administered by male teachers and students. Both exist within institutions where overt and covert gender stereotyping is used to maintain and reproduce the dominant power relations of society in general (Mac An Ghaill 1991). Hegemonic masculinity is inherent in these power relations whereby, through an array of practices, women are subordinated. One such practice includes the placement of homosexual masculinities at the bottom of the gender hierarchy among men, as remarked by this female teacher:

> … the culture of a boys' school is very much along the lines of a single identity of manhood and the exploration of their sexualities is definitely not catered for, in fact it is discouraged because of the subtle culture that says you must be macho, you must be sporting, you must be tough … (Mary, post-primary, denominational)

Depreciated and misunderstood identities

Evidence of how devaluation and misrecognition have been internalised by some lesbian and gay teachers was revealed through the fear that some felt in their everyday interactions with students and the threat of possible accusations of improper sexual behaviour towards students:

> … one of my biggest fears as a teacher, and I think its unfair that I have to say, as a lesbian teacher … that a child will say that they are the victim of some sort of abuse from me – that's my biggest fear and I don't know how the school, the system would back me as a person if that was exposed. (Orla, post-primary, non-denominational)

> I am in situations [PE classes] which could be compromising for me, could be – they're not … … I'm almost doubly aware of it because I just think that, I can imagine the problems that parent might have … (Maeve, post-primary, denominational)

It would seem that these teachers have internalised negative perceptions of minority sexualities communicated through heterosexism. This issue of child sexual abuse is extremely delicate and one that all teachers have to be aware of; however, when probed, both participants said that their lesbian identity made them more aware. Another male teacher felt that it was more a gender issue than a gay issue and stressed his need to

> identify yourself almost unconsciously asexual, in that you don't involve yourself with anything like that because of the whole fear in terms of paedophilia, just that fear of being sexually 'out'… (Paul, primary, denominational)

As highlighted earlier, being sexually 'out' is implicit for heterosexual teachers, it is not for lesbian and gay teachers, therefore one may deduce that this is most definitely a gay issue.

Further evidence of misrecognition in terms of the association of homosexuality with paedophilia was experienced by one participant in the company of an officer from a teacher's union, when he 'jokingly' referred to the inclusion of sexual orientation in the union's equality statement; the following paraphrases this reference:

> … 'what do you think about the paedophile clause?' and I said 'what?' and he [the union officer] said, 'you know, they're protecting paedophiles now …' When questioned further on who exactly he was referring to this teacher reported him as having said '… lesbians and gays … … some of them are paedophiles'… (Sheila, post-primary, denominational)

Inherent in this statement is a direct association between homosexuality and paedophilia and subsequently the devaluation of homosexuality as a perverse form of sexuality. Such messages can lead to internalised homophobia as expressed by the teachers cited above in their fears of allegations of improper sexual behaviour.

Legal rights and discrimination

Whilst Ireland currently enjoys a position at the forefront of homosexual legal rights in Europe due to the Employment Equality Act, 1998, and Equal Status Act, 2000, protection for lesbian and gay teachers is far from strong. In simple terms, openly lesbian or gay teachers may face great difficulties in accessing jobs and promotion under the control of religious establishments. None of the teachers who participated in this research felt completely secure that their sexual orientation, if known, could not be used against them in this regard as evidenced by the following quotations:

> … all else being equal let's [interview board] take the straight person … (Ann, primary, denominational)

> … I think there would be very few schools that would take on a headmaster who isn't married … I think you know if I was going for an interview and if the board knew that I was gay that would be a hurdle to get over. (Tom, post-primary, denominational)

Being open about one's lesbian or gay sexuality is simply not an option for most teachers if they are to protect themselves from suffering negative consequences.

> I think being 'out' is a difficulty and I think that most lesbian teachers are not out in school and not because it doesn't matter but because they think it does matter and it will matter or change something, or because society is so heterosexual, the workplace is so heterosexual, this whole children/family thing is so heterosexual that it just doesn't seem to fit being lesbian or gay within all of this … (Ann, primary, denominational)

The dominance of heterosexuality that this teacher speaks about as a barrier to being out highlights the lack of recognition that lesbian and gay teachers experience. Implicit in all the interviews carried out for this research was the notion of power and the notion that being completely open about one's sexual identity meant leaving oneself powerless in a system where there is no formal support:

> … because of the Employment Equality Act [1998] you've got no protection against the principal using this [knowledge of your sexuality] against you. The principal can legally use it against you. I don't see it ever happening that you'd be fired for it, but certainly in terms of going for promotion … … they're legally within their rights to say, well no actually there's somebody else that has just come in off the street and we're going to give it to them because you don't reflect the ethos of the school. So I think the element of power that's going on, how power is being provided to someone else by telling them of your sexuality is something that would never happen for a straight person … (Paul, primary, denominational)

Within this exploration of the issues that impact on the working and personal lives of lesbian and gay teachers many key issues arose, most of which are a direct result of non-recognition of non-dominant sexual orientation identities, and the devaluation of such identities through the process of heterosexism. Although the interviews revealed some variation in the attitudes and opinions of participants, there was a great deal of shared experiences, despite the different types of schools represented, and range of teaching experience. In the absence of more extensive research regarding the experiences of lesbians and gays in an Irish education context the findings suggest that there are serious equality issues that impact upon lesbian and gay teachers regardless of their teaching situation. At the root of these inequalities is the non-recognition of lesbian and gay sexualities, which is manifested through silence. The silence effectively serves to censure any positive exposure of lesbian and gay sexualities, and condones their disparagement. The result is an enormous drain on the personal and professional resources of the teachers affected, as is evident from the deep-seated anxiety about disclosure in this study. This anxiety evidently varies from person-to-person, and context-to-context, nevertheless it displays a deep sense of social exclusion.

Conclusion

> … if there's anything we owe young people it's the truth, and I feel I'm hiding that from them, and I think that's sad. (Sheila, post-primary, denominational)

The truth that this lesbian teacher refers to is hidden by the silence and fear that surrounds sexual orientation within schools, borne out by this and other research (Griffin 1992, Lynch and Lodge 2002, Woods and Harbeck 1992). The powerful censorial nature of this silence contributes to multiple forms of oppression resulting in psychological, social, cultural and economic stress, as evidenced by the teachers involved in this work. For students identifying as, or beginning to identify, as gay or lesbian, educational disadvantage can be added to this list. The White Paper on Education (1995: 7) established the fundamental aim of education as '… to serve individual, social and economic well-being and to enhance quality of life'. It also cites pluralism and equality as educational principles derived from this fundamental aim of education. Whilst small and tentative steps are being made in some quarters,[5] the evidence from this research suggests that concerted efforts need to be made if these principles and aims are to be met in terms of the recognition and inclusion of lesbian and gay sexualities within education and, ultimately, the equal participation of those students who identify as, or who may be beginning to identify as, lesbian or gay.

An individual's identity is of fundamental importance to their development because, '… we owe our integrity … to the receipt of approval or recognition from other persons … [which is necessary for] … the positive understanding of self … ' (Honneth 1992: 188, cited in Fraser 1995: 71-2). Sexual identity is an essential part of human identity; consequently in being denied recognition lesbian and gay individuals are forced to exist in a reduced mode of being, limiting their freedom and rights as human beings. Silence and disrespect for lesbian and gay sexualities has a negative impact on educational establishments in general. Issues of cultural domination and devaluation are not exclusive to any one minority group; people with disabilities, people of colour, people from lower-socio-economic backgrounds all suffer from similar forms of oppression due to non-recognition and misrecognition (Young 1990). Consequently, schools need to recognise and respect diversity in order to redress the situation and become more inclusive of all their students and staff.

Issues of difference, whether related to sexual identity, ablement, ethnicity, class, gender, etc are issues of equality and plurality. They are also a reflection of the diversity of human life, experience and culture of which society is composed. How any one issue is dealt with, or ignored, reflects how all issues of difference are dealt with. If one is denigrated, then there is a danger

---

[5] For example the Irish National Teachers Organisation opposed Section 37(1) of the Employment Equality Act 1998; The Equality Authority has been proactive in raising the issue of lesbian, gay and bisexual teachers at a joint conference with the Association of Secondary Teachers in Ireland.

that all difference will be equally devalued, for all such issues reflect the operation of power and dominance over powerlessness and oppression. Therefore, the evidence presented in this research provides a response to those who may say that issues of sexual identity have no place in primary schools, in that identity and the recognition of one's identity are fundamental defining characteristics in human beings (Taylor 1931), and sexual identity is central to developing a full interpretation of the self (Inglis 1998). If teachers are so preoccupied with managing aspects of their identities because of fear, how can they be full human beings and therefore provide a broad and holistic education to our young people?

If there is to be any real attempt made to redress the imbalance of dominant cultures in our education system, the silence needs to be broken. The onus is not on those who exist under the blanket of silence to do this alone. Those in positions of power within institutions of education need to start being truthful about the totality of the real world, acknowledging the richness of diversity and celebrating the difference that is an inherent aspect of human nature. We not only owe the truth to our students – we owe it to ourselves and an obvious starting point is in education, however:

> ... in order to educate the kids I think we need to educate ourselves. (Maeve, post-primary, denominational)

We also need to remember that '*... the people that really need it* [education] *are the very ones that probably think they don't need it'* (Sheila, post-primary denominational).

Bibliography

Agnew, P. (2000) 'Pope voices "bitterness" at gay rights festival in Rome', *The Irish Times*, 10.7.00: 13

Collins, E., O'Carroll, I. and Prendiville, P. (1995) *Poverty, Lesbians and Gay Men: The Economic and Social Effects of Discrimination*, GLEN and NEXUS Research Cooperative, Dublin.

Connell, R. W. (1989) 'Cool Guys, Swots and Wimps: the interplay of masculinity and education', *Oxford Review of Education,* Vol 15, No 3.

Cooper, D. (1989) 'Positive Images in Haringey: A Struggle for Identity' in *Learning Our Lines: Sexuality and Social Control in Education,* C. Jones and P. Mahony (eds), London, Women's Press.

Department of Education (1995) *Charting our Education Future: White Paper on Education*, Dublin, The Stationery Office.

Epstein, D. and Johnson, R. (1994) 'On the Straight and the Narrow: The Heterosexual Presumption, Homophobias and Schools', in

Challenging Lesbian and Gay Inequalities in Education, D. Epstein (ed.), Milton Keynes, Open University Press.

Government of Ireland (1998) *Employment Equality Act,* Dublin, Stationery Office.

Government of Ireland (2000) *Equal Status Act,* Dublin, Stationery Office.

Foucault, M. (1981) *The History of Sexuality, Volume 2: the use of pleasure*, Harmondsworth, Penguin Books.

Fraser, N. (1995) 'From redistribution to recognition? Dilemmas of justice in a "post-socialist" age', *New Left Review* 212: 68-93.

Freire, P. (1972) *Pedagogy of the Oppressed*, Suffolk, The Chaucer Press.

Griffin, P. (1992) 'From Hiding Out to Coming Out: Empowering Lesbian and Gay Educators', in *Coming Out of the Classroom Closet: Gay and Lesbian Students, Teachers and Curricula*, K. M. Harbeck (ed.), New York and London, Harrington Park Press.

Harbeck, K. M. (ed.) (1992) *Coming out of the Classroom Closet: Gay and Lesbian Students, Teachers and Curricula,* Binghamton, The Haworth Press.

Inglis, T. (1998) *Lessons in Irish Sexuality*, Dublin, UCD Press.

Lynch, K. and Lodge, A. (2002) *Equality and Power in Schools: Redistribution, Recognition and Representation,* London, Routledge Falmer.

Mac an Ghaill, M. (1991) 'Schooling, Sexuality and Male Power: towards an emancipatory curriculum', *Gender and Education*, Vol 3, No 3.

McNaught, B. (1993) *Gay Issues in the Workplace*, New York, St Martin's Press.

O'Carroll, Í. and Szalacha, L. (2000) *A Queer Quandary: The Challenges of Including Sexual Difference within the Relationships and Sexuality Education Programme,* Dublin, LOT/LEA.

O'Fathaigh, D. (2003) *An examination of the experiences of Gay Teachers in Ireland*, Unpublished MEd thesis, Education Department, UCD.

Rabinow, P. (ed.) (1984) *The Foucault Reader*, New York, Pantheon Books.

Redman, P. (1994) 'Shifting Ground: Rethinking Sexuality Education', in *Challenging Lesbian and Gay Inequalities in Education,* D. Epstein (ed.), Milton Keynes, Open University Press.

Rofes, E. (1989) 'Opening Up the Classroom Closet: Responding to the Educational Needs of Gay and Lesbian Youth', *Harvard Educational Review,* Vol 59, No 4.

Scott, P. (1989) 'Challenging Heterosexism in the Curriculum: Roles for Teachers, Governors and Parents', in *Learning Our Lines: Sexuality and Social Control in Education,* Carol Jones and Pat Mahony (eds), London, The Women's Press.

Taylor, C. (1931) *Multiculturism and 'The Politics of Recognition': an essay by Charles Taylor, with commentary by Amy Gutmann (editor),* New Jersey, Princeton University Press.

Trenchard, L. and Warren, H. (1987) 'Talking about school: the experiences of young lesbians and gay men', in *Gender Under Scrutiny: New Inquiries in Education*, G. Weiner and M. Arnot (eds), Open University Press, London.

Woods, S. E. and Harbeck, K. H. (1992) 'Living in Two Worlds: The Identity Management Strategies Used by Lesbian Physical Educators', in *Coming Out of the Classroom Closet: Gay and Lesbian Students, Teachers, and Curricula*, Karen M. Harbeck (ed.), Harrington Park Press, New York and London.

Young, I. M. (1990) *Justice and the Politics of Difference*, Princeton University Press, New Jersey.

CHAPTER 4

Parents speaking of the educational experiences of their sons and daughters who have Down syndrome

Mercedes Egan

Introduction

Every year approximately one hundred Irish children with Down syndrome[1] are born. Each is an individual with unique appearance, personality and set of abilities. While they have features in common, they also closely resemble their families (Byrne et al 1988; Bérubé 1999). The extent to which a person shows the physical characteristics of the syndrome is no indication of his/her intellectual capacity.[2]

Traditionally, young people with Down syndrome received their education in institutions for those with moderate learning disabilities (Kenny et al 2003). This reflected the tendency both in Ireland and elsewhere to provide education for young people with disabilities in segregated settings (Glendenning 1999, McDonnell 2002). One legacy of this type of provision has been the perpetuation of a segregated mindset, with many teachers, learners and parents believing that those with disabilities are better catered for in

---

1 Down syndrome is a congenital condition that occurs in approximately one out of every 550 live births. In Ireland the prevalence rate is 18.3/10,000 live births (one child in every 546). Survival rate to the age of ten years is 82% (Johnson et al 1996; Hayes et al 1997).

2 Students with Down syndrome experience impairments in some, but not all, domains of learning and development (Dunst 1990). Their development can be asynchronous (Miller 1995). Specific language difficulties may impinge on other cognitive skills (Fowler 1999). Some learning difficulties they experience are caused by sensory, attentional, instructional, environmental and expectational factors and not solely by developmental delays (Combain 1994, Jobling 1994, Falvey et al 1995, Laws et al 1995, Marcell 1995, Wishart 1995, Nadel 1996, Pueschel and Sustrova 1996, Buckley et al 1996, Scheepstra et al 1999).

separate institutions. For example, where post-primary students had no contact with peers with disabilities, they were more likely to believe that special schools were safer and more appropriate places for disabled learners (Lynch and Lodge 2002). The segregated tradition has also encouraged a belief that mainstream schools are disrupted and majority non-disabled students are discommoded by inclusion.

Internationally, in recent years, the number of students with Down syndrome enrolled in mainstream education[3] has increased and a higher proportion continue in mainstream placement throughout their time in school (Scheepstra et al 1996, Cuckle 1997). For example, there has been a noticeable trend towards integration of young people with Down syndrome in mainstream schools and classes in Britain in the last thirty-five years (Cunningham et al 1998). Recent Irish research has indicated that parents of young people with Down syndrome have experienced difficulties in enrolling their children in mainstream schools, in part as a result of the fear and lack of knowledge of educators (Kenny et al 2003). Underpinning the difficulties these parents encountered was the lack of a legislative guarantee of rights that impacts on all people with disabilities in Ireland.

There is a growing body of evidence that students with Down syndrome benefit by attending mainstream schools. They develop academically and socially at least as well as those who attend special schools (Sloper et al 1990, Egan 2000). It has been argued that those young people who have attended mainstream educational institutions have made greater developmental progress than have their peers in segregated settings (Bird and Buckley 1999). Those in mainstream settings also have more social contacts which, in turn, help these learners to make greater progress in communication development (Cunningham et al 1998). It has been suggested that all young people benefit from relationships with peers who have significant learning disabilities. Given opportunity, preparation and support, students in mainstream education reported that interaction with students who have significant learning and communication difficulties was a positive experience (Shevlin and O'Moore 1999). Possibilities for such interaction by most young people continue to be limited by an education system that presumes segregated provision is best for all.

While it is primarily the student whose life-chances are affected by the education he/she receives, parents of students who have

---

3 In this paper the term mainstream education is used to mean the school the parents would most likely send their son/daughter to if he/she was not Down syndrome.

learning disabilities also have to live with the consequences of how well the system accommodates their sons/daughters. Their experience and concerns are important to any dialogue concerning the provision of education for the wider group of students who have special educational needs.

In the study reported on here, a group of Irish parents of students with Down syndrome was interviewed. The parents were asked about their experience of early support services, preschool experience, school placement decisions, in-school learning supports and aspects of student achievement, behaviour and well-being. The families were selected from the Down Syndrome Ireland database.[4] All those listed whose son/daughter was aged sixteen, twelve and eight years were selected. The sample was further refined by selecting the counties of Dublin, Meath, Kildare, Limerick, Galway, Cork and Kerry. Of the eighty-five students thus identified, parents of seventy-eight took part in the study.[5]

Individual interviews took place in the Spring of 1999 at a time and place of the parents' choice. Most chose daytime hours when only the mother was available.[6] The interview schedule included fill-in the response items, fixed alternatives, scales and open-ended questions.

Key findings

Access to preschool and early support services

This study found that initial contacts with education and health service providers affected a child's early development and also influenced future educational opportunities and decisions. However, there was little evidence that multi-disciplinary infant developmental programmes had been provided.[7] A few parents had experienced positive support. However, for most, early

---

4 No comprehensive sampling frame existed for the population. It is estimated that the Down Syndrome Ireland database identified half of all Irish students who had Down syndrome.

5 Forty students were male and thirty-eight female. Twenty were sixteen years of age; twenty-eight were twelve years of age; thirty were eight-year-olds.

6 Sixty-six interviews (85%) were conducted with the mother only; three (4%) were with the father only; nine (11%) were with both parents present.

7 In Ireland, infant and preschool services to children who have disabilities are funded by the Department of Health and Children and the Department of Education and Science. However, programmes are provided through Health Boards and non-statutory agencies. There is no legal entitlement to services. Services vary in different parts of the country and frequently are administered on an ad hoc basis. The Education Act 1998 requires the Minister for Education and Science to provide preschool services to children who have special educational needs. However, the implications of this requirement have not been articulated.

services had failed to provide adequately for the children's need for speech therapy, physiotherapy and educational support. Many of the early services programmes had not met the needs of the children and their families.

> The mother and baby group was initially helpful, but it was difficult to get there on the buses and I found that I could spend the time more valuably at home. There were other problems also. My husband had just lost his job. When I decided to stop going the social worker phoned to ask why. I told her but she was not very nice. She wanted to know if I was pretending that my son was not handicapped.

> I find these groups very difficult. You are put together with a group of mothers and sometimes the only thing you have in common is that your baby has problems. And, they keep going over the same thing. I found that his hearing was the biggest problem he had and we had to go elsewhere for specialists.

Parents commented that early services and preschool were separate entities with little or no continuity.

> They really did not prepare her as such. Really there was only health care, assessment and physiotherapy.

For many, early services had not focused on the skills the children needed and had not supported their child's move to preschool. Two-thirds of the parents believed that their son/daughter could have been better prepared.

> Whatever help we got did not relate to preschool. There was no continuous flow of services or transfer when we moved.

Nearly all the students had attended preschool, approximately half in mainstream placement. Half spent two years in preschool; more than a quarter spent three years. Longer periods in preschool provides time for the children to develop, and parents, teachers and other professionals to observe the children's abilities (Cunningham 1996).[8] This was confirmed by a mother who said:

> It ... [preschool] gave me a great opportunity to see the change in her – her potential, her development – to see the wheel go round. If I had not had that opportunity to see this, I would have abandoned her to the system, to the institution.

---

8 All those who had not attended preschool, or who spent only one year in preschool, then went on to special schools designated for pupils with moderate learning disability. Those who spent longer periods in preschool then went on to a variety of school placements.

Parents whose children attended mainstream preschools rated the experience more highly than parents whose children attended special preschools.

> There was a very good structure. There were the same rules for her as there were for the other children. If she did anything disruptive she was brought back into the activity. She was ready for a bigger situation where she could not just walk around the place and do as she liked. She was interested in taking part in the group's activity. (Parent with a child in a mainstream school)

> He actually developed bad habits through no fault of the other children who were more disabled than he was. He copied their behaviours. (Parent with a child in a special school)

Parents of children attending all types of preschools reported that necessary supports and services, particularly speech therapy, had not been available to their children during their preschool years.

> Speech therapy would have made a huge difference, as it would have increased her ability to communicate with her teachers and peers.

> I felt about his walking that I was in control. I knew that he would walk. I was confident that I could bring him on with time. I was not as sure about his speech and needed much more professional help.

Attendance at special preschool did not guarantee speech therapy. The fact that many children did not attend special preschool has implications for the allocation and delivery of professional supports. Delivery of specialist services in mainstream preschools might be of greatest benefit to the children.

Although nearly all parents reported that a psychological assessment had taken place prior to enrolment in primary school, few expressed satisfaction with the assessment experience.[9] Only one-third of the parents indicated that the psychologist's assessment had influenced initial school enrolment decisions. Only sixteen percent reported that the assessment had been *constructive*.

---

[9] The role of psychological assessment in Irish education has been poorly defined. Department of Health psychologists have usually carried out assessments for the purpose of education *placement*, but these assessments have had little effect on educational *processes*. The Education Act 1998 empowered psychologists, appointed as Department of Education inspectors, to assess the needs of students in recognised schools and to advise in relation to the educational and psychological development of the students. (Education Act 1998, Part I, Sec. 2, Part III, Sec. 13, ss. 2, ss. 4 (a), ss. 5.) In January 2000, the Minister for Education and Science announced the inauguration of the National Educational Psychological Service Agency.

> The psychologist told me of a school that might take J. It had experience of another child who had Down syndrome. The psychologist said that the staff and especially the principal were amenable and supportive. I had to make contact myself. But, I would not have known of the school otherwise.

Nearly half reported that the assessment had been *somewhat helpful.*

> They were assessing her for the services they could provide, or rather those they were providing.

Ten percent reported that the testing had been *unhelpful* and had not reflected the children's abilities.

> When a psychologist sees a child only once a year it is hard to evaluate the child.

Over one-quarter voiced other negative opinions regarding their experience. Their comments typically started with words such as: *upsetting, painful, discouraging, unfair, disappointing, puzzling,* and *a waste of time.*

Parents' choice of school placement

It was difficult for parents to decide where to educate their son/daughter who had special educational needs. Class size, individualised activities, the happiness and protection of the student, the attitude of the teachers, social inclusion, and curriculum issues were cited by parents as important considerations.

> A place that would understand him and not lose their temper with him, because he can be frustrating. I would hate it if anyone would run him down or laugh at him. I would hope they would find something that he was interested in and that he could do.

> A school where he would have the support of the full staff, especially the headmaster. If the headmaster is fully supportive, the rest of the staff come along. A place where he would not be left sitting. A place where he would be progressing at his own pace.

> I want W in school for learning. We don't want minding for him. We can mind him ourselves. What we want from the school for W is education. Otherwise we are all just wasting our time and his.

Some parents were influenced by the existence of a special system. They believed that it was designed to meet the specific educational needs of their son/daughter.

> I felt that there would not be enough resources at the local school to meet his needs. The special school would be familiar with his needs, the teachers there would have special training.

Others felt that, because the special system existed, they were expected to take part in it and were not given alternative choices. For some, there was concern that if they removed themselves from the special system, they would not be welcomed back. There was a perception that special school enrolment was a prerequisite for adult services.

> The agency will continue to provide services, training and employment which makes me feel more secure about his future.

> ... once you are in with an agency they look after you if and when the need arises. We are thinking about this a lot, as his father has not been well lately, he has heart trouble.

Some parents, who would have preferred to have their son/daughter educated in their community, believed the ordinary education system was unprepared, under-resourced, or unwilling to include them. They believed that they could not change the system.

> In my heart I wanted to send him to the local school. I needed help. I felt there was no support for me when I came to make the decision. The other parents seemed to be fiercely sure that they had made the right decision – whatever they had chosen. I did not want to take him from his ... [special preschool friends] and put him in a national school where he might be the subject of ridicule. I could not be sure that he would get the speech therapy he needed if he were to go to the national school. I did not want to send him to mainstream and then have to go back within a few months and say that I had made a mistake, an error of judgement, so, begrudgingly, I left him where he was.

Others felt that segregation was inherently wrong and that specialist provision could not compensate for the inevitable social isolation.

> I feel that it is not natural and very negative to send a child to a special school to educate her with only other children who are disabled. It deprives them of their right to grow up in a normal environment. How does any child learn? They learn from what they see around them. If any of my other children had been sent to a special school, I wonder how they would have come out. If she went to a special school she would be on a bus for at least three hours per day. She would have no time or energy left for family or community life.

In the pursuit of this objective, some parents met serious obstacles, others found willing support from principals, teachers and psychologists. The concept of parental choice is often spoken of as the determining factor in school placement decisions. Until recently, there was often little if any real choice. Necessary supports and services were unavailable except in specialised situations. However, the recent policy of *automatic entitlement* to specialist teaching and childcare in mainstream primary schools may lead to more realistic options for parents.[10]

School placement

For each successive age-group there was a trend away from placement in special schools designated for pupils with moderate learning disability. Students living in Dublin had a wider range of school placement than did those living elsewhere. Those who had attended mainstream preschool, who had received adequate speech therapy, the support of a preschool home teacher and whose parents rated their preschool experience more highly were more likely to enrol in mainstream primary schools.

At the time of interview, of the seventy-eight students, forty-five (58%) attended special schools/classes designated for pupils with moderate learning disability; eight (10%) were in special schools/classes designated for pupils with mild learning disability; twenty-one (27%) were in mainstream schools. Four (5%) were not enrolled in a school programme.[11]

A larger proportion of boys than girls were enrolled in special placements designated for pupils with moderate learning disability.[12] Children from larger families, those in the middle of family constellations, and whose parents had less participation in education themselves, were more likely to attend special schools designated for pupils with moderate learning disability. Most students (88%) continued their education in the initial type of placement. Some transfers occurred. With one exception, all transfers were towards *more restrictive* learning environments. The following are typical reasons parents gave as to why changes had been made.

A parent whose daughter transferred from a special school designated for students with mild learning disabilities to one designated for students with moderate learning disabilities reported that in the first school:

> … many of the students had multiple problems and made it very difficult for the students to get enough help. There was a serious incident of bullying which left A terrified. We decided that it would

---

10 Press Release, Minister for Education and Science, Micheál Martin TD, November 5, 1998. Department of Education and Science Circular Letters: 08/99, 07/02 and 08/02.

11 Two of these four were in Care Units under the Department of Health.

12 Sixty-three percent of the boys and forty-three percent of the girls initially enrolled in this type of school/class.

> be better to send her to a school nearer home that might not be as positive academically but it would be more gentle.

Another student's enrolment in mainstream primary lasted three months. His mother analysed the problems he encountered.

> M first went to a regular primary school for three months. They could not cope with him and he could not cope with them. There were twenty-seven in the junior infant class and the school did not have any experience. He did not feel happy and secure. They need to have the resources there from the beginning. A teacher's aide is necessary from the first day – all day. Especially if the school is just starting off (including students with disabilities). Maybe later they won't need as much help when everything settles, but they certainly do at the beginning or it doesn't work.

Only one girl transferred from a special school to her local primary school. Her mother's reason for the transfer was straightforward.

> I wanted her to be with students who were talking. I thought it would help her speech.

In-school learning support

As might be expected, there was a marked difference in reported class size between special and mainstream schools. This difference should be considered in conjunction with the reported number of classroom assistants. There were assistants in over three-quarters (78%) of special education classrooms but in less than half (43%) of mainstream classrooms.

In mainstream primary schools, specialist teacher support was from a resource/visiting teacher and/or a remedial teacher. The mean amount of specialist teacher support was three hours per week. The amount of specialised teaching ranged from twelve hours to just seven minutes per week. It would appear that support had been allocated on the basis of ad hoc decisions rather than being based on entitlements or policies. Nearly all support teachers worked with the students outside the classroom. Only half of the parents believed that specialist teaching was co-ordinated with the class programme. Ineffective co-ordination between specialist and classroom teachers may have the effect of reducing teacher confidence in her/his ability to teach the individual student, and decreasing teacher perception that the student is in a suitable placement (Ward and Center 1990). Lack of co-ordination may also fragment the student's curriculum.

Inadequate speech therapy again concerned parents of students in all types of school. Less than one-quarter of the students had received what their parents believed to be adequate. Attending a special school did not guarantee speech therapy. All students who attended mainstream school had received at least *some* therapy. One-eighth of students in special education had not received *any* speech therapy. There was limited use of computers by all students. Less than thirty percent of the students used computers on a daily basis. Most students in mainstream schools (76%) were reported to use computers at least once a week; this compared with less than two-fifths (39%) of those in special education.

The supports and services most frequently identified by parents to be deficient were: classroom assistance for students in mainstream schools; speech therapy for students in special schools designated for pupils with moderate learning disability; and computer instruction for students in all types of school.

When assessing the suitability of a school placement, the focus is frequently on the student's academic performance and social behaviour. However, school policy, practice and resources influence the extent to which a student becomes a member of the school community and the degree to which his/her learning needs are accommodated (Martin 1997).

Parents reported that the majority of students were 'delighted to go to school'; a minority were 'agreeable to go'; and a few had negative feelings about going to school. The students reported to have negative feelings all attended special schools designated for pupils with moderate learning disability. One student hated going to school. He had attended a mainstream primary school for three years and then transferred to a special school.

> He only hates going to school since he started at … [special school]. He used to love going. I think that even with all the sports and activities he is bored. He also finds it difficult to be only with other children with handicaps. He will say, 'I don't want to go, I hate it'.

While these students may have been more affected than others, the length of time spent on school transport was a negative feature of the school experience of the majority of students in special educational placement.

Distance and travel-time

The distance from home to school ranged from less than a mile to thirty-five miles. Time spent travelling to and from schools was a negative factor for many students in special education. The mean daily travel-time for students in special schools/classes designated for pupils with moderate learning disability was ninety-six minutes; for students in special schools/classes designated for pupils with mild learning disability it was sixty-seven minutes; for students in mainstream primary and post-primary schools it was twenty minutes per day.

> I do not really know why. It may be because he is on the bus too long – one hour each way. Or, perhaps it is because they change teachers so often.

The distance from the home to school also influenced the quality of communication between school and family. Only one-third of the parents of students who attended special schools/classes of any designation reported that communication between themselves and the school was 'very good', compared with nearly two-thirds of those who attended mainstream schools.

Bullying and student behaviour

Approximately one-quarter of the parents made reference to conditions or incidents that indicated bullying had occurred. The majority of these referred to special schools/classes designated for pupils with moderate learning disability. Parents' concerns were mostly centred on the student's vulnerability.

> They [the school] don't like bullying, but I doubt that it is totally effective. T doesn't speak so I don't know.

> I think they try their best, but some of the older ones have bad behaviour and can be very rough.

Other concerns involved situations on school transport.

> There is only the driver on the bus and no escort. There are big lads and small babies all there together and sometimes it gets very rough. There should be someone on the bus to supervise.

> Now it is OK, for a while there was a problem with one lad, more on the bus than in school. She would sometimes come home with bruises. The bus driver moved her to just behind him. Now the problem is solved, I take her to school in the mornings.

While it was physical bullying that was most frequently experienced by students attending special schools designated for pupils with moderate learning disability, more verbal bullying was experienced by half of the students who attended special schools/classes designated for pupils with mild learning disability.

> … they do their best, but I know from what she says that the 'normal-looking' ones sometimes call her a 'mentaler'.

> He can be blamed for things he hasn't done – left holding the baby. He is not really able to defend himself. He doesn't see it coming.

Only two parents of students in mainstream schools made reference to incidents of bullying behaviour.

> This year for the first time M has said that one of the young fellows was laughing at him, but this is definitely the exception.

> He did come up against one or two incidents, but they were handled very well.

There was evidence that some schools of all categories were taking positive action to prevent bullying. However, fewer than half the parents of students attending special schools/classes of any designation were aware of a school policy on bullying, compared with nearly all of the parents of students in mainstream schools.

Because student behaviour is an aspect of social interaction that affects learning opportunities, behaviour that was considered to be difficult, the conditions under which the behaviour occurred, and responses to problem behaviour, were considered.

Most of the students did not have problem behaviour either at home or in school. Very few of the problems reported were major or continuous. Some had occurred when the student was younger. Several related to language difficulties and resultant frustration. Some in-school problem behaviour could have been prevented or ameliorated with additional support. Other difficulties, as noted above, were precipitated by unsatisfactory school transport arrangements.

Accommodation of students' educational and social needs

Parents were asked to assess how well the school their son/daughter attended accommodated his/her particular academic and social needs and abilities. Eight criteria were identified as indicators of student accommodation. They were: provides a broad and balanced curriculum; provides a safe and caring learning environment; provides individualised learning goals; holds high, but realistic, expectations for the student; includes him/her in a variety of school activities; encourages friendships with his/her peers; provides him/her with role models of acceptable behaviour; encourages his/her individual interests and talents.[13]

---

[13] Parents were asked to rate the degree to which the present schools provided for their sons/daughters in those eight areas. The five options were: *very well, well, adequately, poorly, very poorly*. These were assigned scores from *very well* =5 to *very poorly* =1. The sum of the items was calculated giving a *student accommodation score*. The lowest possible score was eight, the highest possible score was forty. The reliability score (*Alpha*) between the eight items on the scale was .8468.

As a group, the parents rated the schools highly. Parents were most satisfied that their children were in safe and caring environments. Parents whose children were in special schools or classes designated for those with moderate learning disability only expressed the highest level of satisfaction on this item. Parents were least satisfied with the extent to which the schools were providing their children with individualised learning goals. Parents regarded mainstream schools as being most effective in providing role models of acceptable behaviour and in encouraging friendships.

Special schools/classes designated for pupils with mild learning disability were most positively regarded by parents in academic terms. This was the case with regard to four of the survey items – curricular provision; expectations of learners; the provision of individualised learning goals; their encouragement of individual interests and talents.

Academic attainment

The importance of academic skills for students with Down syndrome or other significant learning disability has been the subject of considerable debate. Given the value placed on academic skills and attainment by society, and the evidence that many people with Down syndrome can attain useful levels of literacy and numeracy, arguments against providing the students with adequate opportunities to learn and use these skills cannot be sustained. This is not to give exclusive privilege to such learning, but rather to argue that no student should be precluded from participating in it.

All students with Down syndrome experience difficulties in some areas of learning; some have problems in all areas; however, their ability to learn and build on acquired knowledge has frequently been underestimated. Students with Down syndrome are now attaining higher levels of academic accomplishment than previous generations of students with this disability (Nadel 1992). The study reported here and earlier studies have all found a considerable range in the academic attainments of students with Down syndrome (Cunningham et al 1998). The wide range of observed differences between young people with Down syndrome cannot be adequately accounted for. It has been suggested, however, that learning increases one's capacity to learn (Freeman and Hoddap 2000).

An *Academic Attainment Index* was used to record parent-reported student achievement in reading, number skills and writing (Sloper et al 1990).[14] The findings of the present study were

[14] Neither psychological assessments nor school records were available for comparison.

compared with two other studies that have used the *Academic Attainment Index* (Nye et al 1995, Sloper et al 1990). There was similarity of scores, and patterns of scores, between the three studies. For the study group, mean scores increased significantly with age of student. Although girls obtained higher scores in all three areas than boys, the difference was not statistically significant for any of the three age groups, nor for the study group as a whole.[15]

Analysis of *Academic Attainment Index* scores by number of siblings, order of birth, parent level of education, parent employment status, and health of the student were all found to be not significant. There were, however, significant differences by type of school attended. Students in mainstream schools had the highest mean academic attainment scores.

These differences in reported attainments may have arisen from differences in student abilities, parental perceptions, and/or have resulted from differences in school experience. However, this study did not find a systematic process of assessment prior to or during school. While more able children, who had more positive preschool support, were more likely to be enrolled in mainstream school, there was overlap of student abilities in the various school placements.

Student social involvement

Two measures of student social involvement were explored: the number of activities students participated in, and the frequency that friends came to their home and they went to friends' homes. The students were involved in Special Olympics, team sports, individual athletic activities, drama, dance, art, music, scouting and church activities. The number of activities ranged from zero to five. Individual sporting activities were most frequent. Students who attended special schools designated for pupils with moderate learning disability had the highest mean number of sporting activities. There was low participation in art activities, scouting and church activities such as youth groups or choirs.

The number of contacts with friends reported should be seen as a measure of opportunity for companionship rather than of capacity for friendship. Students who attended mainstream schools had more contact both with friends in their own homes, and in friends' homes than did students who attended other types of school. Distance from home to school was at least part of the explanation for this finding. Parents of students attending special

---

[15] This is in contrast with Sloper et al (1990) who found significant differences by sex of student.

schools for students with moderate learning disabilities reported that:

> He misses out on friends. His school friends live too far away and there is no opportunity to get to know the local children.
>
> I would like her to be in a school in her own area so that she would have contact with the girls in the neighbourhood and they would know her for who she is. She does not have an opportunity to get to know them either.

This can be contrasted to the experience of some of the students who attended mainstream schools.

> He is in his own community. He knows all the children and is great friends with them and can communicate with them.
>
> It is local, she is included. Her friends on the road go to the school. She is known and liked.

This is not to minimise the concerns expressed by some parents of students in mainstream schools regarding friendships. As one mother explained:

> Whenever there is a difference, there may be a difficulty in having a close friend. They are very nice to her, and she has friends to do things with, but she does not have a 'soul mate'.

For the entire study group, contact at home with friends was infrequent. A mother of a young boy expressed her feelings about the lack of friendship opportunities for her son – a sense of longing that was shared by other parents.

> I feel that this is an awful miss in his life. His friend C lives fifteen miles away. It is very sad that no one ever comes through the door for him.

Implications for educational policy

The findings of this study have many implications for educational policy. Five might be prioritised.

- Flexible arrangements for providing adequate and continuous support from early childhood, through preschool and into primary school need to be established and consistently implemented.
- Distance and time spent travelling to special schools need to be examined. Interventions to increase age-peer contact for students in special education should be designed and implemented.

- When a student is enrolled in a mainstream school, adequate support personnel should be available *from time of enrolment*. The student's additional needs should be taken into account for staffing purposes.
- Curriculum initiatives and material resources are needed for students in *both* mainstream and special schools.
- School-based research, in both special and mainstream schools, is necessary, particularly with regard to students' academic and social development, the allocation of resources, and the supports required.

Conclusion

The educational experience reported in this study, for a group of Irish students with Down syndrome, gives positive evidence of advances in aspects of their education. However, some students' needs were not being met. Detailed analysis of student experience is important to ensure that the school experience offered goes towards meeting their educational and social needs, not adding to them.

The provision of education for students who have learning disabilities has evolved and will continue to change. The general principles, which underlie special education, remain valid. However, the extent to which the educational needs of students who have disabilities can be adequately met in separate, special locations needs to be examined further. If a young person is to be removed from his/her community, there must be good reason for so doing.

This study found little evidence that attending special school was more beneficial than attending mainstream school. In keeping with the findings of other studies, there was evidence that students in mainstream settings had higher academic attainment levels and that their parents evaluated their experience more positively (Freeman et al 1999, Cunningham et al 1998). Moreover, the presence or absence of typically developing peers in the learning environment may have a major influence on student development. Students' perceptions of themselves, and their position in the community, are not acquired solely from interaction with the teacher or learning tasks. Other people, particularly the students' age-peers, are an inextricable part of the learning experience.

Bibliography

Bérubé, M. (1999) 'Family values,' in Hassold T. and Patterson D. (eds) *Down Syndrome: A Promising Future, Together*, New York, Wiley-Liss, pp 239-244.

Bird, G. and Buckley, S. (1999) 'Meeting the educational needs of pupils with Down syndrome in mainstream secondary schools', *Down Syndrome News and Update*, Vol 1, No 4, pp 159-174.

Buckley, S., Bird, G. and Byrne A. (1996) 'The practical and theoretical significance of teaching literacy skills to children with Down's syndrome', in Rondal, J., Perrera, J., Nadel, L. and Comblain, A. (eds) *Down's Syndrome Psychological, Psychobiological and Socio-Educational Perspectives*, London, Whurr Publishers, pp 119-128.

Byrne, E., Cunningham, C. and Sloper, P. (1988) *Families and their Children with Down's Syndrome: One feature in Common*, Routledge, London.

Combain, A. (1994) 'Working memory in Down's syndrome: training the rehearsal strategy', *Down's Syndrome Research and Practice*, Vol 2, No 3, pp 123-126.

Cuckle, P. (1997) School Placement of pupils with Down's syndrome in England and Wales, *British Journal of Special Education*, Vol 24, No 4, pp 175-179.

Cunningham, C. (1996) *Understanding Down Syndrome: An Introduction for Parents* (3rd ed.), Cambridge, Mass, Brookline Books.

Cunningham, C., Glenn, S., Lorenz, S., Cuckle, P. and Shepperdson, B. (1998) 'Trends and outcomes in educational placements for children with Down syndrome', *European Journal of Special Needs Education*, Vol 13, No 3, pp 225-237.

Department of Education and Science (1993) *Guidelines on Countering Bullying Behaviour in Primary and Post-primary schools.*

Dunst, C. (1990) 'Sensorimotor development in infants with Down Syndrome', in Cicchetti, D. and Beeghly, M. (eds) *Children with Down Syndrome: A developmental perspective*, Cambridge, Cambridge University Press, pp 180-230.

Egan, M (2000) *Students Who Have Down Syndrome: A study of their school placement, educational supports and parental evaluation of their education*, Unpublished PhD thesis, NUI Maynooth.

Egan, M (1995) *Getting to Know You: An Introduction to some Irish Children and Adults with Down Syndrome and their Families,* Dublin, DSAI.

Falvey, M. and Rosenberg, R. (1995) 'Developing and fostering friendships', in Falvey M. (ed.) *Inclusive and Heterogeneous Schooling: Assessment, Curriculum, and Instruction*, Baltimore, Paul H. Brookes, pp 267-283.

Fowler, A. (1999) 'The challenge of linguistic mastery in Down Syndrome', in Hassold, T. and Patterson, D. (eds) *Down*

Syndrome: A Promising Future, Together, New York, Wiley-Liss, pp 165-182.

Freeman, S. and Hoddap, R. (2000) 'Educating children with Down Syndrome: linking behavioral characteristics to promising intervention strategies', *Down Syndrome Quarterly*, Vol 20, No 3, pp 143-151.

Glendenning, D. (1999) *Education and the Law,* Dublin, Butterworths.

Government of Ireland (1998) *Education Act,* Dublin, Stationery Office.

Hayes, C., Johnson, Z., Thronton, L., Fogarty, J., Lyons, R., O'Connor, M., Delany, V. and Buckley, K. (1997) 'Ten-year survival of Down Syndrome births', *International Journal of Epidemiology*, Vol 26, No 4, pp 822-829.

Jobling, A. (1994) Physical education for the person with Down syndrome: more than playing games? *Down's Syndrome Research and Practice*, Vol 1, No 2, pp 31-35.

Johnson, Z., Lillis, D., Delany, V., Hayes, C. and Dack. P. (1996) 'The epidemiology of Down Syndrome in four counties in Ireland 1981-1990', *Journal of Public Health Medicine*, Vol 18, No 1, pp 78-86.

Kenny, M., McNeela, E., Noonan Walsh, P. and Shevlin, M. (2003) *In the Morning – the Dark Opens,* Dublin, The National Institute for the Study of Learning Difficulties, Trinity College, Dublin.

Laws, G., Buckley, S., Bird, G., Mac Donald, J. and Broadley, I. (1995) The influence of reading instruction on language and memory development in children with Down's Syndrome, *Down's Syndrome Research and Practice*, Vol 3, No 2, pp 59-64.

Lynch, K. and Lodge, A. (2002) *Equality and Power in Schools*. London, Routledge Falmer.

Marcell, M. (1995) 'Relationships between hearing and auditory cognition in Down's syndrome', *Down Syndrome Research and Practice*, Vol 3, No 3, pp 75-92.

Martin, M. (1997) *Discipline in Schools*, Report to the Minister for Education, Niamh Bhreathnach, TD.

McDonnell, P. (2002) 'Regulating Problem People: Discourses in Disability', Public Lecture, Equality Studies Centre, UCD, Dublin, February 7.

Miller, J. (1995) 'Individual difference in vocabulary acquisition in children with Down Syndrome', *Progress in Clinical Biological Research*, Vol 393, pp 93-103.

Nadel L. (1996) 'Learning, memory and neural function', in Rondal, J., Perrera, J., Nadel, L. and Comblain, A. (eds) *Down Syndrome Psychological, Psychobiological and Socio-Educational*

Perspectives, London, Whurr Publishers, pp 21-42.

Nadel, L. (1992) 'Learning and Cognition in Down Syndrome', in Lott, I. and McCoy, E. (eds) *Down Syndrome: Advances in Medical Care*, New York, Wiley-Liss, pp 37-39.

Nye, J., Clibbens, J. and Bird, G. (1995) 'Numerical ability, general ability and language in children with Down's Syndrome', *Down's Syndrome Research and Practice*, Vol 3, No 3, pp 92-102.

Pueschel S. and Sustrova, M. (1996) 'Visual and auditory perception in children with Down Syndrome', in Rondal, J., Perrera, J., Nadel, L. and Comblain, A. (eds) *Down Syndrome Psychological, Psychobiological and Socio-Educational Perspectives,* London, Whurr Publishers, pp 53-63.

Scheepstra, A., Nakken, H. and Pijl, S. (1999) 'Contact with classmates: the social position of pupils with Down's syndrome in Dutch mainstream education', *European Journal of Special Needs Education*, Vol 14, No 3, pp 212-220.

Scheepstra, A., Pijl, S. and Nakken, H. (1996) '"Knocking on the school door": pupils in the Netherlands with Down's syndrome enter regular education', *British Journal of Special Education,* Vol 23, No 3, pp 134-138.

Shevlin, M. and O'Moore A. (1999) 'Fostering positive attitudes towards people with the severest disabilities', *Irish Educational Studies*, Vol 18, Spring 1999, pp 165-179.

Sloper, P., Cunningham, C., Turner, S. and Knussen, C. (1990) 'Factors related to the academic attainments of children with Down's Syndrome', *British Journal of Educational Psychology,* Vol 60, pp 284-298.

Ward, J. and Center, Y. (1990) 'The integration of children with intellectual disabilities into regular schools: results from a naturalistic study', in Fraser W. (ed.) *Key Issues in Mental Retardation: Proceedings of the 8th Congress IASSMD*, London, Routledge, pp 354-365.

Wishart, J. (1995) 'Cognitive abilities in children with Down Syndrome: developmental instability and motivational deficits', in Epstein, C. (ed.) *Etiology and Pathologenesis of Down Syndrome: Proceedings of the International Down Syndrome Research Conference*, New York, Wiley-Liss, pp 57-91.

CHAPTER 5

A partnership of care: an evaluation of a Department of Education and Science initiative to combat early school leaving – the 8 to 15 Early School Leaver Initiative

Clare Ryan

Introduction

This chapter presents key findings from a qualitative evaluation of site-specific practice in three distinct areas of the 8 to 15 Early School Leaver Initiative (ESLI). The study analysed, from the perspective of the author, who was also the National Coordinator of the initiative, the development of ESLI by examining in detail three particular ESLI projects representing the geographical urban, rural and town spread. The chapter focuses on two essential issues that permeated the study, namely the urgency for collaboration in responding to the needs of pupils and families 'at risk' and the simultaneous urgency for school change particularly within the remit of individual care.

The initiative

Established as a pilot scheme in 1998, ESLI was premised on the core principles of collaboration, spanning primary and post-primary schools and relevant voluntary and statutory bodies. It emerged as a district-based response to early school leaving and was established in the context of government policy to tackle social exclusion, targeting pupils identified as at risk of leaving mainstream education before certification and also those pupils who may already have dropped out of formal education with a view to supporting their return.

In May 1998, invitations to submit proposals were extended to designated schools serving areas of disadvantage and schools in areas appointed under the Operational Programme on Local Urban and Rural Development. Significantly, applications for funding would be considered from consortia of primary and post-primary schools working in collaboration and with relevant voluntary and statutory bodies and appropriate community interests. A cohort of young people was to be identified, using locally agreed criteria, and a specific programme of activities, involving in-school and out-of-school provision, was to be designed to support their retention in or return to mainstream education or appropriate training. Seventeen projects, representing rural, town and urban consortia were selected from 117 proposals, for participation in the two-year programme, and they commenced in September 1998.

The project from the outset therefore was designed in such a way as to extend the school day through a redefinition of education, recognising that learning itself emanated from and extended into a range of milieux. The coalition of formal and non-formal provision was actively encouraged, particularly in the out-of-school environment, which gradually began to percolate into the formal arena. This was assisted from the outset through the employment of personnel from diverse backgrounds such as youth and community development, childcare, psychology and social care.

The district-based approach espoused is critical in that the initiative was very much designed as an organic process, supporting Burkan's philosophy that 'organisational change must be led top-down but must be engineered bottom-up' (Burkan 1996:190). Fullan similarly argues that top-down only structural change does not work but that 'Systems change when enough kindred spirits coalesce in the same change direction' (Fullan 1993: 143). This way of working is clearly aligned with the concept of partnership and empowerment and in essence seeks to legitimise the contributions of the local community and in particular the family, in relation to pupil learning. In Freirean terms, promoting empowerment through '... striving so that those hands – whether of individuals or entire peoples – needed to be extended less and less in supplication ... they become hands which work and, by working, transform the world' (Freire 1972: 21-22).

The inception of the Early School Leaving Initiative

Early school leaving and educational disadvantage are incontrovertibly bound. Kelleghan et al (1995) detail instances in the environment, home and school, which contribute to disadvantage such as how time and space are organised and used in the home, the relationship between parents and children, exposure to acute stresses, low expectations of teachers for children coming from poor socio-economic backgrounds, grouping practices and an inability to integrate the home and school experience. The problems inherent in disadvantage translate into difficulties adjusting to school, repeatedly resulting in poor educational experience and performance. 'Signs of difficulty are usually in evidence from an early age and, as children progress through the system, the achievement gap between students from advantaged and disadvantaged backgrounds tends to widen' (Kellaghan, Weir, Ó hUallacháin and Morgan 1995:30). The extreme consequence is leaving the system prior to certification.

Poverty has been consistently linked with poor educational achievement and prospects. Schorr (1998) cites poverty as being the most potent risk factor of all. Kellaghan et al (1995) similarly contend that poverty restricts and limits educational participation for that population who are socially and economically marginalised. The multiplicative effects of disadvantage demonstrate that where poverty persists it will combine with other factors resulting in detrimental long-lasting outcomes for the child.

The relationship between social background and educational achievement is the focus of a significant body of international research. A wealth of research documents the poor child's progress in the school system compared to that of his more privileged peers. Under-performance, poor educational qualifications, early school leaving, under-representation at third level and poor marketability in terms of employment and careers are predictably synonymous with poverty. It is universally recognised that the most marginalised group features those who have left school with limited or no qualifications.

In Ireland, the late 90s witnessed increased resolve to curb educational disadvantage and early school leaving. Department of Education and Science commitment to increasing retention at second level as well as a more global deepening awareness of social exclusion expedited increased attention to disadvantage. Simultaneously, the growing recognition of the multi-dimensional nature of educational disadvantage prompted the exigency to employ innovative and creative means incorporating a collaborative response. Thus, the 8 to 15 Early School Leaver Initiative was launched.

The research

For the purposes of the evaluation, from the seventeen ESLI sites, three were independently selected for analysis. The core objective was to attempt to evaluate specific practice in these three sites (Urban, Rural and Town) operating under the aegis of a national scheme. It described the goals that were set in each site and then evaluated these in terms of the outcomes at site level and in relation to the objectives at national level. In particular, the study sought to establish in each of the sites, the impact of the scheme on pupil retention and participation.

A second strand of the study examined specific elements of the 8 to 15 ESLI at national level, namely parental and family involvement and the employment of non-formal methodologies, and examined how these were addressed in the individual sites. It sought to establish what level of parental involvement existed in each site and to what extent it was being developed. Simultaneously, the non-formal methodologies employed in each site were analysed and attempts were made to ascertain their impact on pupil retention and participation.

Methodologies

In examining the 8 to 15 Early School Leaver Initiative, it was vital to employ the correct combination of methodologies to reflect the diversity of the three sites whilst simultaneously providing a valid and reliable reflection of the overall initiative. The research concentrated on the embryonic period and represents only the beginning of an evaluation process. The astute reader will also be acutely aware of the dangers associated with the author's close involvement with the initiative. The series of steps taken to ensure objectivity are documented throughout the dissertation (Ryan 2001) and were strictly adhered to during the research period. There were also inherent benefits of the National Co-ordinator assuming the role of evaluator, a position much espoused in emancipatory research. These included allowing the reader to become privy to an 'insider view' of the scheme from its inception, and facilitated access to Department of Education and Science philosophy and thinking as the initiative evolved. Having been present from the initial stages she was in a pivotal position to provide information otherwise inaccessible. The author's position ordained that she had direct access to written quarterly progress reports from each of the seventeen sites and was thus able to assess the practice of the three sites within the national framework. Confidentiality and protocol were meticulously observed and the privilege of position, which permitted access to these data, was not abused.

To substantiate and humanise the wealth of information, the opinions and perceptions of the stakeholders were essential. In total, thirty-two interviews were conducted and featured 113 participants. Interviews were structured in order to gain reasonably comparable data. Figure 1 presents a breakdown of the participants.

Figure 1: Categories of Interviewees

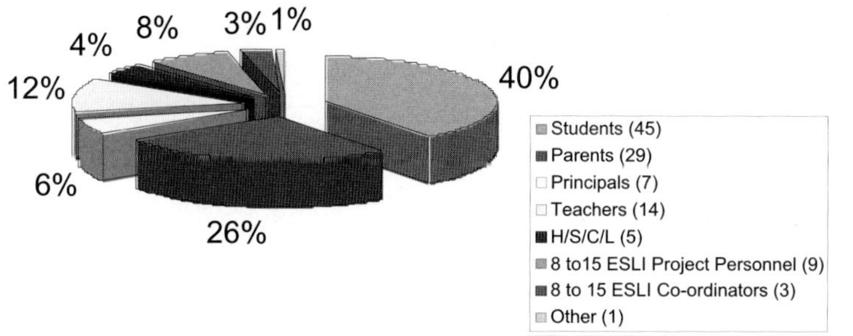

The breadth and variety of perspectives drawn from the interviews forms a substantial body of material and enables the emergence of a comprehensive picture of the initiative as it presented in each site. The primary stakeholders were significantly represented and served to provide a broad and balanced range of opinions, views and attitudes relating to pertinent issues. The spectrum further authenticates the research process. The interviews were in turn correlated by additional methodologies and procedures including participant and non-participant observation, a reflective journal maintained by the author since the inception of the initiative, the gathering of extensive documentation and memoranda relating to the initiative, photographic, video and auditory evidence of practice from each site, attendance and participation at consortium meetings as well as regular structured visits to sites and to the participating schools

At the very core of the study was the voice of the client – the child – and this is encapsulated in the broad spectrum of analyses. Significantly, the interviews provided the opportunity of exploring in depth the opinions, thoughts, hopes, fears, expectations, values and experiences of a substantial range of stakeholders. They clearly and audibly confirm the need for a changed way of working. Their personal stories form the core of this contribution and allow us to listen to and hear the perspective of the key stakeholders, which regrettably is so often excluded from analyses of early school leaving. It is important to remember that ESLI, being a targeted initiative, allows us to hear the voices of the most marginalised children and their families. These voices rarely, if ever, are represented on Boards of Management, Parents' Committees or Student Councils and for this reason alone the message is all the more powerful.

The practice

ESLI is primarily about a changed way of working. This implies a changed perception of those who reject formal education and change in how we respond to them. One avenue of change is that of school improvement. The other relates to the improvement of the broader social and economic context of the child through effective multi-agency practice. Conventional analysis of early school leaving tended to centre on the young person as the victim of circumstances, where outside influences such as family and socio-economic background were unquestionably accepted as the chief reasons for failure and dropout. Such analysis was often accompanied by a sense of fatalism and low expectation. Wehlage et al (1989) contend that the child who leaves school is actually rejecting a system he perceives to lack validity. They argue that those pupils whose experience of formal education culminates in physical rejection, entered the system with hopes and aspirations to complete schooling just like the majority of children. 'Generally, there is evidence that even those students who drop out of high school initially enrolled believing in the legitimacy and efficacy of education and expecting to graduate' (Wehlage, Rutter, Smith, Lesko and Fernandez: 1989: 118).

Interestingly, the initial aspiration to complete school was corroborated by each of the 113 interviewees in the research. All of the parents and children interviewed spoke animatedly of their respective dreams and aspirations. Parents invariably wished their children to remain in and complete school, even if they themselves had left school early. One Traveller mother spoke of her aspirations for her three children who were targeted, saying that if they completed their Leaving Certificate 'that would be my reward'.

Each of the children interviewed was acutely aware that staying in school constituted currency for the future. Their responses in the three sites as to why they believed young people should stay until Leaving Certificate included 'to get an education', 'to get a good job', 'to go to university', 'to have a better life'. Three Traveller children incorporated 'learning to read and write', 'Communion' and 'Confirmation' as reasons for going to school. A fifth-class pupil responded that staying in school keeps you out of trouble: 'it's like to stay in school, not to be out there sleeping. Going out to learn, not just sitting in your house and all or using drugs'. The practicality of staying in the system, however presented multiple obstacles.

The younger children interviewed in particular were passionate in terms of their future ambitions. Future careers included 'a solicitor', 'a footballer', 'an air hostess', 'a boxer', 'a doctor', 'a dancer or a singer' and 'a rugby player'. As the children progressed in age, the initial dreams gradually dissipated and tended towards the bland and practical. Many of the older children interviewed had no particular career in mind. Of those that had, these tended to be aligned with their favourite subjects in school. Hence, 'bricklayer', 'carpenter' and 'mechanic' featured prominently amongst the responses of second-level pupils.

Innovation as a response

A criticism of school improvement research through the years has been that it leans towards exaggerating the extent to which individual schools can instigate positive lasting change in the midst of chronic disadvantage. Whilst acknowledging the realities of a society that maintains successfully its social divisions and hierarchies, this study proposed that individual schools engaged in collaborative work *can* redress much of the balance. Also highlighted are the manifold ways in which individual teachers can themselves become agents of change and in doing so actualise their initial motivation for entering the teaching profession, '... to make a difference' (Fullan and Hargreaves 1992). In each of the three sites studied, teachers, principals, home school community liaison co-ordinators and project personnel were pivotal in the targeting, support and maintenance of 'at risk' children and their families. The courage of the schools in these areas to collaborate with outside personnel, particularly with non-teachers, allowed innovative practice to take place. The willingness to expand the definition and location of education bore testament to their commitment to alleviating educational disadvantage. In one of the interviews, with a group of primary teachers, a clear message as to the value of ESLI was collectively enunciated.

> It's hugely valuable I would say. I mean the children in the 8-15, they are the most marginalised in the school. I mean we could have the 8-15 for every single pupil in the school for one reason or another. But the pupils we have highlighted, we have highlighted them because they are out there on the edge and they are the kids who just won't respond to the simple curriculum as it is. They are the children who respond to a nod in the morning. They come in and they have breakfast, they might have ten minutes individual reading with [project staff]. They might get to go to some club or other and, fine, the others may say 'they are getting every thing' and 'they are the ones who cause trouble', or 'they are the ones who don't attend school'. But if it has that small impact for that length of time with those children it has to be of benefit.

Whilst not every school is at this level, there is a need to acknowledge those who *do* strive to provide a truly educational and caring environment for the children in their charge. Their practice is possibly the most transferable learning to be extracted and needs to be recognised and affirmed.

ESLI was expressly designed to maximise the contributions of significant others in the child's life. The argument for coalition is based on the realisation that no institution, least of all schools, can resolve all of society's ills. That responsibility must be apportioned and assumed accordingly. However, schools are obliged to constantly engage in searching for ways of minimising the negative societal impacts on the teaching and learning process. Central to that quest is the mobilisation of partners in education. The process of schooling itself must also engage in active restructuring, aware of the many elements of its make-up, which are implicated in exacerbating and prolonging disadvantage. This restructuring is all the more crucial in the context of early school leaving. In defence of teachers and teaching, it is vital to acknowledge the arduousness of the task, particularly in areas of concentrated disadvantage. Regarding potential early school leavers or children 'at risk', the demands on teachers are even more onerous than in the normal course of events. However, this is also the area where the person of the teacher is most crucial.

The rural project co-ordinator views the educational system itself as one of the major blocks to progress. 'I understand where the inflexibilities are coming from and I understand that sometimes the young people that we work with are the very ones that can cause awful hassles for people every day, I acknowledge all of that.' She refers to some of her target children and feels that often teachers only see the child in front of them and never see or want to see the person that could be there. 'It doesn't matter that they might be a brilliant person, the one that would do all the messages for all the old people in the area' or the person who 'is struggling at home'. Another project co-ordinator admits that school is not always the optimum environment for a child. 'I have to say that the inflexibility of the curriculum does not suit every child. Now that is a really hard thing to gauge because I fundamentally believe that the best place for a young person is in school but at the same time maybe sometimes it is just a waking hell for them. And, hand on my heart, I have let one or two people go because I know that is what it is for them, a waking hell.'

Listening to children and parents

Bernstein (1970) argued that school cannot compensate for society. That accepted, it behoves us in schools to constantly hone and refine one of the most powerful contributions in combating exclusion: education. We must be especially wary that we do not contribute to further marginalisation of an already peripherised cohort. Schools can be places of great joy or they can, for a significant number, be places of abject failure. MacBeath noted that the pattern of failure often assumed by dropouts commences very early on in school: '... every failure at school is seen as another assault, another confirmation of low self-worth, another piece of evidence that school learning is difficult, threatening, irrelevant' (MacBeath 2000:248).

In the interviews with the children, those who clearly disliked school associated it with failure. Reasons cited by pupils for their being targeted by ESLI encompassed a range of behaviours such as 'bullying', 'bashing other kids', 'angry', 'spitting', 'tripping others up'. 'Cause I used to be very bold in school', 'I used to be running over against the window and banging me head against the wall and I kept on cursing at the teacher' and 'I ran off on me teacher'. Their experiences of school were generally negative. One boy admitted that if an opportunity presented he 'would be out the door'. Each of the three focus groups was asked what the word 'school' conjured up for them. Responses varied according to age but the sentiments were similar: 'boring' just 'sitting in the same classroom for six hours', 'homework', 'prayers', 'hard' and 'trouble'. One pupil did not like his teacher and got 'into hassle' almost every day. His feelings around school were prefaced continually by the word 'hate'.

In the interview with Nancy, a Traveller mother, memories of her own exclusion in the classroom remain painfully clear. She remembers thinking 'why doesn't she (teacher) actually sit down and start learning me to read and write. I wanted her there, beside me, learning me. That's the way I felt as a child and I did say to her: "I want to learn how to read". And she said, "you'll have to learn how to start listening then". But I was listening, I don't know what it was, but I found it hard, very hard.' Nancy describes the loneliness and the rejection she felt 'in the middle of a load of educated children' but she still had a hunger to learn. Her home circumstances militated against her ever having that opportunity. 'I remember another time, we travelled around like and I remember pulling in near a settled school and I seen them playing in the yard. You would see them going in the mornings and I would say "God, why isn't it me? Why didn't I get the chance to learn?"' Her greatest battle however was not being able to help her own children because of her personal difficulties. She tried to encourage and support them. 'I did encourage them, 'cause they often came to me saying, "Mammy, you don't know how to read and write and it didn't make much of a difference in your life". And I said, "yes, it did".'

Remaining positive

Schools and teachers can make a difference, of that there is little doubt. Paradoxically, the difference can be either/both negative and positive, a veritable double-edged sword. A core strand of ESLI involved facilitating pupils to have positive experiences of school. Positive Reward systems, educational trips, positive notes home, Discipline for Learning, reward ceremonies, outside speakers, out of school activities, family days out etc combined to allow pupils to both positively contribute to and extract from the educational experience. Out-of-school activities and holiday programmes in particular lent themselves to positive affirmation as well as a sense of personal achievement and gratification. The reason for the inclusion of this element is firmly grounded in practice and research. The challenge educationally is to integrate the learning back into the formal system. Hargreaves et al argue that engagement in extra-curricular activity 'provides opportunities for the school and for teachers to demonstrate caring. The often informal atmosphere that characterises these settings provides both students and teachers with opportunities to interact without constant reference to the usual hierarchy that generally sets the stage for student-teacher relationships' (Hargreaves, Earl and Ryan 1996: 67).

A crucial feature of ESLI was that there was no cost attached to additional provisions such as holiday programmes or breakfast support. Parents were very appreciative of this and were in no doubt as to their value. Nancy remarked on how she would not have been able to afford extras for her children. She says that money was tight with a 'big family and you trying to keep food on the table and the bills paid' and that being able to go 'made them happy and it didn't make them feel left out'. Before that, the children couldn't go anywhere and she describes them coming pleading to go but she had to refuse. This 'makes you feel bad. It makes you feel like you have failed.' Throughout the interviews with parents, out-of-school activities were cited as being crucial in maintaining their children. 'The holidays are so long and you are trying to keep them off the street and keep them occupied. You can't afford to bring them everywhere – it's so expensive'. One mother who accompanied her children on the trips spoke of how this activity supported her as a parent: 'It's good that you are out enjoying yourself with them and not screaming and shouting at them'. After-school trips to the theatre and pantomime were appreciated. 'Now the likes of that was lovely at night time because my kids don't go out at night. Well they play on the road and that's where the trouble starts.'

The availability of holiday programmes, during school vacations is well received by pupils, schools and families. They were used as a means of promoting family involvement (family trips, family picnics, reward ceremonies), allowed pupils go to the Gaeltacht, abroad, on residentials, and participate in community programmes otherwise inaccessible to them. Educationally, they facilitated remediation, the continued contact with education and learning, prepared pupils for re-entry to the mainstream system after a holiday period and helped to alleviate some of the trauma associated with the transfer from primary to post-primary. One of the project co-ordinators is very pragmatic about the long-term value of holiday programmes: 'The holiday provision is crucial. If there is no contact with them over the summer, the development that has happened can be lost. Alcohol and drug abuse and crime soar over the summer. They can limit the development that has taken place over the year. It is important for them [target children] to have the structure in their lives over the holidays.'

Although openly animated about the various out-of-school supports, the pupils themselves were also quite positive about academic support such as individual tuition and homework clubs offered in each of the areas.

> When we get the help with the maths and stuff it builds you up in yourself that you are doing well in it.
>
> When you go home from school and you have to think, aw! I have to do my homework, that will take longer. But when you're in the homework club you can do it and you have the teachers to help you.
>
> Because at home some children's Mas help them but some children's Mas doesn't. And if you go to a homework club I think it helps you more because you have the teachers there.

Supporting the primary carer

Complementary work with parents was an essential component of ESLI. This happened primarily through the Home School Community Liaison co-ordinators or through project personnel. Formal personal development for the parents was an integral part of the pre-test site's intervention and was facilitated by the project co-ordinator whose background was in psychotherapy. Parents were unanimous in their support of such a programme and one could sense that these mothers were involved in a process of personal growth. They could see how they themselves were being empowered and in turn empowering their children.

> Every child needs it [ESLI] and we know now through our own problems and how long and hard it is for adults to be brought out that it has to be harder for the children. Because they are brought up wrecked because of what we have been through.

> Yes I found it great, the homework club, because my little one, it was very hard to get her to sit down and do it. It would go on for hours and I remember picking the books and throwing them at her. Just giving up and roaring at her.

> I felt as if they (teachers) were blaming me. I felt as if they were blaming me for abusing him at home and that he was going into school and reacting with the school.

> None of mine have wanted a day off for the last three years. Before they would have, but since the project started they enjoy it so much there's no problem

Building relationships with children

Key to all of the interventions seemed to be the person of the project co-ordinator or key worker. In describing an 8 to 15 project co-ordinator, four fifth-class children succinctly describe their relationship. 'She could have chosen the good ones, but she didn't, she chose us'. They described how they used to bully other children in the class and in the yard and now they have given that up and 'all because of Mary' (project co-ordinator), One boy demonstrated their relationship with Mary, which was visibly close. He extended his two hands and said 'when she gives, we give'. He retracted one hand and continued 'when we don't give, she still gives'. In relation to targeting the most 'at risk', this child obviously valued the notion of being chosen and being maintained. Key work and intensive personal development through formal and informal interaction had greatly improved these boys' behaviour, attendance and sense of belonging. They were determined to repay the co-ordinator for having stuck with them and this sense of loyalty was overwhelmingly strong. The power of relationships to maintain children on the edge was crystallised in the actions and words of these boys. The challenge to replicate the same bonds in a classroom is unquestionably difficult.

The teacher as innovator

Ruddock et al, in their interviews with pupils outlined a series of teacher behaviours judged most likely to increase pupil commitment to learning. These included teachers who: 'enjoy teaching their subject, enjoy teaching their students, make their lessons interesting and link them to life outside school, will have a laugh but know how to keep order, are fair; explain things and go through things students don't understand without making them feel small; and don't give up on students' (Ruddock et al 1997, cited in Cox 2000). Fullan also chooses the individual teacher as the commencement point, noting that if 'you scratch a good teacher you will find a moral purpose' (Fullan 1993: 10). The potential of individual teachers to make lasting educational reform is real. If the will and skill of the teacher is mobilised, then the possibility of translating potential into practice for students becomes increasingly tangible. 'There are few professions other than teaching where gaining personal meaning through improving the lives of others for years and even generations to come is so palpable and so profound' (Fullan 1999: 82).

Schools can make a substantive difference to pupil achievement, participation and retention. When combined with the efforts, resources and commitment of others, the difference can be far-reaching and permanent. The work of Comer (1980) and Coleman (1998) fully support the outcomes associated with schools' promotion of parental and community involvement and its consequent impact on academic achievement. Their respective studies emphasise the capacity of such collaboration to connect the child to school, and in doing so respectfully, to maintain and validate cultural values and interests. The interviews conducted with the pupils corroborate the literature in postulating that all pupils want their teachers to care. In the urban area, one child admitted he never did homework. Another child immediately pleaded with him to change his ways because his teacher would not 'be friends' with him. '... cause if you are not going to do your homework and she's not going to bother with you. If you want to get friends with her you should start doing your homework. She is not going to bother with you and she is not going to talk to you.'

Young people who have dropped out of school refer to the fact that what may have precipitated the event was a negative encounter with a teacher. Equally, what may have reversed or delayed the decision, was a more caring teacher (Wehlage and Rutter 1986, Boldt (1994a, 1994b). Hargreaves et al outline the case for care, arguing that the academic will happen only when care is intrinsically linked to learning. 'Many young people ... will lose attachment to their learning, if they feel isolated, lost and uncared for in their schools. And without learning the skills, responsibilities and rewards of caring for and co-operating with others, all the intellectual advancement in the world will not make them better people or more moral citizens. Care matters. We cannot afford to neglect it' (Hargreaves, Earl and Ryan 1996: 59). The town project co-ordinator defines her role very clearly in the context of relationships. When asked what motivates her in her work she replied: 'I suppose it is the belief of the good in every person and every child. The belief in the potential in every child. A belief that I have, that even with the Celtic Tiger the gap is becoming wider between the haves and the have-nots. A belief in being with people or kids who are marginalised or pushed aside. And it's just about caring really.'

The ethic of care

Schrage's definition of collaboration as a 'process of shared creation' (cited in Fullan 1993) is essentially the vision of ESLI, resulting, if effective, in innovative and creative practice across the board of service provision as well as a more profound understanding of role, responsibility and contribution. In practice, integrated delivery of service implies seamless provision. This is not merely desirable but imperative for young people and families at risk. In the area of education, integrative practice relates to both the internal processes in a school (collegial support, cross-curricular networking, shared vision etc) and the school's links with the universe outside. The ability to influence societal development through educational reform depends on the capacity of the teacher and the school to strategically collaborate both internally and with the wider environment.

> Schools pursuing a systemic agenda have a 'client orientation'. They maintain a sustained focus on strengthening the involvement of parents with the school and their children's schooling. They also actively seek to strengthen the ties with the local community and especially those resources that bear on the caring of the children (Fullan 1999: 46).

We recall the words of one of the project workers who epitomised his role in change agentry: 'I feel privileged that in some way I am able to effect change, change that I think over time will affect hundreds of children and their parents and maybe the rest of their lives'. Equally, the words of the school principal who remarked that ''I think if we bring about a generational change. Many of the parents of these children have failed in school; they don't have very positive images of school. The involvement of parents is in my opinion what changes the whole notion of schooling in the home. That is what brings about change. Maybe a generation down the line, the children of the children we have at the moment won't be targeted.'

ESLI represented one attempt at changing established practice. Despite the difficulties, the weaknesses and the challenges, this initiative has provided an example of change where disaffection can be translated into engagement. The formal evaluation undertaken by The Children's Research articulates the sometimes intangible outcomes. 'There is a strong sense within the projects that these mechanisms have had positive impacts on participating children. Personnel speak of important behavioural changes and gradual improvements in inter-personal skills, such as beginning to make eye contact with certain adults, smiling and talking, simply "looking happier", having the confidence to put their hand up in class, remembering to bring their pens and books to school and so on ... other impacts included positive changes in patterns of attendance and punctuality, interest in school and project activities, and reading and writing levels' (Cullen 2000: 48).

The significance of relationships within the educational remit of care was undeniably the most conspicuous element in each of the three sites. In the context of disaffection, 'the ethic of care' is paramount. All pupils, irrespective of background or bent, want their teachers to care. Care matters! We cannot afford to neglect it. Indeed, as Noddings (1992) argues, no genuine school improvement is possible without placing care at the centre of educational experience for all learners and teachers.

Bibliography

Bastiani, J. (1989) *Working with Parents: A Whole School Approach*, Berkshire: NFER-Nelson.

Bernard van Leer Foundation (1986) *The Parent as Prime Educator: Changing Patterns of Parenthood (Summary Report and Conclusions)*, The Hague, Bernard van Leer Foundation.

Bernstein, B. (1970) 'Education cannot compensate for society', *New Society* 387, pp 344-347

Boldt, S. (1994a) *Hear My Voice: A longitudinal study of the post-school experience of early school leavers in Ireland*, Dublin, Marino Institute of Education.

Boldt, S. (1994b) *Listening and Learning – A Study of the Experiences of Early School Leavers from the Inner City of Dublin*, Dublin, Marino Institute of Education.

Boldt, S. (1998) *Showing The Way: Responses and approaches to the needs of students and early school leavers*, Dublin, Marino Institute of Education.

Burkan, W. (1996) *Wide Angle Vision,* New York, John Wiley and Sons.

Coleman, P. (1998) *Parent, Student and Teacher Collaboration: The Power of Three,* California, Corwin Press.

Combat Poverty Agency (1998) *Educational Disadvantage and Early School-Leaving,* Dublin, Combat Poverty Agency.

Comer, J. P. (1980) *School Power: Implications of an Intervention Project,* New York, Free Press.

Conaty, C. (1999) *Partnership in Education, through Whole School Development with Parent and Community Involvement: A Study of a National Initiative to Combat Educational Disadvantage – the Home, School, Community Liaison Scheme,* Unpublished PhD thesis, NUI Maynooth.

Cox, T. (ed.) (1999) *Meeting the Needs of Vulnerable Children,* London, Falmer Press.

Cullen, B. (2000) *Evaluation of 8 to 15 Early School Leaver Initiative*, Dublin, Department of Education and Science.

Department of Education (1995) *Charting Our Education Future: White Paper on Education,* Dublin, Stationery Office.

Department of Education and Science (1998) *8 to 15 Early School Leaver Initiative Projects' Specification,* Dublin, Department of Education and Science.

Devlin, M. (1998) 'Youth And Community Work and Early School Leaving', in *Prevention of Early School Leaving: The Youthstart Experience, Conference Papers,* Dublin, Youthstart National Support Structure.

European Social Fund (1996) *Early School Leavers Provision,* Dublin, European Social Fund Programme Evaluation Unit.

Freire, P. (1972) *Pedagogy of the Oppressed*, London, Penguin.

Fullan, M. (1993) *Change Forces: Probing the Depths of Educational Reform*, London, Falmer Press.

Fullan, M. (1999) *Change Forces: The Sequel,* London, Falmer Press.

Fullan, M. and Hargreaves, A. (1992) *What's Worth Fighting for in Your School?,* Buckingham, Open University Press.

Government of Ireland (1997) *Sharing in Progress: National Anti-Poverty Strategy,* Dublin, Stationery Office.

Government of Ireland (1997) *Early School Leavers and Youth Unemployment: Forum Report No 11,* Dublin, National Economic and Social Forum.

Hargreaves, A. (1996) *Changing Teachers, Changing Times: Teacher's Work and Culture in the Post-Modern Age*, London, *Cassell.*

Hargreaves, A., Earl, L. and Ryan, J. (1996) *Schooling For Change: Reinventing Education for Early Adolescents,* London, Falmer Press.

Kellaghan, T, Weir, S., Ó hÚallacháin, S and Morgan, M. (1995) *Educational Disadvantage in Ireland,* Dublin, Department of Education: Combat Poverty Agency: Educational Research Centre.

MacBeath, J. (1996) *Success Against the Odds: Effective Schools in Disadvantaged Areas*, London, Routledge.

MacBeath, J. (2000) 'Support for Lifelong Learning', in T. Cox (ed.) *Combating Educational Disadvantage,* London, Falmer Press.

National Youth Federation (1998) *Opening Horizons: A progressive policy of inclusiveness for young people who leave school early*, Dublin, Irish Youth Work Press.

Noddings, N. (1992) *The Challenge to Care in Schools: An Alternative Approach to Education,* New York, Teachers College, Columbia University.

Ryan,C. (2001) *The Perpetual Paradox: Opening Doors of Opportunity for Children 'at risk'. A Study of a National Initiative to Combat Early School Leaving – the 8 to 15 Early School Leaver Initiative,* Unpublished MA thesis, NUI Maynooth.

Schorr, L.B. (1998) *Within Our Reach: Breaking the Cycle of Disadvantage,* London, Doubleday.

Seidman, I. (1998) *Interviewing as Qualitative Research: A Guide for Researchers in Education and the Social Sciences*, New York, Teachers College Press.

Smyth, E. (1999) *Do Schools Differ? Academic and Personal Development among Pupils in the Second Level Sector,* Dublin, The Economic and Social Research Institute.

Wehlage, G. and Rutter, R. (1986) 'Dropping Out: How much do schools contribute to the problem?', *Teacher's College Record,* 87/3, pp 374-392.

Wehlage, G., Rutter., Lesko, N. and Fernandez, R. (1989) *Reducing the Risk: Schools as Communities of Support,* Sussex, Falmer Press.

Wolfendale, S. (1993) *Parental Participation in Children's Development and Education*, London, Gordon and Breach Science Publishers.

Wolfendale, S. (1992) *Empowering Parents and Teachers: Working for Children*, London, Biddles Ltd.

CHAPTER 6

Travellers and education: a personal perspective

Winnie McDonagh

A personal educational history

My family always travelled when I was very young. From the time I was born until I was five or six years old we had a completely nomadic life. Then in the early sixties my family travelled over to Manchester, mainly for economic reasons. The men took up building site work and the women would have gone out begging or selling just as they did at home in Ireland, the intention was to save or put by as much as you could and return to Ireland as soon as possible.

A number of my family group moved to England at this time, as did many other Traveller families. Four or five families shared a rented house and again like at home in Ireland the families moved from house to house when the need arose or when they thought they had been too long in the same place, it was just like moving from camp to camp at home.

The sharing of a house by a number of families provided company as well as a sense of support. There was a feeling of safety and support in staying close together in a strange country and as many of the Travellers did not have an education or training (many could not read or write) this would also have been a factor in remaining close together.

Gradually over a period of time as they became more confident and familiar with their environment and surroundings a single family would move into their own rented house, but never far from the other members of the extended family, so you would have five or six families living in adjacent houses or streets within easy reach or contact with each other. There was very little if any mixing or socialising with the settled Irish people who had moved over to England, the Traveller families kept very much to themselves.

All this time there would be regular travelling over and back to Ireland and this would always be an occasion for sending home or getting news from family and friends, those going home would get a big send off, with a great welcome for those coming over. Funerals in particular were events not to be missed under any circumstances and great efforts were made to ensure that close family in particular were able to go home for such sad occasions.

My own family travelled between Ireland and England from the time I was about four or five years old until I was ten or eleven years. I went to three-four different Catholic primary schools in Manchester during that time and I also attended a convent school in Mullingar for a short while during one of those return trips.

The very first school I remember attending was a Catholic primary school in Manchester from the age of four or five until I was seven. I went to this school with my older brother, sister and cousins. Depending on how often the families moved or 'travelled' around Manchester or England you could be sent to a number of schools in a short length of time.

My family moved back to Ireland permanently when I was about ten/eleven years old. That year we travelled around for the summer months and after about six to nine months my parents applied for a house in Mullingar. We lived in Mullingar until I was fifteen or sixteen years of age. I went to primary school there on and off and made my Confirmation. By the age of fourteen I had completed my schooling, which had not been very regular or consistent at the best of times.

My longest period in school was in Manchester. There was a legal requirement that children must go to school in England and Traveller families were afraid of doing anything that would attract the attention of the authorities or social services which could result in the children being taken away by the 'cruelty man', i.e. School Attendance Officer or social workers.

The adults saw authoritarian figures in England very differently than they regarded them in Ireland. In England, the threat or fear of the unknown seemed greater, while in Ireland there was a sense that they were 'among our own'. Families 'put up' with sending children to school in England because it was the law and it was expected of you, whereby in Ireland it did not appear to matter too much, if at all.

It was useful too, it could be seen as a sort of childminding service, as the fathers were out of the home every day working on the building sites and the mothers went out begging or selling paper flowers and clothes pegs as they had done in Ireland. In Ireland a number of adults would always be around the campsite, the men making tin cans, saucepans, looking after the horses or other women who did not need to go out selling or begging that day.

When we returned to Ireland, schooling wasn't regarded in the same way. There wasn't the same sense of threat or fear and school wasn't really necessary as members of the extended family could share childminding responsibilities or the children would be brought out with the mothers.

My older sister, brother and I went to school in Manchester. The three of us learned to read and write fairly quickly. I was a very good reader by seven or eight and developed a love of reading, which has stayed with me and 'educated' me down through the years. A younger sister had stayed at home in Ireland with my grandparents when the rest of the family had first moved to England. She didn't go to school until she joined us later on. She and my younger sisters did go to school in England for a short while, but she never learned to read or write to the same standard.

Perhaps the difference in our reading abilities is a reflection of how well the three of us were taught or the age at which we learned. I'm not really sure, or if there were other factors involved. I went to the convent school in Mullingar before special classes had been introduced or set up. They did not have segregated or special classes in the schools I attended in Manchester. I was always in mainstream classes throughout my time in school.

We had a good experience of education in England and Ireland in mainstream classes. In England we were treated as being Irish, and although some would describe us as gypsies we were identified mainly as being from Ireland. I have no recollection of experiencing prejudice in England as a child. Similarly, in Mullingar I have no clear experience of prejudice. My experiences of education and relationships with others at that time were generally positive.

At times like when we made our First Holy Communion and Confirmation, the nuns gave poorer parents a 'helping hand', it was generally done sensitively and privately. Settled and Traveller children got free books. There wasn't a feeling in that sense of being different to other families, whether they were Travellers or settled people. There was a lot of shared poverty in both the settled and Traveller communities in Ireland from the 1950s to the 1980s. We knew that there were poor and disadvantaged children families in the settled community too.

Mullingar was a small country town where rural and urban children attended the schools. In general, relationships between Traveller and settled children were mainly okay, or so it appeared to me as a child anyway. We walked to and from school from our camp on the side of the road with other Travellers and with settled children from the country area and then the town when we were housed.

There were of course incidents at times, name-calling or teasing by the settled children, but this was not a big deal to us, as we gave as good as we got, there was a big enough group of us in school to watch out for each other. I and the other Traveller children were aware that we were different from the settled boys and girls, we could not say how but we knew!

The teachers also treated us differently, sometimes unfairly, other times more positively. I suppose looking back with hindsight as an adult, one could describe some of this as discrimination, prejudice, but as children we could not name this.

I do remember that there was one black girl who was in my class for a short while, whose father was from Africa. The teacher did a geography project on the country where her father came from. This was very interesting and I can still remember how proud the girl was, and even some of the work we did for the project. Compare this to how the more negative delivery of an Irish lesson entitled 'Campa Tincéiri', using the old Cómhra pictures, was for me in the same class. Because most of my early schooling had taken place in Manchester, I had no Irish at all and I didn't understand what was being said or the context of the lesson.

I do remember that I felt very uncertain and uncomfortable about the pictures and story and I can clearly remember the awkward or uncertain way and manner in which the other children were looking at me. There was no positive affirmation or celebration of Travellers, their customs, lifestyle etc in the same way as for the African girl – everyone knew you were a Traveller but it was unspoken, something best left unsaid. No one ever did tell or explain to me what the story was about!

As Traveller children we were 'educated' within the family or community. This was an informal and practical life-skills education. We observed the cultures and practices in our own family and community. This education didn't include reading and writing. Girls mainly learned domestic and child minding responsibilities and boys learned 'outdoor' duties. You learned by listening, observing and a very much hands on experience rather than following written instructions or reading 'how to'.

The gender differences were I suppose similar to those in the farming and country communities of the time. But it wasn't everyone's experience. My mother grew up in a mainly female family and so had to do a lot of the boys or 'outdoor' duties that would be done by males in a family where there were sons and daughters.

I spent a lot of time minding younger brothers and sisters. I can remember sitting around fires hearing music on wind-up gramophones and stories, my granny lilting or singing songs. Travellers made their own entertainment. The adults would recall or tell about things that they had been told as children, stories, happenings or the history of the family.

Contact and communication with the extended family was very important – families didn't lose touch when they went away. Information was passed between people by those who were travelling around the country, or between Ireland and England, for funerals or weddings. It was very important for people to maintain a contact with home.

My family moved to Finglas, Dublin, in the early 1970s. It was a much bigger place than Mullingar and there were better opportunities at the time to make a living or go out begging or selling, i.e. more houses/people!

But things were changing in Ireland and there were also growing fears and concerns. Traveller parents were reluctant to let their children or young people wander too far away. We always went out begging or selling in groups of three or four, and we didn't always tell our parents that we sometimes went further than we were told.

On a few occasions while we were out with the other girls, men pulled up and tried to entice us into their cars. We had all been taught to run away if something like that happened. These people probably thought we were vulnerable because we were not in school or were out on the roadways without adult company.

My own mother became more cautious about my younger siblings going out on their own. She was fearful of who might be in a house or on a road and worried about their safety in a big city like Dublin, full of strangers. Later the pattern of begging/selling changed. There was always at least one adult with children for safety and eventually the begging slowly died out among most of the families I know.

Some of the women today would have what they call 'callbacks' whereby they are regular callers to certain houses that they have been calling back to over a number of years, most of the younger people would not now go out begging or selling. Developments such as part-time or full-time work, the setting up and availability of women's groups, training courses and training allowances particularly for the women, and improved conditions also had an impact and reduced the necessity of begging.

Traveller experiences of and attitudes towards begging have changed. This is partly due to legislation as well as other social changes. It was part of the Traveller way of life and was an important skill in the past. For my mother's and previous generations, you really needed to be a good beggar or seller. It was an essential skill. When Traveller families were very nomadic there was no alternative for most.

The men were dependent on seasonal work and settled or regular work wasn't available or suitable to them. Knowing how to sell, beg or 'hawk' meant that a woman's family would not go hungry. My family accepted begging as an essential part of life in the same way that other Traveller families did – it wasn't seen as degrading or being downtrodden, but as an important life-skill.

When I was seventeen I got married and spent the next twenty years rearing a family of four children. In this time I did voluntary work and also a number of short educational and training courses. I attended the local Traveller training/education centre for a year and during this time I got involved as a trainee representative with the training/education centre representative committee. I worked for this committee for a number of years producing a community type magazine, which was a publication for and about Travellers and is still being produced.

I decided to use my knowledge and experience to apply to Maynooth University to do a three-year course in youth and community work. I completed this in 1997 and that year I started to work with a Barnardos Traveller education project as the education development worker. I have been working with this project for the past number of years and have seen lots of changes and developments regarding the Traveller community even in this short space of time.

People have many different opinions and views regarding their understanding of education, what it is and its value. For myself something as simple as learning to read and write well at an early age and which was to a standard that I myself could then continue to develop and improve has had numerous rewards and outcomes for me personally.

I have completed a number of third-level certificate and diploma courses in subjects such as computer studies, group facilitation skills, equality studies, addiction studies, family literacy and adult literacy tutor.

It has allowed me to develop and challenge myself personally, given me life and work skills, increased my confidence and self-esteem, broadened and increased my interest, understanding and knowledge of people and the world about me, given me employment and financial security, opportunities for further education and training, so many, many experiences that I otherwise would not have done or even attempted. In short, I suppose it has played a major part in making me the person I am.

I have always encouraged my own children to develop a love of reading and learning and to see the value for themselves in this, without pushing them too hard or putting too much pressure on them. Sometimes you have to let these things develop gradually.

I would like in the near future to do a university degree. I have some ideas in mind that I would like to explore and I will probably do this in the next while. I believe strongly in the principle of life-long learning and that you are never too old or late to learn or achieve something.

Recent changes in the Travellers' experiences

Things have really changed for the Traveller community in the past thirty to forty years. There have been huge developments in all aspects of Travellers' lives, you have only to read and compare some of what has been written and recorded from the early sixties to the present, i.e. *Report of the Commission on Itinerancy* (1963), *Report of the Task Force on the Travelling Community* (1995), to be aware of this. Of course there remains a lot more to be done before Travellers are really equal citizens in this country.

Most young Travellers today haven't travelled, they haven't lived as nomadic a life as their parents or grandparents have. Younger people in their thirties and forties can remember travelling but it hasn't been as central a part of their lives as it was for their parents. It could be said that young Traveller people have lost the skills and maybe the necessity or inclination for travelling or living a nomadic lifestyle.

Settled people are always making the assumption or mistake that the identity of Travellers is only possible or applicable if the person is travelling or living on the side of the road. They believe that housing Travellers automatically changes them, Travellers themselves don't see it like that at all. They still belong to the Traveller community and identify themselves very clearly as Traveller. Even very young children know who they are and are aware of their identity and that their family links to other Travellers are very important to them.

My mother sometimes says that the younger generation aren't real Travellers at all! Like most people from another or older generation she thinks that they don't know anything! But they don't *know* the kind of life and experiences that she and others of her generation have lived.

The way of living and society has changed completely from her childhood and youth, and the current young generation of

Travellers are trying to live in the ever-changing world of today while also trying to hold on to and maintain what their understanding and perceptions of being a Traveller are for them.

They have to live in a very different time and society than the one that their parents or grandparents lived in and they have to try to cope with that reality and also with what their families and community expect of them and this can at times be at odds. It is very difficult and confusing for them.

Their grandparents and parents may want them to live a life, as much like what they themselves did, this can seem to the young people that they are caught between two worlds. On one hand they want and need to live and survive in today's society and on the other they are expected to continue to live like Travellers from another time and place and with the best will in the world this is neither possible nor, I would say, is it appropriate.

The older generation would love if time had stood still! They are concerned and fearful about some of the more negative influences and developments that affect young Travellers today and yet don't really know how to deal with them or even prepare or support the young people to cope themselves with these issues or concerns.

The young people want to be like their peers – they are living closer than ever to and with the settled community. They see consumerist culture on television and in the media. Many young travellers are starting to work, socialise and go to school for longer with the young people from the settled community and so are more exposed to outside influences. This can be confusing and frustrating for young and old. I even find it confusing myself!

Some of the community traditions and practices can seem to them to be very old fashioned, out of date and not relevant to them. The option or opportunities to keep distance and space between the Traveller and settled people is no longer possible or even desirable.

You can't change things overnight – but it is a struggle and challenge for all to figure out how to adapt and bring about positive change and developments, not just make the best of things. The question is how this can happen in a balanced way without causing too much grief and hurt for all concerned.

The Traveller community and education

Due to various causes and, most significantly, the inappropriateness of an education system which ignores the distinct cultural identity of the Traveller community, Travellers fare badly within the existing mainstream education/training system.

There are many books and a lot of documentation in evidence regarding the Traveller community and the Irish education system.

These deal with a wide range of different aspects or perspectives, among which are discrimination, participation, social, economic, political and cultural and so on. The vast majority of these are written by settled people with little or no real input from Travellers.

The history of Traveller participation in the formal education system is relatively new and there has been a sizeable improvement at primary level. According to the *Report of the Commission on Itinerancy* (1963) there were 144 children attending primary schools at that time. At present, there are 5,240 Traveller children registered with extra capitation status at this level (Pavee Point 2004). In the school year 1997/1998, 737 of these children were aged twelve years and over.

Travellers have never seen formal education or training as a way of improving either themselves or their community. Self-sufficiency has always been the choice of most Travellers. For the older and many of the current Traveller population the connection between school, book learning and making a living was never really clear or seen as relevant.

Most Traveller parents would agree that education is important to an extent – they believe that today people need to be able to read and write to do well (this also is a matter of opinion, some say that you can make a living just as well without!). But the majority at present are certain that post-primary schooling is not necessary or important to help prepare their young people for life or at least the life that they as young Travellers will lead.

For Traveller parents some of the subjects or materials taught or used by the teachers are seen by them as not being suitable or appropriate for their children to learn about in school, i.e. programmes such as drugs and sex education. Even some schools, especially secondary co-ed, are suspect, boys and girls together!

I find that in some ways I have more in common with Asian or Muslim people that I have met than I have with many settled Irish people. There are certain values or practices we have in common that are not necessarily shared with the majority Irish population, i.e. close family kinship, extended family, arranged/inter family marriages etc.

Travellers feel it is alright to send young children to preschool or primary school, at lower primary school age they are still seen as children and not yet expected to contribute to the family income or be preparing for the more grown-up roles that they will be expected to fill during their teenage years. Confirmation is still seen as an important transition in the life of the young Traveller, a time to leave childhood behind and become a more responsible and grown-up person who is preparing for the more important things in life such as earning a living, marriage and raising a family.

Many Travellers today are living or located on the margins of localities or communities that are in the main working class or designated disadvantaged; they see that continuation or participation in education is not very important or vital to the settled communities among which they themselves reside, many of whose children too drop out of school or don't continue on in the education system. Many of these young people want to get jobs, earn money, get married, enjoy themselves rather than stay on in school or go to college or university. Travellers can see this as further confirmation that formal education is not all its made out to be. If it's not important or necessary to these young settled people what are our youngsters going to use it for or gain from it?

Traveller parents in the main are familiar and more comfortable with primary education and schools. The subjects the children learn or are taught make sense to them – they can see the value in learning reading, writing and maths. It is also simpler to deal with one teacher per year and a school principal. If families have a number of children attending one or the same school, the children get similar type homework and, while a majority of parents themselves have a poor education standard, the children manage to get through primary school adequately, although from my experience and work this can be a matter of the individual succeeding rather than the system.

I see far too many Traveller children still coming through the primary system who literally cannot read or write, and this despite all the extra or increased funding and resources that are available to schools for Traveller children. This of course has a knock-on effect on the transferring of the child and their ability or skills for participating or progressing at secondary school.

I can see from my current work and involvement with Traveller parents and the schools how much segregated education – special classes, segregated withdrawal etc has impacted on the current generation of young Travellers. Their parents own very negative experience, poor expectations and outcomes have coloured and influenced their own fears, concerns, ability to support and expectations of their own children's education prospects today.

My own younger siblings and other younger Travellers with whom I work and have spoken to have awful stories about being taken out for enforced showers, separate lunches and playtime, separate Communion and Confirmation ceremonies, special segregated learning etc. All of this segregated provision stigmatised Travellers and made them feel different and inadequate compared to other children. It also influenced how they were assessed and taught by teachers.

I know there were some positives too – that individual schools and teachers had better and equal teaching practices for Traveller children. But in my view the many negative experiences far outweigh the positives and have had a lasting and ongoing effect.

Post-primary education

The experience for Travellers at post-primary level is not so positive and the figures bear this out. In the 1999 school year there are 650 traveller children registered/attending post-primary schools out of a total of 3,000 eligible. There is evidence too that there is a dramatic fall off within the first two years of registration.

There are many and complex reasons for this low level of participation and continuation, among which from the Traveller point of view/perspective are: family concerns, age appropriate transfer, history of non-participation, nomadism, customs and traditions, value of formal education, low expectation or achievement, costs, discrimination and racism.

Table 1: Retention of Travellers in post-primary 1997/1998

School Year	Numbers	%
1st Year	314	100
2nd Year	175	55.73
3rd Year	91	28.98
4th Year	20	6.36
5th Year	22	7.00
6th Year	15	4.77
P.L.C.	1	0.32

Source: Presentation Paper by Peter Kierans, VEC representative, Department of Education Advisory Committee on Traveller Education

While there have been increasing numbers of young Travellers transferring to post-primary schools in the past number of years, how many are still attending in the final term? Retention and continuation in the system of these young people are two of the major challenges for parents and education providers.

As Traveller children get older and move on to post-primary, the situation for Traveller parents is completely different from the primary system: now the school is bigger, there are more teachers to deal with and there are new and strange subjects and Traveller parents are unsure of the value of this wider curriculum.

Many young Travellers, who may be the first in their family or group to transfer to post-primary, can feel isolated and unsure without the presence or support of other young Travellers, their lifestyle, social mores and values are different than the settled students. Young Travellers can feel they have to submerge their identity in order to participate or survive at this level.

Teachers at second level are in the main expected to teach and prepare the young people in their care for state exams, future employment and to contribute positively to their community and society. All too often this is a preparation for life in the settled or majority community, it doesn't make allowances or take into account young Travellers or other minority groups or communities, and the positive contribution they can make to themselves, their communities and the wider society.

Because there are so many more teachers involved in their child's education it is difficult for parents to connect with all of them. Attendance at parent-teacher meetings is a struggle and parents are confused and uncertain about the purpose of much of what their children are being taught or what the end result or outcomes will be. The structures, expense, exams, longer day etc at second level all contribute to the uncertainty and worry about the usefulness or need of this additional education to Traveller parents.

Concerns, challenges and hopes for young Travellers

There are many concerns and challenges that must be met in regards to Traveller education both by the Traveller community, the government, the teaching profession and education providers if we are to have hope or give hope to future generations of Traveller children.

The mindset and thinking of the Traveller community about education and training needs has to change if their young people are to be equipped to provide for their future. They cannot expect to continue to live the inadequate self-sufficient, hand to mouth existence which previous generations of Travellers accepted and thought would never change. They cannot depend on social welfare or low paid temporary jobs, or live on the margins of society because they are Travellers rather than being able to make their rightful contribution to society.

Because of parental fears and concerns, some genuine, some misplaced, Traveller children have not been given opportunities to be open to or experience positively other cultures, customs, socialising etc. Parents express concerns that they may change or be negatively influenced by the settled community and so lose their identity, values, etc. Other communities or societies who have been marginalised or who have similar customs, practices and traditions to Travellers have always seen education and used educational advantage as the way forward for the betterment of their own and their communities' futures.

I have never believed or felt that any one of the educational or training experiences I have gained has made me any less of a Traveller or removed me from my family or community; on the contrary it has made me more sure of my identity both as a Traveller and as a woman. Any difficulties I have experienced have arisen out of the negative attitude and behaviours of others, both Traveller and settled.

The segregated and negative mindset of the past still exerts an influence in schools and with teachers today and must be addressed. The legacy of special classes and segregated education continues to have an impact.

Teachers very often lack an awareness of the realities of Travellers' lives. The training of teachers in intercultural teaching methods or curriculum is totally inadequate. In light of the societal changes that have occurred in Ireland over the past ten years it is unbelievable that this has been allowed to continue.

Teachers who are interested in learning, increasing their knowledge or improving their teaching practice have had to do this in their own time or at short in-service training courses, when it should be an integral part of all teacher training and ongoing career development. Prejudice and racism against Travellers and other minorities is still very much alive in Irish society and has an impact on how Travellers are perceived and treated by the settled community and teachers can go a long way in addressing and combating this.

The principal of respecting other cultures and identities is one of the most important areas to be addressed if we are to make any headway in the other areas of Traveller education. There must be a respecting and understanding that other people's cultures and identities are of equal value. I believe that until we achieve this in respect to Travellers and other ethnic or minority groups and peoples we will always be trying to play catch up.

I know of a teacher who during Confirmation preparations handed back a Traveller girl her baptismal certificate, with the words that 'you will be needing this soon as you will be getting married soon'. This particular girl liked school and was a good student who intended to go on to secondary school. In this instance she was challenged by the prejudice she had experienced. However, once she had completed her Junior Cert, there was family and community pressure to take her out of school.

This is how some of the misplaced or misinformed internal factors and practices of the Traveller community and schools help maintain and perpetuate inequalities for Traveller children in the education system.

Parents, grandparents, the extended family and community all have a huge influence, but they don't always have the confidence, the ability or the skills to support and encourage their young people to explore or fulfil their true potential or explore other opportunities or options that could be open to them. Many don't see that not all children develop or mature at the same rates or ages. There is a lack of knowledge or understanding of the life chances that a good education can offer or make possible.

There can be huge pressure on the individual Traveller who does attempt to succeed through the formal education or training system because they are under scrutiny from the rest of the community. Lack of instant success or outcomes, failure, the length of time or the number of years it takes to finish a particular course of study or training are seen as affirming and/or confirming all the misgivings and doubts Travellers have about post-primary or further education and their value or usefulness.

Traveller Education Centres can and do provide young Travellers with some options but these too can be limited and restrictive. The young people may not be adequately prepared or challenged to look beyond the centre to further their education, training or work prospects. Some of these too are Traveller-only centres and so continue with another form of segregated education or training provision or service. The young people need huge support to have their self-esteem affirmed and developed to enable them to participate and work outside these centres. These centres can become a comfort zone where people are reluctant to move on.

Not all Travellers are the same. As in the settled community, there is much diversity. Within the Traveller community there can be an expectation that everyone will do the same thing and go in the same direction. The educational limitations that many young Traveller people experience coupled with the limitations coming from the family and the community can smother the individual.

Young Travellers do what they can within the boundaries of the Traveller community, some of these young people are attempting to push back the boundaries, they are questioning some of the practices and traditions within the community and their relevance to their current lives. If someone does something different and succeeds, this can result in a lessening of the more restrictive and negative control or influence of the family, the community and the wider society.

There are real and genuine fears in the Traveller community regarding young people and children – parents want the best for the younger generation but these may be very new or unfamiliar things. It is difficult at times for Traveller parents to name or describe what they want for their children and even for themselves – will they cease to belong fully to the Traveller community, will they still be accepted as Travellers? This is very important to both the old and young.

I would hope to see young Travellers of the future being sure and confident in their identity, being the recognised role models and professionals of their own community in whatever field they choose and making a valid and positive contribution to their community and to the wider society in which they will live and participate.

Bibliography

Commission on Itinerancy (1963) *Report,* Dublin, Stationery Office.

Department of Education (1995) *Charting Our Education Future, White Paper on Education,* Dublin, Stationery Office.

Kierans, P. (1999) Presentation paper by VEC Representative on Department of Education Advisory Committee on Traveller Education, 23 April, 1999.

Pavee Point (2004) Information leaflets on the Traveller community, Pavee Point, Traveller Centre, Dublin. www.paveepoint.ie

Task Force on the Travelling Community (1995) *Report,* Dublin, Stationery Office.

SECTION 2

Prioritising the life-worlds of children

Chapter 7

School matters – listening to what children have to say

Dympna Devine

Introduction

When asked to consider the position of children in Ireland today, adults often respond ambiguously. They may cite improved economic and social conditions and the positive impact on children's welfare, alongside concerns over children's emotional and social well-being in light of changing parental work patterns, materialism and increasing family breakdown (Devine et al 2003, Beck 1992, Jensen and McKee 2003). How we, as adults, think about children and childhood is open to change however, with subsequent implications for the way in which we intervene in children's lives. In modern times, psychological and medical perspectives have dominated how adults think about children. More recently however, questions have been raised about the tendency of such perspectives to emphasise the innocence and vulnerability of children, over and above their capacities as thinking, critical and reflective beings (James et al 1998, Mayall 2002).

This chapter explores these contrasting ideas about children and childhood with reference to primary-school children's views of school. It begins by tracing the changes in how we, as adults, think about children and how issues of power, rights and equality are increasingly entering into discourse on children and childhood. This sets the context for considering the discourses of childhood that have informed practice in Irish primary schools. Research documenting children's views on their status in primary schools is presented and conclusions are drawn with reference to the implications for practice in primary schools.

Changing constructs of children and childhood

Socio-historical analyses point to the evolving nature of childhood and how children's lives change in line with economic and social development (Gillis 2002, Hendrick 1997, Jencks 1996). Central to this change is the role accorded children by adults in society. Curtin (1984), speaking in an Irish context, points to the traditional use accorded children in Irish society: as a source of cheap labour, a form of generational continuity and security in old age. More generally in modern western society, the traditional role of children as a source of labour on farms, in factories or in the home has gradually been replaced by their compulsory placement in schools.[1] Childhood in modern western societies is synonymous with schooling, with the length of time spent in school increasing with each generation. Children's school labour (Qvortrup 2001) is intimately tied to long-term goals of economic productivity and prosperity and it is no coincidence that societies which seek to modernise themselves prioritise compulsory schooling as a key component in the project of modernisation (*Investment in Education* 1965, OECD 1964).

Religious and psychological constructs of childhood cut across these changing societal conditions. Evangelical concepts of the child as being born with the stamp of original sin compete with more romantic conceptions that deem the child to be innocent and vulnerable. Psychotherapeutic perspectives emphasise the importance of adults remaining in tune with the voice of their 'inner child'. This child of the 'unconscious' reinforces the importance of sensitivity to children and of the complex interaction between emotional/psychological development and the child's social environment. This social environment is in turn becoming subject to global influences, as children all over the world participate more than ever before in a shared culture of music, sport and fashion and the boundaries between adult's and children's lives becomes increasingly blurred (Buckingham 2000, Postman 1994).

Added to these evolving concepts of children and childhood are those which are informed by sociological perspectives. Such perspectives, spearheaded by the new sociology of childhood, assert the importance of considering children as a distinct social category, to be considered independently of the more dominant adult group.[2] The absence of considering the position of children as

---

1 Of course child labour is still a major issue world wide (Mizen 2001) and it is estimated that about ten million children in the world are bound in slavery.

2 Traditional categories within sociological analyses relate to gender, social class, dis/ability, sexuality and ethnicity. While there are differences between children in respect of each of these characteristics, the perspective that is being described

both separate from and relative to adults has been attributed to the adult-centred nature of much social research. (Lynch 1999, Qvortrup 1994). This has had potentially negative implications for safeguarding both the rights and welfare of children in areas as diverse as the distribution and allocation of wealth, the protection of children's rights in the law, and the manner in which children's time and space is organised in society.[3] Such adult centredness often derives from paternalistic assumptions that adults will act in the best interests of the child (Archard 1993).

By focusing on children as a distinct social category, however, such assumptions are open to question, as issues of their rights and status relative to other groups (such as adults) begin to emerge. This is especially well reflected in the enactment of the United Nations Convention on the Rights of the Child (1989)[4] which specifies the rights of children in a series of Articles which span all aspects of their lives. Two articles are relevant to the remainder of this chapter in that they signal a recognition of the rights of children not only to be protected from discrimination and abuse but also to have a voice in matters that directly affect them. Thus Article 12 states:

> 1. State parties shall assure to the child who is capable of forming his or her own views the right to express those views freely in all matters affecting the child, the views of the child being given due weight in accordance with the age and maturity of the child.

While Article 13 states:

> 1. The child shall have the right of freedom of expression; this right shall include freedom to seek, receive and impart information and ideas of all kinds, regardless of frontiers, either orally, in writing or in print, in the form of art, or through any other media of the child's choice.

This rights-based concept of childhood is one which challenges adults to act not only in the best interests of children but also to incorporate children increasingly into decision making about their lives. It draws on assumptions that while children may be different

---

2 *contd.* here is part of what is termed inter-generational analysis, examining differences in power, status etc between differing age/groups and generations (see for example Mayall and Zeiher 2003 for further discussion).

3 For further discussion see for example Devine 2003 and the Constitution Review Group (1996) discussion on the rights and status of children in the Irish Constitution.

4 A child is legally defined as every human being below the age of eighteen years, unless under the law applicable to the child, majority is attained earlier.

to adults, they must be respected by them, providing children with the opportunity to voice their opinion on matters directly of concern to them. Issues of respect and recognition are central to current work in the area of equality studies (Fraser 1995, 2000; Lynch and Lodge 2002) and apply no less to relations between children and adults. The emphasis within such work on the importance of recognition and voice in relations between majority and minority status groups ties in usefully with the analysis of differences in power and voice between children and adults in society. Devine (2003) outlines how such differences are supported by discourses that construct children as 'other', incapable of acting responsibly in matters of concern to them. Conversely, discourse that stresses children's capacities as active agents (also a central feature running through sociological analyses of childhood) asserts children's critical and reflective skills and challenges traditional patterns of dominance/subordination in child/adult relations (see for example Connolly 1998, Davies 1991, Deegan 1996, Devine 2003, Lodge and Flynn 2001).

The move towards a greater recognition of rights and voice in discourse about children in Ireland is also evident in the publication of the *National Children's Strategy* (2000). The strategy attempts to provide a unified and coherent direction to government policy on children and childhood in Ireland into the new millennium. Central to the vision underpinning the strategy is a discourse on children and childhood which emphasises voice, respect and recognition:

> An Ireland where children are respected as young citizens with a valued contribution to make and a voice of their own; where all children are cherished and supported by family and the wider society; where they enjoy a fulfilling childhood and realise their potential (NCS 2000: 4)[5]

Notwithstanding criticisms that have been made in relation to the strategy (Devine et al 2003), what is important for our purposes is the recognition given to children's right to voice their opinions as well as the connection that is implied between listening to children, respect and children's citizenship. Given the amount of time children spend in school, an obvious forum within which children's voice should be heard is that of the organisation of their school lives. Previous analysis has stressed the importance of such

---

[5] Specific measures identified for improving the voice of children in Irish society include the establishment of Dáil Na nÓg, an office of Ombudsman for Children and national and local services for children.

practice in the induction of children into citizenship in a gradual and age-appropriate manner (Devine 2002). Whether or not the current primary school system is structured towards the inclusion of children's voice in a meaningful way however is best considered in light of discourse on children/childhood informing primary school practice to date.

Educational discourse on children and childhood

Devine (2003, 1999) notes that traditional concepts of children's rights and schooling in Ireland have tended to focus on children's right to schooling rather than on their rights as a group within the school system itself. Rights to voice and participation in decision making have tended to focus on hearing adult voices within the system, such as teachers, Department of Education officials, patron bodies and increasingly the voices of parents. This exclusion of the child's voice has its roots not only in discourse which defines children as immature and incapable of participating effectively in decisions about their lives but also, and by implication, differences in the power and status of adults and children in Irish society.

A socio-historical analysis of the primary school system highlights how conceptions of children and childhood in the broader society directly influenced policy and practice in relation to children in schools (Devine 1999). The socialisation of children in line with both political and religious goals prior to the 1960s was reflected in a primary curriculum that was subject-centred and authoritarian, geared toward the consolidation of a Gaelic and Catholic Ireland (Akenson 1975, Devine 1999). With the advent of membership of the European Union and a radical shift of economic policy from the 1960s onward, patterns of childrearing began to change to incorporate more child-centred perspectives. Coupled with a gradual decline in family size, increasing attention was paid to the individual child and the need for the state, through education, to maximise individual talent and ability *(Investment in Education* 1965). Such perspectives were reflected in the new curriculum of 1971 where explicit consideration is given to the recognition of childhood as a distinct period of human development and of children having distinct and individual needs. In its implementation in practice however, the 'new' curriculum was mediated not only by the reluctance of the state to invest heavily in primary education (itself indicative of the lower status accorded to children) but also by the assumptions and perspectives of teachers themselves, many of whom were reluctant to move away from the more traditional didactic approaches to teaching (INTO 1985, O'Sullivan 1980, Department of Education 1990). While children now had access to a more broad-based curriculum that was implemented in a less authoritarian manner, issues to do with children's rights and voice were overshadowed by a discourse which stressed their needs.[6]

The 1990s witnessed an intensive period of educational reform that included widespread consultation with the education partners, culminating in legislation (Education Act 1998) and curriculum reform at all levels. Such reform included a greater focus on equality issues than heretofore, the latter emphasising children's right to access and participation in the education system irrespective of their social class, gender etc. While children were not included as one of the education partners in the process of consultation leading to either the Education Act (1998) or the Revised Primary Curriclum (1999), there is ironically evidence in both documents of an awareness of discourse related to the inclusion of children's voice on matters affecting them.[7] Such discourse clearly derives from government commitments under the United Nations Convention on the Rights of the Child (1989) as well as stated policy in relation to children in the *National Children's Strategy* (2000).

With respect to the Education Act (1998) for example, children are accorded rights to be informed about school activities and to greater involvement in the operation of the school (Section 23 (No 1 and 2) and Section 27 (No 3)), as well as to be consulted on the setting and monitoring of school objectives. That such rights are conditional however on adults within the system (principal, teachers, Boards of Management and parents) deeming children to be of an appropriate age and experience for such consultation, may limit the effect of such provisions in practice. The fact that the Act also allows for the establishment of student councils at second level (again subject to adult defined conditions) but not at primary level (Section 27, 3 (a)) is indicative of a discourse which perceives younger children in a paternalistic light, incapable of participating in such structures.[8] Within the Revised Primary Curriculum (1999), the capacity of children as active agents is acknowledged (Ibid: 8)

---

6 For a discussion of some of the complexities that arise in relation to child-centred education see for example Woodhead 1990, Sugrue, 1997.

7 The absence of including children in these discussions while acknowledging the importance of their voice raises questions about the serious intent of adults to pay more than lip service to the inclusion of children's perspectives on policy development in education. As a contrary example children were invited to make submissions to the development of the *National Children's Strategy* (2000).

8 That primary school children can contribute effectively to school life through participation in a student council is evident from the research conducted by McLoughlin and outlined in Chapter 8 of this volume.

as is the importance of developing citizenship through active and critical reflection in the SPHE programme. Again however, partnership in education appears to be defined in adult-centred terms, with children's voice confined to independent initiatives in schools rather than through any prescribed obligation to include their voice on policy decisions made.

While changes in educational discourse have brought benefits in terms of a less authoritarian approach to children's education, coupled with a broadening of their curricular experience (as in for example the Revised Primary Curriculum 1999), children's own views and perspectives on their school experience have been markedly absent from policy debates and discourse in education.[9] This absence of children's voice is no longer tenable in light of discourse and legislation, both national and international, which stresses the rights of children to have a voice in matters that directly affect them. The remainder of this chapter presents research conducted into children's own perspectives on their status in school as well as their perspectives on having a greater say in school matters.

Listening to what children have to say

The research was conducted with a sample of primary school children on their views of school (Devine 2003). In total three primary schools were involved, all co-educational with contrasting socio-economic intakes: 'Churchfield' which was predominantly middle/upper middle class, 'Hillview' which served a lower middle class population and 'Parkway' which was a designated disadvantaged school. A mixed methodological approach was utilised, consisting of qualitative fieldwork over a period of one school year, continuous observations of classroom practice, open-ended questionnaires and semi-structured interviews with 133 pupils in first/second and fifth class. Interviews were conducted in friendship groups of three and four, the children free to select with whom they wished to be interviewed. Semi-structured interviews with the teachers of these pupils (five in total) as well as their school principals (three) were also conducted. For the purposes of this chapter the analysis focuses on two main themes:

- children's perspective on their status in school
- school matters – giving children a say

9 A notable exception, perhaps signaling the way forward, is the active inclusion of children's voice and perspective at the National Forum Proceedings on Ending Disadvantage at primary level (Zappone 2002).

Children's perspective on their status in school

When asked to comment on their relations with their teachers in school, the children voiced mixed views that were significantly linked to their gender, age and social class. A majority of children (60%) for example indicated that their teacher was kind to them, with girls, younger children and those from a working class background most positive in their views. Being praised by the teacher for doing their work, cared for in terms of getting a good education and being kind in their dealing with children were important signifiers of these positive relations with teachers:

> She's very nice and doesn't give out a lot. She's never uptight and she listens when you have something to say. Also she's very clever. (5th class girl, Churchfield)

> I feel happy when I get everything right and the teacher says good boy. (2nd class boy, Churchfield)

A more conditional response was reflected in the views of many of the older children however, especially when issues of respect for children were raised. Only 18% of children agreed with the statement that 'children are treated with respect in school' while 48% disagreed, with a significant proportion of this latter group from the older fifth classes (P<001). Clarification of the children's views was sought during interviews where a number of subthemes related to the children's perception of their status in school emerged. These themes centred principally on the control of children's learning and the organisation of school rules. The analysis suggested a link in the children's minds between respect for children and the recognition and inclusion of their voice on decisions related to the organisation of their learning and the making of school rules.

Respect and recognition of children's voice in school learning

While there were aspects of the school curriculum that the children both enjoyed and disliked,[10] they recognised for the most part that what they learned in school was necessary for their future adult lives. Criticisms they expressed centred on how this learning was organised (as they saw it in terms of adult priorities) and the absence of choice given to them over the order and emphases of learning in school:

---

10 For a fuller discussion of the children's experience of the school curriculum (prior to the Revised Curriculum 1999) see Devine (2003).

> Teachers sort of choose the subjects they like … so they do that a lot … like our teacher loves Irish or when we had nuns they did a lot of religion. (5th class girl, Churchfield)

> I'd like to be able to choose more … 'cos everyday we do the same thing and it gets boring … and if you want to do say history she wants to do maths or something … she sticks to the same routine all the time. (5th class boy, Hillview)

Annoyance was also expressed over the undue emphasis that was placed on work over play in the organisation of the school timetable:

> We should be allowed choose about PE or going out to the yard … we'd mix work and play more … like at the beginning of the year we could decide the timetable and have half an hour of work and an hour break. (5th class girl, Churchfield)

> Children should be respected more … we should have more things to do than work and more work and we get so tired. (5th class girl, Churchfield)

Their absence of control over how learning is organised is epitomised in the comment of one younger child (to a chorus of agreement from the other children) who stated:

> Sometimes it feels a bit like being a robot … as if the teacher is in the middle of the room with a great big remote control and you have to do everything she says or you will get into trouble. (2nd class girl, Churchfield)

In making such criticisms what the children were asking for was a rebalancing of work time and playtime in school, as well as consultation on how their time should be spent in school:

> I'd make learning more fun and stop all the rules … and I'd have work followed by football and give the children an hour where they could decide what to do. (5th class boy, Churchfield)

> Do some school work but not as much, like geography, Irish, Maths, Science, History and English in the same day, because we deserve a break too. (5th class girl, Hillview)

These children's comments not only indicate their dissatisfaction over aspects of their learning experience but also how such experience can indicate an absence of recognition of their priorities in school. An interlinked concern relates to the view expressed by a number of children, most particularly those in the older classes, that adults do not fully understand what it is like to be a child in school. This they connect to issues of respect and status:

> Some teachers don't understand what it's like … how hard it is … like they might say do the next six questions and they might be the hardest in the book … and twenty minutes later they say have you got them done even though they would take you half an hour … if they had to be children for just one hour they would know it was hard and find out what it was like to do a question in five minutes. (5th class boy, Churchfield)

> Children should be respected more … we should have more things to do than work and more work and we get so tired. (5th class girl, Hillview)

A lack of empathy with children was also commented upon in relation to the difficulty of learning tasks and the absence of individual attention when children found the work they were doing difficult to understand:

> I hate the way if you don't understand something and you say you don't. … the teacher just explains it the same way all over again … they don't change the way they explain so you still don't understand. (5th class boy, Hillview)

> In maths she might explain something by doing two sums and if you didn't understand them then tough … she'll say I'm not taking any more questions after this so you better all listen and even if you did listen and you tried to understand but couldn't she wouldn't' answer you … she has no patience. (5th class girl, Churchfield)

Children held more ambiguous views however regarding their involvement in decisions about other aspects of their learning. Evaluation and assessment for example was generally perceived to be the preserve of the teacher and an area where most children did not have any great wish to become more directly involved. Marking their work, reporting on progress to parents was seen to be something which belonged to the 'adult world' of checking and monitoring.[11] Control over the organisation of classroom space was also perceived to be firmly in adult hands, justified in the main by adult ownership of the school and classroom:

> It's her classroom so she can do it whatever way she wants. (5th class girl, Churchfield)

Where children expressed the view that they should have a say, this centred on deciding with whom they should sit, with older children again most likely to express their desire to be consulted in this way:

---

[11] See Devine (2003) for a more detailed discussion of the children's perception and experience of evaluation in school.

> You should be allowed to sit beside your best friend ... she tells everyone to stand up and then she picks two boys and two girls for each group. (5th class boy, Churchfield)

Respect and recognition in the making of school rules

Systems of surveillance permeate school practice so that children themselves constantly monitor their behaviour in light of school norms. Jackson (1968) in typifying the work of schools speaks of them as places of 'crowds, praise and control' and much has been written in the sociological literature on the socialising functions of schooling through adherence to a series of rules and regulations (Bernstein 1975, Bowles and Gintis 1976, King 1978/1989, Lynch 1989, Pollard and Triggs 2000). This aspect of the exercise of power between adults and children in school is epitomised in the comment of one child in the study who stated:

> I'd put the teacher's desk as far away as possible ... outside the classroom door ... 'cos she's watching over your every move. Every time you even look in your bag she's watching over you and even if you want to get a head start in your homework she sees you. (5th class girl, Hillview)

While the above quote indicates an extreme sense of control perceived by that child,[12] all children in the study recounted rules related to how they spoke, how they moved, what they ate, how they interacted with one another and their teachers, what they wore and how they were to behave for learning. On the whole however most children recognised the need for some form of discipline in school, citing reasons of safety, the facilitation of learning and the need for self-discipline:

> They have rules so children won't hurt themselves and to teach them discipline ... 'cos if you learn discipline the older you get, the wiser you become. (5th class girl, Churchfield)

> If there were no rules there would be no discipline or order ... you have to have order so it will be easier for the teachers to do their work ... just think of it without the rules ... it would be impossible! (5th class boy, Hillview)

However there was some discrepancy evident in children's attitudes toward the fairness of rules, with older children, especially

---

[12] While children do experience high levels of control over their behavior in school, as agents they are critically able to reflect upon this control and negotiate spaces with their teachers where control is less complete (Devine 2003).

middle class boys, most critical of the exercise of power and control by teachers. For these children, school rules interfered with their capacity to have fun and exercise some freedom over what they did in school:

> School rules aren't fair 'cos we should be allowed have fun sometimes ... rules do make school safer but they make it too safe ... they shouldn't stop you from running or eating what you want. (5th class boy, Churchfield)

For other children, especially younger girls, rules were perceived as being there for children's own good and there was an acceptance that their behaviour should be curtailed in school:

> If there wasn't school rules then children would end up in hospital. (5th class girl, Hillview)

> There are rules in school 'cos children are bad. (2nd class girl, Parkway)

These differences in views were also reflected in the children's attitudes toward having a voice in the making of school rules. Eighty six percent of children in the study stated that the teacher decided what the rules would be, and just over half (52%) were happy with this situation. Boys and older children, especially those who were middle class, were most likely to assert their right to be consulted about school rules:

> It would be better to share decisions about rules with children ... at the start of the year he just comes in with a long list and says now abide by the rules ... it's like being in boarding school but we're here in an ordinary school. (5th class boy, Parkway)

Older children were also more likely to draw comparisons between their own status in school and that of teachers, who appeared to be able to circumvent school rules by virtue of their adult status:

> The teachers are allowed smoke ... they're allowed walk around the classroom whenever they want ... they're allowed talk whenever they want ... they're allowed have cups of tea in the middle of school when we're not allowed even a drink of water ... they should have to follow the rules they make ... the same ones as us. (5th class girl, Parkway)

> No way are the children respected ... let us have more say in having rules over them ... we should have a say in making rules for us and our clothes ... I hate this uniform. (5th class girl, Hillview)

Younger children however were highly ambiguous about questioning teacher authority, encapsulated in the comment of one young boy that 'teachers are allowed to do everything they want' and by implication, children are not. Part of these children's discourse also included a perception that children were not capable of making responsible decisions relating to school rules:

> We're too young to be in charge ... we're smaller than the big people (2nd class boy, Churchfield)

Overall what the data suggests is that there are two competing discourses which children draw upon in their attitudes toward having a voice in school. The first, expressed most often by younger children and girls, coincides with a more paternalistic view of children and childhood. In this discourse, children are viewed as dependent and vulnerable, in need of adult guidance and protection. School is a space controlled and owned by adults and within which children must comply and do what they are told. This serves their best interests. An alternate discourse, posited by older middle class children, especially but by no means exclusively boys, is one that asserts children's right to be consulted on what they do in school. While older girls were more accepting of teacher authority than their male peers, dissatisfaction they expressed tended to focus on the manner in which rules were implemented rather than the existence of rules per se.

School matters – giving children a say

These children then are keenly aware of differences in power and status between themselves and teachers in school. They acknowledge for the most part that teachers need to take control and be 'the boss' if learning is to take place. However, the children, especially as they get older, seem to question the extent of control that is exercised. Where this arose in discussion during interviews, being taken seriously as children was central to the children's perspective, as reflected in the comments below:

> When adults are treated unfairly they stand up and object to it ... but they don't kinda take children seriously ... they think they are just messing or looking for attention. (5th class girl, Churchfield)

> Sometimes children should have a say ... if something is really hard for children and they might feel scared ... if they have a say the teacher might understand more ... but you need to know they won't say: 'oh listen to this and listen to that' ... that's what they do sometimes at staff meetings with the black book.[13] (2nd class girl, Churchfield)

---

[13] The 'black book', notorious among the children as an instrument of control, was the notebook in this school in which teachers took account of children's misdemeanors – mainly in the schoolyard. It comprises part of the system of surveillance used in schools and alluded to earlier.

However, not all children subscribed to these views, and factors such as social class and age level influenced the degree of dissatisfaction expressed. This was especially the case in relation to children's desire to exercise a greater voice in school, with fifth-class children and children who were middle class most likely to assert their right to be respected and to voice an opinion on matters which concerned them in school. Fairness was central to the views expressed – that to exclude children's views was to treat them unfairly. Suggestions made to give greater recognition to children's views included the following:

> If I was a teacher I would take the pupils' opinions as serious as they took mine because it wouldn't be fair if it was just my opinion all of the time. (5th class girl, Hillview)

> If I were a teacher I would make sure all the teachers in the school were kind but strict and let the children have their own point of view before making a decision that included them. (5th class boy, Churchfield)

These older children had some sense of adult democratic practices and mentioned the importance of being allowed to vote on issues of importance to them:

> I think there should be a vote over rules … 'cos we live in a democracy … if we could have different lunch times that would be brilliant … we should be allowed vote about whether or not we want to go to the choir. (5th class boy, Churchfield)

> I think the children should get a say in deciding rules … well there are votes for Presidents or whatever so we could put our vote in the box … she'd have her rules and then we'd vote for them. (5th class girl, Churchfield)

For some children, being given a say involved having a more open relationship with their teachers, where they were less part of the 'crowd' and given recognition for themselves as individuals, with their own feelings and views. This was often equated with the relationship of care and empathy that they had with other significant adults in their lives, such as their parents:

> If I was to change one thing about teachers it would be their anger … everyone at some stage in my class got given out to by the teacher … I would try to be kind and sweet like Mary Poppins. I wish at school we could act ourselves in the same way at home – everyone different, everyone special in a way. (5th class girl, Hillview).

> At home they care about you more and you have more freedom … there's fewer children at home. (5th class boy, Churchfield)

From the children's perspective this care and empathy should cut across all of their school lives, enabling them to be listened to without risking rebuke or criticism.[14] This appeared to be mostly mentioned with regard to understanding what they are learning and the fear of making mistakes:

> Your teacher should be your best friend. She should understand your mistakes and help you fix them and make them easier to understand the next time. (5th class girl, Hillview)

> I think they only listen to you when you do something to get attention … like excuse me I've cut my arm or something like that … you're told to sit down and wait your turn … 'I'll come down and talk to you later' and then she doesn't. (5th class girl, Churchfield)

Conclusions

This chapter began by presenting an outline of the changes which have taken place both nationally and internationally on discourse relating to children and childhood. Central to such change, and enshrined in both national and international legislation, is the recognition that children have a right to have their views heard in relation to matters which directly affect them. Developments such as the Ombudsman for Children and Dáil Na nÓg signal the increasing attention being given to this area by policy makers. School matters to children, not only as a space within which they acquire the skills to compete effectively as adults in the economic system, but also as one where they develop the social and personal skills to become active contributors, not just to the economy but to society itself. Given the changing context of children's lives in the broader society, where negotiation with children and recognition of their voice is increasingly incorporated into public discourse and policy, it seems both opportune and necessary to include the perspectives of children in the organisation of primary schools.

By exploring children's perception of their status in school and their attitudes toward having a greater say in school, this chapter has raised questions about the location of children as persons with the right to be heard in school. The children in this research are keenly aware of differences in status between themselves and adults in school, although varying views were expressed on the

---

[14] For their part, teachers also spoke of their wish to have stronger interpersonal relationships with the children but felt constrained by resource pressures, including time itself. For a more detailed discussion about the dynamics of teacher/pupil relations see Devine (2003).

legitimacy of such differences. The views they express in this and the following chapters demonstrates their ability to reflect both critically and constructively on what happens to them in school. They also challenge overly paternalistic discourses which can limit and constrain children's opportunity for more active engagement in decision making. Teachers, as adults, can harness this capacity in their classroom and school practices. However, listening to children, exploring their lifeworld, prioritising their perspectives presents challenges and opportunities to both teachers and children themselves. At its core is a re-evaluation of the dynamics of power and control that currently prevail in primary schools, where children, as is increasingly the case with parents, are perceived along with teachers, to be partners in education with a voice to be heard and expressed. Educating children about democracy, justice and inclusiveness, about rights and responsibilities will be most effective where children themselves are afforded greater responsibility through active involvement in school. International research on school effectiveness and improvement supports such development (Teddlie and Reynolds 2001) as part of the creation of an inclusive culture in schools. In school matters, children's voice, no less than that of teachers or parents, deserves to be heard.

Bibliography

Akenson, D. (1975) *A Mirror to Kathleen's Face: Education in Independent Ireland 1922-1960*, London, McGill-Queen's University Press.

Archard, D. (1993) *Children, Rights and Childhood,* London, Routledge.

Beck, U. (1992) Risk Society, London, Sage.

Bernstein, B. (1975) *Class, Codes and Control: Towards a theory of Educational Transmission* (Vol 3), London, Routledge Kegan Paul.

Bowles, S. and Gintis, H. (1976) *Schooling in Capitalist America,* London, Routledge Kegan Paul.

Buckingham, D. (2000) *After the Death of Childhood: Growing Up in the Age of Electronic Media,* Cambridge, Polity.

Connolly, P. (1998) *Racism, Gender Identities and Young Children*, London, Routledge.

Corsaro, W. A. (1997) *The Sociology of Childhood*, London, Pine Forge Press.

Curtin, C. and Varley, A. (1984) 'Children and Childhood in Rural Ireland: A consideration of Ethnographic Literature', in Curtin, C. et al (eds*), Culture and Ideology in Ireland*, Galway University Press.

Davies, B. (1991) 'Friends and Fights', in Woodhead, M. and Light, P. (eds) *Growing up in Changing Society*, London, Routledge.

Deegan, J. (1996) *Children's Friendships in Culturally Diverse Classrooms*, London, Falmer Press.

Deegan, J. (2002) 'Early Childhood Discourse: Problematising Some Conceptual Issues in Statutory Frameworks', *Irish Educational Studies*, Vol 21, No 3: 77-88.

Department of Education (1990) *Report of the Primary Review Body on the Primary Curriculum*, Dublin, Mount Salus Press.

Devine, D. (2002) 'Children's Citizenship and the Structuring of adult-child relations in the primary school', *Childhood*, Vol 9 (3): 303-321.

Devine, D. (1999) 'Children: Rights and Status in Education – a Socio historical Perspective', *Irish Educational Studies*, 18:14-29.

Devine, D., Nic Ghiolla Phadraig, M. and Deegan, J. (2004) 'Time for Children – Time for Change?: Children's Rights and Welfare in Ireland during a period of economic growth', in Jensen, A., Ben Arieh, A., Conti, C., Kustar, D., Nic Ghiolla Phadraig, M. and Nielsen, H. (eds) *Childhood in Ageing Societies, Country Studies on Children's Welfare in Everyday Life*, Vol 1, Trondheim, Norwegian Centre for Child Research and Tartu University Press.

Devine, D. (2003) *Children, Power and Schooling – How Childhood is Structured in School, Stoke on Trent*, Trentham Books.

Fraser, N. (2000) 'Rethinking Recognition', *New Left Review*, 2, 3: 107-120.

Fraser, N. (1995) 'From Redistribution to recognition? Dilemmas of justice in a "post-socialist" age', *New Left Review*, 212: 68-93.

Gillis, J. (2002) 'Birth of the Virtual Child: Origins of our Contradictory Images of Children', in Dunne, J. and Kelly, J. (eds) *Childhood and its Discontents*, Dublin, Liffey Press.

Government of Ireland (2000) *The National Children's Strategy*, Dublin, Stationery Office.

Government of Ireland (1999) *Revised Primary Curriculum*, Dublin, Stationery Office.

Hendrick, H. (1997) 'Constructions and Reconstructions of British Childhood: An Interpretative Study 1800 to the present', in James, A., Prout, A. and Jencks, C. (eds) *Constructing and Reconstructing Childhood: Contemporary Issues in the Sociological Study of Childhood*, London, Falmer Press.

INTO (1985) *Primary School Curriculum – Report and Discussion Papers*, Dublin, INTO.

Investment in Education (1965) *Report of the Survey Team*, Dublin, Stationery Office.

Jackson, P. (1968) *Life in Classrooms*, Chicago, Holt, Rinehart and Winston.

James, C., Jenks, C. and Prout, A. (1998) *Theorising Childhood,* London, Polity.

Jenks, C. (1996) *Childhood*, London, Routledge.

Jensen, An-Magritt and McKee, L. (eds) (2003): *Children and the Changing Family: Between Transformation and Negotiation*. London, Routledge Falmer.

King, R. (1989) *The Best of Primary Education? A Sociological Study of Junior Middle Schools,* London, Falmer.

King, R. (1978) *All Things Bright and Beautiful? A Sociological Study of Infants' Classrooms,* New York, John Wiley and Sons.

Lodge, A. and Flynn, M. (2001) 'Gender Identity in the Primary School Playground', in Cleary, A., NicGhiolla Phadraig, M. and Quin, S (eds) *Understanding Children,* Volume 2, Dublin, Oak Tree Press.

Lynch, K. (1989) *The Hidden Curriculum: Reproduction in Education: A Reappraisal*, Lewes, Falmer Press.

Lynch, K. (1999) *Equality in Education*, Dublin, Gill and MacMillan.

Lynch, K. and Lodge, A. (2002) *Equality and Power in Schools,* London, Routledge.

Mayall, B. and Zeiher, H. (2003) *Childhood in Generational Perspective*, London, Institute of Education.

Mayall, B. (2002) *Towards a Sociology for Childhood,* Buckingham, Open University Press.

Mizen, P. (2001) *Hidden Hands: International Perspectives on Children's Work and Labour*, London, Routledge Falmer.

NCCA (1990) *Report of the Review Body on the Primary Curriculum*, Department of Education, Dublin, Stationery Office.

OECD (1964) *Papers from a Conference on the financing of Education for Economic Growth*, Paris, OECD.

O'Sullivan, D. (1980) 'Teacher Socialisation and Teaching Style in an Irish Cultural Context', *European Journal of Education,* Vol 15, No 4.

Pollard, A. and Triggs, P. (2000) *What Pupils Say: Changing Policy and Practice in Primary Education*, London, Continuum.

Postman, N. (1994) *The Disappearance of Childhood*, London, Allen.

Qvortrup, J. (2001) 'Schoolwork, Paidwork and the changing obligations of childhood', in Mizen, P., Pole, C. and Bolton, A. (eds) *Hidden Hands: International Perspectives on Children's work and Labour*, London, Routledge Falmer.

Ovortrup, J. (1994) 'Childhood Matters: an introduction', in Qvortrup, J., Bardy, M., Sgritta, G. and Wintersberger, H. (eds) *Childhood Matters: Social Theory, Practice and Politics,* Aldershot, Avebury.

Sugrue, C. (1997) *Complexities of Teaching: Child Centred Perspectives*, London, Falmer Press.

Teddlie, C. and Reynolds, D. (2001) *International Handbook of School Effectiveness and Improvement*, London, Falmer.

Woodhead, M. (1990) 'Psychology and the Cultural Construction of Children's Needs', in James, A. and Prout, A., *Constructing and Reconstructing Childhood*, Basingstoke, Falmer Press.

Zappone, K. (2002) 'Achieving Equality in Children's Education', in *Primary Education: Ending Disadvantage – Proceedings and Action Plan of National Forum*, St Patrick's College, Drumcondra.

CHAPTER 8

Citizen child – the experience of a student council in a primary school

Owen McLoughlin

Introduction

Underpinning any research into participation in society is a particular group's status as citizens. Traditionally ignored in citizenship studies, children are recently more frequently recognised as citizens with rights and responsibilities, as indicated by the publication of the *National Children's Strategy* (2000), the establishment of Dáil na nÓg (2002) and Comhairle na nÓg (2003). While these initiatives are welcome, they provide for a limited number of children to participate directly in decision making in matters that affect them. As outlined in the previous chapter, the Education Act of 1998 provides for second-level pupils to be given opportunities to form a student council. The concept of these student councils has been recognised and endorsed (Humphreys 1998, O'Gorman 1998). However, no such recognition is given to primary school children.

Citizenship can be embraced as a possible vehicle for the extension of rights to children and student councils in primary schools are proposed as ideal fora to frame a redefinition of children's citizenship. The chapter outlines the findings of a case study into the establishment and operation of a student council over one school year. Utilizing Hart's (1992) framework, it explores the citizenship status of the pupils in St Paul's NS as they grapple with the challenges and opportunities as a result of their membership of the student council.

The chapter is divided into three sections: children's citizenship and pupil participation in primary schools are initially explored. This is followed by a review of previous research related to the establishment and functioning of student councils at primary level.

An outline of the main findings related to the establishment of this Irish primary school student council is then presented.

Children's citizenship and participation in primary school decision making

Traditional studies of citizenship have tended to preclude consideration of children as citizens (e.g. Marshall 1950) and, as with women, they have been conferred with subordinate status. While Marshall's work *Citizenship and Social Class* (1950) has been highly influential in debates over citizenship, the citizenship of children is considered incomplete in this work, adding to their invisibility as a social group in society. Bulmer and Rees see this neglect of children in Marshall's work as a major oversight:

> Children are largely invisible yet it is they and not their parents who are the direct users of the school system, and who may well have strong views of their own about their education (Bulmer and Rees 1996: 276).

Many social theorists are now placing a higher value on children, further enhancing their social citizenship (Alton 2001, Delanty 2000). This is also notable in research in Scandinavia and New Zealand, both regarded as a benchmark in children's citizenship studies (Qvortrup 1996, Wyness 2000).

A difficulty in researching children's citizenship is the significance of age (Bytheway 1995, Hill and Tisdall 1997). While there are many new civil rights introduced in the UNCRC (United Nations Convention on the Rights of the Child 1989) within articles 12-15, it is not specific regarding age applicability (United Nations 1991). It has been shown that the United Kingdom is in direct breach of a number of articles within the convention (Wyness 1999). Similarly, in Ireland, relevant groups have not promoted the fact that children *must* have a say in matters that affect them, although with recent publications (Department of Health and Children – *Children First* and *National Children's Strategy* (2000)) this is beginning to change. Involving children in decision making, which is fundamental to their citizenship, is unknown to many professionals. Practices of speaking to and listening to children in a democratic fashion are rare (Roche 1999, Hart 1992).

Few people are arguing that children have the same citizenship as adults. What is being argued is that children are active, social beings and citizens in their own right. The world has always been defined in adult terms and, for effective change, adults will have to do things differently (Davie and Galloway 1996). The language of children's rights (UNCRC, Children's Rights Alliance – CRA

(1996, 1997 and 1998), *National Children's Strategy* (2000)) is a starting point and not the end. It is about respecting and valuing the contribution that children make and have to make to the world that they share with adults. Many western nations think of themselves as having achieved democracy fully. However, they teach the principles of democracy in a pedantic way in classrooms which can themselves be models of autocracy (Hart 1992).

Figure 1: Hart's Ladder of Participation

Rungs 1-3: Degrees of non-participation
Rungs 4-8: Degrees of participation

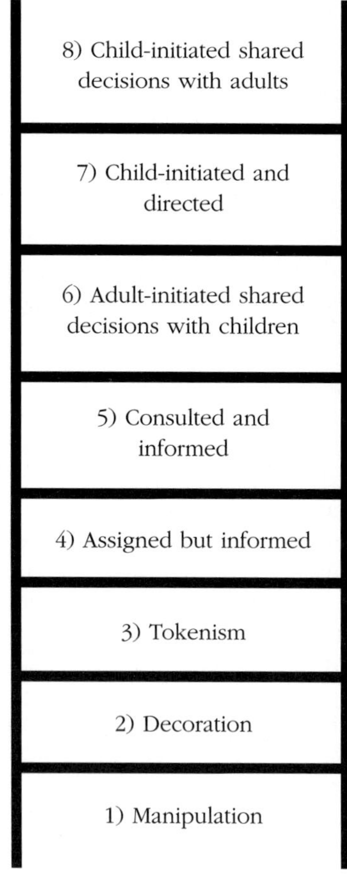

Adapted by Hart (1992) from Sherry Arnstein (1969)

The theoretical framework underpinning this chapter to articulate a vision of children's citizenship status is Hart's Ladder of Participation (Figure 1). If participation is the fundamental right attached to citizenship (Hart 1992) then children, as citizens, should be stakeholders in the day-to day decisions that affect their lives (Devine 2002, Murray and Hallett 2000). Applied to the operation of a student council, Hart's analysis provides a marker of the citizenship status of children in a primary school, through the decisions made by the elected members of a student council and shared by the teachers and management of that school.

There is a direct link between the rungs of this ladder and the level of social citizenship achieved in the school. If children are consulted on matters that affect them and their views are taken seriously by other (adult) stakeholders in the school, then school-based projects can be better developed than before. As will be shown, in the findings presented in this chapter, some original proposals by children in the school were agreed to by teaching staff and subsequently ratified by the Board of Management. Without the formal structures of the student council, this higher-order citizenship (level 8 on the ladder) could not have been achieved.

Within the United Kingdom, Wyness (1999) and Wade and Moore (1993) look pessimistically at the opportunities for reform in children's participation in schools. In a survey of 115 mainstream primary and secondary schools, Wade and Moore found that less than one-third took account of pupils' views. Wyness (1999) recognises that there are so-called 'child-centred' reforms in education and a move towards control of schools locally but he states:

> there are little grounds for thinking that present education systems treat children as competent social actors (Ibid: 1999, p. 354).

The indictment of the present system results from the few chances for creativity offered to children in schools. Children are subdued by curriculum requirements and discipline structures. They move through the system as temporary guests, while schools remain the world of teachers (Wyness 1999). The consumers of education are parents and not children. All information regarding children is addressed to their parents. Pupils are not involved in policy consultation and school choice is the preserve of parents. In fact, all information regarding children places adults at the centre. By making curricula teacher-centred, education reforms in Britain in recent years prevent or, at least, impede the possibility of pupil involvement.

Student councils in primary schools

Student councils in Britain had greater popularity in the 1980s than the 1990s. A survey carried out in 1989 found that 97% of second-level schools had student councils while a similar survey in 1993 discovered that only a seventh of primary schools and 50% of secondary schools had councils (Willow 1990). Reasons given for the recent demise of the councils include curriculum demands and moves away from pupil-focused practice in the United Kingdom. Willow (1990) found rare examples of worthwhile student councils, particularly one at Highfield Junior School, Plymouth. In this school the council had a budget and was involved in the recruitment and selection of staff. However, this seems to be the exception as most other councils were identified as relatively weak.

There is scant research documenting the experiences of and attitudes towards student councils in primary schools in Ireland. Brennan (2000) conducted research with teachers in primary schools on the potential of student councils. While there was a positive response in general to the idea of student councils in primary schools, only two schools in the sample reported having a student council. Some of the teachers felt that it was solely for public relations purposes and did not serve as a mechanism for children's participation in decision making. Many teachers felt that student councils in primary schools would be better confined to senior classes. Teachers were reluctant to get involved in such an initiative as it might fall to them to organise and supervise the work of the council. Teachers had resistance to the notion of consultation with children because of the continuing extra work involved. Further, they felt that consultation could be dangerous as it could undermine the teacher's authority. They felt that teachers should always make the final decisions. Such findings were also identified by Devine (2003) where teachers in her study met the notion of participation by children in active decision making with both suspicion and incredulity.

Positive comments made by teachers regarding student councils (Brennan 2000) included the benefits of responsibility being accorded to children: pride, happiness of children involved, a sense of belonging, increased confidence and self-esteem and a growing sense of partnership. The problems that arose included the resistance by teachers to the idea of consultation and the emergence of leaders in the project committee with squabbles over who was 'in charge'. O'Gorman (1998) notes that the post of co-ordinator of the student council is not suitable for all teachers and that whoever undertakes to operate it must believe in it. Because it is a recent innovation, she recommends that the development of the council be gradual, with progress being constantly evaluated.

For examples of successful action research projects on student councils we must look further afield. *Involving Pupils in Practice* (Jelly, Byers and Fuller 2000) was an action research programme in special education in the United Kingdom. Its main aim was to increase student autonomy through empowerment. The project (involving six schools with student councils) suggests that we should be re-framing what constitutes the product of education and redefining success from a pupil perspective. To achieve this, it contends that leaders articulating their vision and having action plans is not enough when the essence of a successful school is the communication within. The project encourages risk-taking from teachers in terms of positive initiatives to help transfer control of learning to pupils. These risk-takers equate with the 'emergent citizen' of Hart's (1992) writing. The schools involved all reported improvements and positive results for staff, pupils and the organisation. The approaches used included allowing pupils to lead; listening to pupils' views; affording pupils respect; treating pupils as partners, while maintaining boundaries and framing questions from a pupil's perspective. Involving students in developing policies, such as codes of discipline, is encouraged and has reduced discipline issues in some of the schools. The idea of a model of a student council as a tool for participation in decision making in education and as an aid to redefining social citizenship for children is central to these projects. The development of a citizenship curriculum in 1999 for British schools is also pivotal and lays the foundation for similar work in Irish primary schools.

A student council in an Irish primary school

The school in this case study, St Paul's[1] is a vertical mixed school of Catholic denomination. In an urban area of mixed housing, it is designated disadvantaged. There are twenty-five members of staff. The sample population of the study consisted of representation from all classes in St Paul's NS from 3rd to 6th class (including three special classes). The children were elected in class elections organised by their class teachers. There was advice given to teachers on preliminary circle-time, running elections and ensuring fairness in the selection procedure. Extracts were given to teachers from the NYCI (National Youth Council of Ireland) manual on advice towards setting up a student council (2001). Elections were held in ten classes and fourteen children were deemed elected. The

1 St Paul's NS is a pseudonym for an Irish urban primary school.

student council was formally introduced to the school's principal and the children were presented with certification. The ten organised student council meetings in the St Paul's case study followed the NYCI recommended format. Officers were elected (Chairperson, Secretary, Treasurer and PRO) and the basic duties of council members were adhered to. Student council members were afforded status in the school by peers, management and staff and were considered representative, communicators, listeners, leaders and organisers. Meetings followed an agenda that evolved throughout the year. The content of the agenda was generally simple and not overly ambitious.

Agenda for student council meeting

Dear members, please note that there will be a council meeting in the parents' room on Wednesday, 24th October, 2001 at 2:35 pm.

The following will take place at the meeting:

1. *Minutes of last meeting – J. K.*
2. *Matters arising from minutes*
3. *Chairperson's letter from BoM*
4. *PRO – ideas for L. F.*
5. *Notebooks – new suggestions*
6. *Decisions for next meeting*

The methodology of data gathering was qualitative (Greig and Taylor 1999, Graue and Walsh 1998, Lewis and Lindsay 2000). It involved the use of taped council meetings, a field diary by the researcher, questionnaires to the relevant stakeholders before and after the case study and an open forum of senior children in the school. A central part of the data gathering was the taped meetings. All ten council meetings were conducted in circle time fashion with a microphone offered as the mode to take the 'floor'. These taped meetings were subsequently transcribed. With only one voice possible through taking the microphone, the method allowed for few interruptions to a child's comments or suggestions. Communication of council matters in St Paul's took the form of a brief verbal report at each staff meeting. This enabled staff members to be kept fully informed of the development of the student council and to communicate the suggestions of the children.

Staff concerns regarding the one-way path of communication (i.e. from children to staff) were noted as the case study progressed. Therefore, it was decided to send a response to the student council from the staff after each monthly staff meeting. Other difficulties encountered included communicating the progress and decisions of the council to the pupils within the school, given the restricted opportunity for children from different classes to engage and interact with one another during the school day. However, contrary to previous findings (Brennan 2000), there appeared to be little opposition to the initiative by the relevant stakeholders in this case study. Parents of children who were elected to the student council commented on their interest in the council and its development, through questionnaires. No parent was opposed to their child's participation in the venture and their reaction after the case study was singularly positive. The Board of Management endorsed the venture, replied to council members in writing and was kept fully abreast of developments.

Teacher perceptions of the student council

Data that emerged in relation to the teachers' perceptions (through whole staff questionnaires before and after the case study), related to their approval/disapproval of the initiative, their opinions on the rights of children's voice to be heard and their views on children's potential participation in decision making. Although in favour of a student council, the teachers were nervous at the challenge of concessions that may have to be granted to children. Overall however staff members took the views and concerns of the children seriously, and expressed surprise at the level of coherence of the views expressed:

> What worked well was the follow-through on issues that have arisen. The staff have listened and by-and- large acted upon the wishes of the council. The children have learned to request reasonable, workable solutions. (senior class teacher)

> It was great to hear how the children think – their priorities and concerns. (junior class teacher)

The tokenism shown to be present in many student councils was absent in this particular case and real progress in the stakeholding of children in this primary school was realised through many examples of participation in decision-making. These included a policy change deriving from children's suggestions (related to the allocation of homework), formal negotiation on issues like litter, yard behaviour, shop openings, etc, and a formal opportunity for the student body to voice *any* concerns and teachers' willingness to implement suggestions.

Concerns from teachers over student control were present at the outset of the student council and language like potential 'bad-mouthing of teachers by children' (staff member of St Paul's) was raised in the preliminary discussions about the initiative. A development of more positive attitudes towards the student council occurred throughout the case study when it became obvious that children's suggestions were both practical and respectful of the adults. In relation to communication, teachers felt that there was a lack of opportunity for council members to report back to the student body, a diminishing importance of the student council report at staff meetings over the course of the school year and a lack of information provided to younger children. Proposed development of the student council communication procedures by teachers included examples such as children organising assemblies, children being invited to speak to staff, children helping to draw up the code of conduct and children editing school magazines with information for children by children.

Findings from teachers also indicated an over-burdening of curriculum requirements (Revised Curriculum – Department of Education and Science 1999), discouraging them from active involvement in new initiatives in keeping with the findings by Brennan (2000). Further, the teachers noticed children's difficulty with the slow pace of change. Children's frustrations were perceived by teachers as innocent and naïve rather than as a concern to be taken seriously, reiterating findings noted by Devine elsewhere in the previous chapter. This is perhaps indicative of the novelty of the initiative in primary education. Teachers also felt that the younger representatives were unsuitable for council membership. In addition, teachers felt that certain roles (secretary) should not be given to children with special needs as they may be unable to cope with such duties. Although these concerns are valid, they do not negate the work of the student council and further emphasise teachers' appreciation in St Paul's that it is now necessary and beneficial to consult with children on matters affecting them:

> A very good idea for opening up lines of communication with both staff and pupils. (junior class teacher)

> Getting the students' perspective on things was really interesting. Sometimes they saw things in a completely different way to the teachers. Other times the staff at their meeting and the student council were discussing the same things simultaneously. (senior teacher)

The children's voice

Children's perceptions and experiences of a council centred on the themes of communication and rights.

Communication

Findings of the case study in St Paul's indicate a number of concerns experienced by children in relation to communication in the school. These centred around the absence of communication in relation to school-based projects and the working environment of children. The establishment of the student council provided the children with a forum in which to document their concerns. Those particularly highlighted included food (consistency among teachers to implement policy), sport (provision of adequate goalposts and new football gear for girls, etc), homework (concessions desired for half days) and working environment (hardness of seats and positioning of tables, etc).

School lunch provision, shop and school policy on food featured at each council meeting:

> I got two suggestions. One was the shop should be bigger and another one says that there should be rolls like salad and bread to be served. (Dan – senior special needs)

> You know the milks we're getting now, the ones from Donegal, they're not really as nice as the other ones we used to get 'cos they're kinda watery and they taste disgusting, my class was saying. (Rita – 5th class)

> People came and they said stuff like, em, they want Pat to accept Irish punts until, until you're allowed, you know 'cos he's only taking euro and I'm not sure if he knows how to convert it much 'cos like the prices are going real far up, on some things. (Sam – 6th class)

The issue of sport and its development in the school was also very common among children's suggestions. Most notable were the purchase of new equipment and the delays in action being taken by teachers:

> A lot of people said 'new goalposts' since ours have been taken down, because at the moment my Mam and Dad are giving out because my jumpers are getting dirty by putting them down for goal-posts because everybody keeps trodding on them and rolling over them. (Rita – 5th class)

> Loads of people in my class said we should get new football gear for the girls because the boys and girls have to share and, one time, eh, the boys were playing a match before the girls and they just threw off the jerseys and gave them to the girls. They have to wear everything, like the shorts and everything. (Kate – 6th class)

> Me and Joan went to her. She said she'd get this sorted, she'd get crests and all … never happened. It was about two months ago,

> wasn't it? We'll go to her and we'll ask her did she forget and remind her. She must have forgotten. (Bill – 6th class)

Children's views on homework included the notion of a concession by staff once a month that was subsequently agreed upon by the adults:

> you know the way we have staff meetings once a month on a Wednesday, well, people were saying it would be nice not to have homework on those half days. (Sarah – 6th class)

> em, it'd only be once a month and we could do all our homework properly on the other days. (Bill – 6th class)

Among the most interesting suggestions from the children were the practical adjustments to their physical environments they felt were necessary to improve conditions. Rarely would school-wide suggestions as these have been previously listened/responded to:

> I have a suggestion that you should knock off the radiators on hot days. (Bill – 6th class)

> It's really stupid now but my class said that, em, the seats are really hard and they want cushions or something on them. (Maria – 4th class)

Sarcasm by representatives was not uncommon and highlighted frustrations of children in situations where they feel helpless:

> We have soap dispensers and somebody said we should put soap in the soap dispensers. Teacher would say 'go in there and rub your hands with soap' and he doesn't know there's no soap in it. The only soap there is, is the one in the sink in the classroom and when they were going they were trying to rub it all off with their hands but they made it kinda more soggy and they went out and told teacher there was no soap and he just said 'oh, just sit down'. (Joan – 5th class)

> How we supposed to play chasing walking? You'd be going at the same speed and catching everybody! Yeh, it's different if it's on the corridor but outside … that's basically what outside is for. Just say someone is having a race in the field, they'd be walking, a walk race. (Sam – 6th class)

Absent from the findings was any mention by council members of aspects of teaching and learning. It appears that, from the children's perspective, curriculum content and teacher styles were non-negotiable. This may be because of the novelty of the initiative whereby children were beginning to explore the parameters of the student council and were nervous talking about individual teachers. Alternatively, the presence of the researcher at all meetings may have influenced children not to voice their concerns about educational matters.

Findings also indicated the difficulties of effective communication of the content of meetings of the council to the student body. The attempt to communicate with the general body of teachers and pupils in the school was inadequate. Thus, the children perceived a lack of interest developing among their peers over the course of the school year. There were some discussions at assemblies and some publicising of council business but there was no formal structure of communicating decisions and actions to the general student body. 'Circle-time' sessions were proposed as a possibility for the review of meetings but were not formally timetabled (Mosley 1993, 1996). The study also noted how the dynamics of peer interaction could be influenced by student council membership. An example of this was the accusation by classmates of favouritism by teachers toward some council members, resulting in the resignation of one of the members during the course of the year.

Power and rights of children

The study also indicated that children's perceptions and experience of their rights was a frequent element of student council discussions. The issues in relation to rights emerging in St Paul's included the desire by children for fair play between adults and children, the children's demands for extra concessions for themselves, their frustration at the slow pace of change and the perceived poor utilisation of children's capacities in school-wide projects. Further, some of the children's definitions of concepts relating to citizenship (democracy, freedom of speech, etc) indicate a higher level of political understanding than may have been previously assumed by adults in the school. Some examples of children's responses to why adults should listen to their voice include:

> Because we know the right things for children. (12-year-old)
>
> Well children do have a wisdom about them. Whether they like to admit it or not adults can learn from us! (11-year-old)
>
> Because sometimes children need and want things that are very important. They might not be important to the adults. (12-year-old)

It is clear from their comments that children perceive adults in the school as having had no consciousness of the need to consult with them. The children stated that they had rights as well as teachers, that children have a valid, responsible voice and should not be 'bossed' around by people, confirming findings previously noted by Devine (2003) in her study of primary schools. They also suggested that their elected representatives to the council were both mature and worthy. Furthermore, the children verbalised the 'adultism' they felt was present in schools. They stated that one or more adults (teachers) could ultimately veto a student's suggestion to the student council, no matter how valid the suggestion:

> I thought it was more like the teachers working together with the students but the teachers still act like they are older … (murmurs of 'they are') … yeah, I know but they're supposed to work together with the kids on the council but the teachers still act like they're older so that if they disagreed about anything, the students aren't getting it. (6th class boy)

Children verbalised perceived adult control in the data, by talking about adults 'owning' them. Children felt that adults wielded power in St Paul's by threatening sanctions. They felt that they had not previously been given a valid forum to redress this power imbalance. The children proposed structure to their days and timetables with adult overview but not outright control:

> It doesn't matter how old you are. You cannot just say 'you have to do this/you can't do that' because I'm a teacher. I agree with Mary. You have to have like order. You can't just have people running around and all because you'd grow up and you'd be like on the street or in a horrible flat or something but, like, every single school should have the student council. It's not fair if they don't. It should be part of the curriculum. It should be like just there. (6th class girl)

The children involved in the various elements of the case study did not use the student council as a 'talking shop' or token initiative. They had genuine concerns and suggestions. They wanted recognition for their suggestions from the teachers and frequently became annoyed at the slow pace of change:

> I'd try to get more things done faster. I'd suggest ideas to raise money for things we didn't get done by now. (11-year-old)

The fact that so many of their suggestions were truly taken on board by the teachers and management over the course of the year shows a potential willingness among educators to contribute actively towards realising children's rights in schools. Furthermore, the seriousness with which the children in the council took the initiative indicates that some adult perceptions (prior to the experience of the council) that children would be out of control were unfounded. However, much progress is needed in raising the consciousness of teachers to accept the opinions of their students, to empathise effectively with them.

The study also confirmed the development in children's understanding of a student council. At the outset of the initiative the children in both the student council and the student body in general were enthusiastic. However, it is clear that the consultation alone wasn't enough. The frequent discussions on the slow pace of change and the political negotiation necessary for change (between members of the council and individual members of staff) show an increased awareness among the children of the intricacies of collaboration and consultation. Difficulties over lack of communication and rights' negligence were central to the children's perceptions throughout the case study of the student council. They benefited greatly from the experience of voicing their opinions and gave many suggestions towards the refinement of the procedures for student councils in primary schools in Ireland.

Conclusion

If fora like student councils become commonplace in Irish education, the language of children's citizenship should evolve within these new structures. The reality of children's present subordinate and 'incomplete' citizenship status presents Irish educators with an immediate challenge. Token student councils should not be tolerated, whereby they perpetuate this subordination. The future 'child as citizen' should participate in decision making in all aspects of school life. The importance of educating and supporting teachers should not be underestimated, as children and adults will need to learn to negotiate in a new way (Devine 2002). Teacher Unions, parent bodies and Boards of Management also need to be educated in the area of consultation with children. Children need to be trained to understand the incoming democratic structures and potential membership of a council. Children may then take part ownership of the schools they attend and cease to be just the temporary guests.

Bibliography

Alton, D. (2001) (ed.) *Citizen 21 – Citizenship in the New Millennium,* London, Harper Collins.

Brennan, A. (2000) *Teachers' Perspectives on the Child's Right to be Heard,* Unpublished Thesis, Education Department, University College Dublin.

Bulmer, M. and Rees, A. (1996) *The Contemporary Relevance of T.H. Marshall,* London, UCL Press.

Bytheway, B. (1995) *Ageism,* Buckingham UK and Bristol USA, Open University Press.

Children's Rights Alliance (1996) *Seen and heard – Promoting and protecting Children's Rights in Ireland,* Dublin, Genprint.

Children's Rights Alliance (1997) *Small Voices: Vital Rights,* Dublin, Genprint.

Children's Rights Alliance (1998) *Children's Rights, Our Responsibilities,* Dublin, Children's Rights Alliance.

Davie, R. and Galloway, D. (1996) *Listening to Children in Education,* London, Fulton Publishers.

Delanty, G. (2000) *Citizenship in a Global Age,* Buckingham and Philadelphia, Open University Press.

Department of Education (1992) *Education for a Changing World: Green Paper on Education,* Dublin, Stationery Office.

Department of Education (1995) *Charting our Education Future: White Paper on Education,* Dublin, Stationery Office.

Department of Education and Science (1998) *Education Act,* Dublin, Stationery Office.

Department of Education and Science (1999) *Primary School Curriculum: an Introduction,* Dublin, Stationery Office.

Department of Education and Science (1999) *Primary School Curriculum: SPHE Teacher Guidelines,* Dublin, Stationery Office.

Department of Health and Children (1999) *Children First: National Guidelines for the Protection and Welfare of Children,* Dublin, Stationery Office.

Devine, D. (2002) 'Children's Citizenship and the Structuring of Adult/Child Relations in the Primary School', *Childhood:* Vol 9 (4), London and New Delhi, Sage.

Devine, D. (2003) *Children Power and Schooling – How Childhood is Structured in the Primary School,* Stoke-On-Trent, Trentham Books.

Greig, A. and Taylor, J. (1999) *Doing research with Children,* London, Sage.

Graue, E. and Walsh, D. (1998) *Studying Children in Context: Theories, Methods and Ethics,* London, Sage.

Hart, A. (1992) *Children's Participation – From Tokenism to Citizenship,* Innocenti Essays, No 4, Florence, Unicef.

Hill, M. and Tisdall, K. (1997) *Children and Society,* London and New York, Longman.

Humphreys, T. (1998) *A Different Kind of Discipline,* Dublin, Gill and MacMillan.

Jelly, M., Fuller, A. and Byers, R. (2000) *Involving Pupils in Practice,* Wilts, Cromwell Press.

Lewis, A. and Lindsay, G. (2000) *Researching Children's Perspectives,* Buckingham, Open University Press.

Marshall, T.H. (1950) *Citizenship and Social Class,* Cambridge, Cambridge University Press.

Mosley, J. (1993) *Turn your School Around,* Wisbech, Learning Development Aids.

Mosley, J. (1996) *Quality Circle Time in the Primary Classroom,* Wisbech, Learning Development Aids.

Murray, C. and Hallett, C. (2000) 'Young People's Participation in Decisions Affecting their Welfare', *Childhood* 7 (1), London and New Delhi, Sage.

National Children's Strategy (2000) *Our Children – Their Lives,* Dublin, Stationery Office

National Youth Council (2001) *Youth Participation, Citizenship, Democracy – learning the skills of active democratic participation,* Dublin, NYCI.

O'Gorman, A. (1998) 'Student Councils – Why bother?', *Issues in Education,* Vol 3, Dublin, ASTI.

Qvortrup, J. (1996) 'The Continued Intergenerational Interdependence', in *Children on the Way from Marginality to Citizenship,* Eurosocial report 61, Vienna, European Centre.

Roche, J. (1999) 'Children: Rights, Participation and Citizenship', in *Childhood* 6 (4), London and New Delhi.

United Nations (1991) *The Rights of the Child,* Fact Sheet No 10, Geneva, United Nations.

Wade, B. and Moore, M. (1993) *Experiencing Special Education, What young people with SEN can tell us,* Buckingham, Open University Press.

Willow, C. (1990) *Hear! Hear! Promoting Children's and Young People's Democratic Participation in local government*, London, Local Government Information Unit.

Wyness, M. (1999) 'Childhood, Agency and Education Reform', *Childhood* 6 (3), London and New Delhi.

Wyness, M. (2000) *Contesting Childhood,* London, Falmer Press.

CHAPTER 9

'Big mad words' – schools, social class and children's perceptions of language variation

Gerry MacRuairc

Introduction

The analysis of language variation in schools presented in this chapter is based on the widely held notion that language is central to the individual, to the group and to society in general (Richardson 1991). As an individual goes through the process of socialisation the language of the social group is acquired in a range of speech situations and through a highly specific network of speakers. The words we use and the grammatical patterns that shape and hold them together come entirely from outside ourselves. Our social context teaches us our language and language makes us ourselves by controlling the way we experience, understand and manage our lives (Milroy and Milroy 1991). The differences between speakers are the focus and site of a range of sociological study. As a modern stratified society has a variety of ways of living within it, so too does any language encompass a wide variety of ways of speaking it. 'If the society is stratified, then as language enters into the life of that society to shape, cement and reproduce it, it too will display stratification.' (Montgomery 1995: 64). However, within this linguistic stratification all language varieties are not regarded as being of equal value. Each variety is accorded a different prestige, with the greatest social and economic value being reserved for that variety that is validated and promoted by the dominant class and the institutions that uphold its dominant position (Bourdieu 1991). This 'standard' language variety will exert overt pressure on all other varieties to conform to the norm. This pressure is reflective of the power that the dominant group holds within society. Montgomery (1995: 178) argues that we should not be misled into believing that it represents some absolute standard of correctness. Neither should we suppose that the language of the lower status member of the society is deficient because the linguistic patterns are not identical to the standard (ibid). The arbitrary nature of language allows no absolutes and the social power of specific high-status language varieties relates directly to the notion of discourses which empower some and disempower others (Foucault 1979).

The language variety used by an individual can have a significant impact on success or failure within society generally and within the education system specifically. The prestige associated with the standard form of the language is part of the cultural capital of the dominant middle class (Drudy and Lynch 1993). The dialect of lower socio-economic groups often stands in marked contrast to the standard prestige variety (used by the middle classes) in terms of pronunciation and grammar. The speech community that exhibits non-standard varieties of speech is subject to the lack of prestige associated with the distance from the dominant norm. Bernstein's theory of class-based linguistic codes (1971, 1973, 1975) was the first formal sequential theory that linked language to social class and disadvantage. His theory outlined the existence of an elaborated code and a restricted code which were reflected in the positional and closed role systems in society. These role systems give characteristically differing orientations towards language, with a pressure on language to be more specific the more personal or open it becomes (Montgomery 1995). There is little doubt but that Bernstein's theorectical perspective was often misunderstood (Edwards 2002: 528). In this guise he became the prime source of 'verbal deficit' theories. Some of the strongest attacks came from socio-linguists, Labov (1969) in particular, intent on defending non-standard language against being misheard as substandard. The validity of dialects of groups from disadvantaged social groups and the central role of such dialects in defining the meaning systems of these groups emerged as a main finding from the socio-linguistic school of thought.

This present paper upholds Labov's perspective but it also accords with the more recent reading of Bernstein's work and his assertion that social class, with all its constituent factors of which language system is but one, remains the dominant cultural category that penetrates schools so as 'to position pupils differentially and insidiously … legitimising the few, invalidating the many' (Bernstein 1990: 98). It examines language climate created in schools by teachers, textbooks and testing and explores children's perceptions of this climate. It takes as a core principle Bernstein's central message in relation to the

> previous histories of discursive participation different groups of children bring to school and how this history might impinge on learning in school given the nature of official pedagogic systems (Hasan, 2002: 547).

Methodology

In order to explore this difference in relation to children's attitudes to language, a sample of children was chosen from a variety of schools across the social class spectrum. Sample selection was based on the researcher's knowledge of the socio-economic background of each school through personal contacts in each school. At the time the study was conducted the researcher was a teacher in one of the schools, i.e. School D. The main aim of the research was to explore the children's ideas and perceptions in relation to language variation. This focus on children's perspectives is in line with the developing trend within the sociology of childhood to view children as individual social actors who reflexively shape their own biography and are responsible for their 'project of self' (Devine 2003, Edwards and Allard, 2000 : 436). The title of this paper itself is a direct quote from the children in one of the working class schools who considered school language to consist of *all big posh hard words … big mad words.*

The sample used in the research consisted of all of the children in one sixth class in each of the six schools selected from across the socio-economic spectrum. The researcher spent two and a half hours with each class. The format used with each group was similar. The aims of the study were outlined, the vocabulary section of the Drumcondra Primary Reading Test was administered and a class discussion took place during the remaining time (MacRuairc 1997). A summary of the socio-economic profile of each school is given in Table 1.

Table 1: Socio-economic classification of schools in sample

School A	Working Class
School B	Working Class
School C	Working Class
School D	Lower Middle Class
School E	Middle Class
School F	Upper Middle Class

Selections from the transcribed discussions will be used through the chapter to outline and support the issues arising out of the data. While the phonological differences between children of the various social class groups are not the chief focus of the study, the interviews are scripted to reflect the differences in the children's language varieties. A simple non-phonetic style of scripting is used to best represent the children's pronunciation (e.g. dis for this, sayn' for saying). Where included, the language variety used by the researcher will be transcribed in a similar fashion. Interviews with teachers (six in total) were also conducted to support and lend greater understanding to the perspectives and voices of the children.

The children's views are reported under two broad headings. The first section entitled 'Language and the school' examines children's attitudes to the language of tests and texts and their views on the use of a text containing vernacular Dublin dialect. The second section entitled 'Correction and the politics of choice' details children's views on the language climate of schools, the impact of dialect correction policies and the rationale underlying the children's choice of language register.

Language and the school

> We say he doesn't *Steveo* ... you say he doesn't *Steven* ... you're different, even there. (excerpt from School D)

One of the clear issues that arise from this data is the high level of awareness that the children have of language varieties. This demands that more attention is paid to what children have to say about this aspect of school life. In order to explore children's attitudes to language and the school three broad areas were discussed. The first of these was children's experience of the language of standardised tests, the second referred to the children's attitudes to the discourse of textbooks while the third examined what the children feel about alternatives to the routine, standard language environment of the school. Such an alternative is offered for discussion in the form of an English language text book entitled 'Get a Grip' developed for use in an inner city school project in the 1980s. Finally the perceptions of children regarding the implications of each model of language and the school are examined.

Language variety and standardised testing

The method used for assessing children's ability in English is of considerable importance especially where judgements are made about the children's general ability based on linguistic scores. Much has been written on the cultural bias in standardised tests (Edwards 1989, Milroy and Milroy 1991) and on the powerful influence these test results have on curriculum priorities (Pollard 2000). The result of the standardised test used in this research (MacRuairc 1997) reveal a marked difference between the scores of the children in the working class schools and those in the middle class areas. It is clear from the results of the test and the reactions of the children to the administration of the test, that such assessments do not favour the working class child. All of the schools taking part in the research used standardised testing irrespective of social class background of the children. Since this research was conducted the profile of standardised testing in school has been enhanced by the recent Department of Education and Science (DES) guidelines for deciding on children who require learning support. Selection of children for learning support based on standardised test results is now recommended practice (*Learning Support Guidelines* 1999). If the results of these tests are used as criteria for general assessment of children the problem for the working class child is worsened. If teachers feel that the language variety of a child is inadequate, this has implications for general assessment. Literature on this area points to long-standing findings of research that supports this link and points to lower levels of expectations among teachers, based on attitudes to language (Edwards 1989, Corson 1994). When the level of perceived correspondence of linguistic ability and general ability was examined for the purposes of this research there was a large degree of consensus on the issue. This consensus is articulated clearly by one of the teachers interviewed:

> Teacher F (comparing her present middle class school to her previous working class school)
> If they are good at languages they'll be good at maths 'cause they can read the maths too. I always found that a huge problem in my other school was that I had to sit down with the maths book to read the questions … here you just say open at page 213 and away they go. The instructions had to be explained out there, the reading wouldn't be as good. You also run into problems with History and Geography if reading isn't strong.

It is evident from comments such as this that the working class child is not served well by a system that is not prepared to take the language and culture of the working class child on board.

The Drumcondra Reading Test is a standardised test that is used widely in Irish primary schools. For the purposes of this research the first part of the test, i.e. the reading vocabulary test, was administered and the results are tabulated below. While the sample used in the research is not statistically significant, the trends indicated in the data are noteworthy and merit further research and investigation. When the results of the mean scores of the test are compared, the stratification of the results reflect the stratification of the schools with respect to their socio-economic position. The patterns outlined in Table 2 echo the patterns observed by Garwood (1992).

Table 2: Drumcondra Test Results

School	**A**	**B**	**C**	**D**	**E**	**F**
Mean score (Percentile)	18.4	34.4	32.1	50.8	69.4	70.2
SES		Working Class		Lower Middle Class	Middle Class	

Many of the children in the working class schools found the test very difficult and were visibly uncomfortable and frustrated with the process. There was very little difficulty experienced by the children in any of the three middle class schools. This concurs with the views expressed by teachers in the middle class schools who supported the use of the tests and felt that they were an adequate reflection of the children's ability. Conversely, the teachers interviewed in the working class schools identified the need for administering some form of standardised test but saw limitations to using such tests because of the widespread low scores among the children and the cultural bias of the test in favour of more middle class children.

Teacher B Sometimes I'm almost disappointed ... no not disappointed, almost surprised with the results ... I think sometimes there should maybe ... then again I don't know ... different tests for middle class and working class children ... I don't know do these tests illicit their language.

Researcher Would you be disappointed in their tests?

Teacher B Some yeah ... I think that they do worse than I would have thought. I may be totally wrong but I think that they have more than these tests show.

A selection of comments outlined below reveal the children's attitude to a test upon which many judgements are made about ability. The letters A, B, C, D, E and F used in the extracts correspond to the schools as outlined in Tables 1 and 2.

Comments from working class children

Child A	I don't know 'cause I couldn't understand them.
Child B	I can't read the words, I don't know what the words are so I wrote down anythin.
Child A	I think the words were rock hard.
Child A	The word were confusin'.
Child A	I didn' know what most of them meant.
Child A	Yeh can use other words instead a' them.
Child B	It's not doin' it's job 'cause there's more to English than them kinda words.
Child B	Nobody uses them words here.
Child B	It only finds out if we're good at hard words.
Child B	We don't use them sort of words.
Child C	I jus' wouldn' think of it.
Child C	It's too long … its' real long.
Child C	Because like, there's all different kinds of English.

Researcher	Do you understand everything your teacher says to you?
Children	Chorus of 'no'
Researcher	Why don't you understand her?
Child A	'cause she's a culchie
Child A	She's posh as well.
Child A	She talks real posh.

Researcher	Do you think that you have got better words than the words in the test?
Child A	Yeah, 'cause other people can understan' us.
Child A	Easier to say when yeh don know what it sez.
Child A	Yeh can understan' it bet'er by using our own words.
Child A	(our words) are not huge
Child A	If you're in a hurry yeh can write them (our words) down faster.
Child A	If yeh say big words your more educational.
Child A	'more educational' ooh (MOCKING TONE)
Child B	They're easier to say.
Child B	They sound better to your friends.
Child B	You'd sound tougher to yer posh cousins.
Child B	They'd be afraid of yeh cause we're all common people.
Child B	Down in all the poshie places they call us ***** heads and they slag us about the way we talk.
Child B	They're all muppets' there, all stupi'.

Comments from lower middle class children

Child C	People around would not understand.
Child C	People would not like you for usin' big mad words like the test.
Child C	They just think you're trying to show off.
Child C	If I went up to a person and said (tone here is of ridicule) 'Ireland is such a picturesque country' or 'the incident was fresh in my memory' they'd slap you in the face and run away.
Researcher	Why would they do that?
Child C	Because we don't speak like that.
Child C	They're just too big. You wouldn't go out in the street an' say he spoke in a sarcastic voice.
Child C	(interrupts in a negative tone of voice) That's the way they speak.
Researcher	Who's 'they'?
Child C	Poshies.
Child C	It sounds sad, nobody would hang around with ya.
Child C	We don't say those words because we weren't brought up that way ... my Da wouldn't say 'the recurrence of the event at work'.
Teacher	What would he say?
Child C	He'd say ... am ... that fella who was caught robbin' those engines or whatever ... was doin' it again.
Child C	Big long word don't suit our voices.

Attitude to language of textbooks

There was notable agreement among the children irrespective of their social class about the language used in textbooks. On the whole, they find the words and descriptions uninteresting and the stories boring. The children in the working class areas find the words and sentence structure very confusing and therefore they tend not to like the book. The children in School D – the lower middle class school, also consider the textbooks to be difficult. The other middle class children, however, have no difficulty understanding the stories but feel that the content and descriptions make them boring.

Comments from working class children

Researcher	When you see words like this in your books what do you think? How do you feel?
Child A	Weird.
Child A	'What does tah' mean?'
Child A	Yeh get confused.

Researcher Do you like the stories in your English books?
Child A No, some of them are boring.
Child A I like the poems though.

Comments from lower middle class children

Child D They have a weird way of saying some word that we never heard of … how are we meant to know what it means?
Child D The way they describe things confuses ya.
Child D It's real borin' it is.
Child D It's too longwinded … ya could say it all in a few sentences.
Child D If people say, wrote stories say about football or somethin' do ya not think people are gonna ta get better marks and everythin' cause writin' like that (textbooks) who wants to read it?
Child D It's education an ya don't wanna t' read it, like it has ta be about somethin' not learnin' or anythin'. If we look at a book an' in education we jus' close it bu' if it's about somethin' we enjoy …

Comments from middle/upper middle class children

Child E They're like fairy tales and we don't want fairy tales, we want real life.
Child E No one ever dies and it's all happy ever after.
Child E A lot of it is easy, there are very few words that we actually don't know.
Child E There's never any unhappy endings … they don't look like life.
Child E A lot of them go on and on and we don't really want to read them.
Child E The stories are boring and if there are facts in them then you don't want to learn the facts 'cause the story is not exciting.
Child E If it's printed by C.J.Fallon that's enough.
Child F Sometimes like in History there should be more action … it should be described using better words … more action words. Some of the words are boring words … It's kindda adult words.

It is clear that language of texts and tests poses difficulty for all the children. The unanimity of the objection to the language used in the school books and test is notable. The comments of the children reveal a strong negative feeling towards the language of the textbooks and a distinct lack of interest in such language variety.

This attitude is not specific to children of any of the socio-economic groups. However, the working class children have more of a problem in relation to understanding the language in the text-books, which may be one of the causes of failure. The language register used in textbooks is very different and contains structure and vocabulary not included in these children's language repertoire. This puts them at a distinct disadvantage educationally. The lack of difficulty experienced with the language of the textbooks by the middle class children is further evidence of the predominance of middle class linguistic capital in schools (Bourdieu and Passeron 1977).

Correction and the politics of choice

It was clear that the language associated with school work was not the same as that used by the children in other areas of their lives. This issue is highlighted forcibly in the selections below. In particular, the definite prestige among the working classes for their own language and the difference between this language variety and that of the school serves to highlight aspects of discontinuity highlighted previously.

Comments from working class children

Researcher	Do you ever use words like this in your textbooks?
Child A	No excep' when yeh have to use them.
Child A	If yeh say big words your more educational.
Child A	'More educational' ooh!
Researcher	Do you ever use them in your own life outside.
Child A	There's a language for school and a language for home … callin' nicknames.

Correction

Children differed in their response to the issue of correction depending on the practices that occurred in schools. The children are corrected a lot in school A and, as a result of this, the issue is very relevant to them.

Comments from working class children

Researcher	Do you like being corrected?
Child A	No!
Child A	We should say our own words.
Child A	Say if ye'd said compu'er she'd make yeh say computer (posh voice).
Child A	If yer tellin' her a story or somethin' an ye say somethin'

	wrong, she turns round and sez, she butts in on the story, it wrecks yer head.
Researcher	Why does it wreck your head?
Child A	Yeh want tell your story.
Child A	Yer talkin your way an' she butts in an yeh forget where yeh are.
Child A	They should jus' let yeh finish.
Child A	She always tryin to correct us the way we talk like, when we say 'me Ma' she changes it.
Child A	You pronounce yer 't's', you talk like her.
Researcher	If you keep getting corrected, why don't you change the way you talk?
Child A	'Cause we don't want t'.
Child A	That's the way we talk.
Child A	That's the way everybody talks around here. If you were to say computer you'd probably get a baytin' or somethin'.

The children in School C are not corrected by their present teacher. They have a different view on the issue of correction. They are far more positive about the teacher and their language variety.

Comments from working class children

Child C	Our teacher never says anythin'.
Child C	Our teacher never tells us wha' way t' speak properly an all that.
Child C	Yeah our teacher doesn't, but all others, the head an' all, they do.
Child C	Miss O ***** she was always sayin' it.
Child C	One teacher in second class was tryin' to tell us to do different words … real poshie words.
Researcher	How do you feel when they try to change things?
Child C	Yeh jus' pretend and then when yer ou' yeh say wha' yeh like.
Researcher	How is it different with this teacher who doesn't correct you. Is it nicer?
Child C	Yeah much!

In School D (lower middle class school) the children view correction in two ways. Some object strongly to it, while others feel that the school has a role in changing and improving language. This would concur with studies of language and lower middle class groups in both Norwich (Trudgill 1974) and New York (Labov

1977). Some individuals in this class grouping seem to be particularly conscious of their language variety. They are more careful of their pronunciation in certain formal situations than groups immediately above them on the social scale. This 'hypercorrection' or over production of prestige forms is consistent with their marginal position in the social stratification. This is seen as being indicative of the 'linguistic insecurity (of a group) … who identify with the patterns of the group they aspire to join' (Montgomery 1995:68). It is also interesting to note that in the three working class schools this idea was never mentioned.

Comments of lower middle class children

Child D	Do ya know the way teachers, they correct ya most of the time an if ya say 'me an' me friend' they jus' go 'My friend an I' but if yer teacher said somethin' like tha' an' you corrected them they'd give out heck t' ya.
Child D	Sur, its like the people from ****** were here before the school and the school came in and expect you to change your language.
Child D	They have a cheek.
Child D	What's the point in goin' to school then, ya have t' learn somethin'.

There is a difference in the way the children are corrected and in their reaction to it in School E. The correction here is far less extensive and is not viewed by the children with the same degree of hostility.

Comments of middle class children

Child E	She always makes us say 'Susan and I' and not 'me and Susan'.
Child E	She always corrects for words like 'poor' instead of 'pour'.
Child E	Or po-er.
Child E	She always gives out to me for tha'.
Researcher	How do you feel then when you get corrected?
Child E	Annoyed.
Child E	Frustrated because you can't correct the teachers.
Child E	People might like being called by their second name and if the teacher corrects them she might be doing the wrong thing.
Child E	It annoys yeh 'cause you can't speak yer mind.
Child E	You can't use slang … she gets so cross when you use slang.
Child E	Teachers encourage slang not to be used.

Child E	They think that if you're writing a book or something that people won't accept slang.

The children in School F are not corrected for the way they speak in school. They are corrected for issues relating to good manners and for using 'slang'. However it is worth noting that the children's version of slang in this school is much different to the slang used by the children in the working class schools. For example, the children in School F did not understand a slang word used in working class areas and used by the researcher (underlined below).

Comments of children who are upper middle class

Child F	If you go … say you turn around to talk to someone and she goes 'what are you doing?' and you go 'I was just talking to her' she goes 'her has a name'.
Child F	Say if we wrote 'cop on' in an essay, she'd always give out to us for writing that.
Child F	For using too much slang.
Researcher	What do you think of slang … do you use a lot of slang?
Child F	Yeah … sort of … word like 'cool'… 'sound'… 'groovey'.
Researcher	Would you say things like '<u>stall it</u>'?
Children	WHAT?
Researcher	Stall it?
Child F	No … what does that mean?
Researcher	It means stop it.

The main issue arising from these extracts is the difference in terms of type of correction policy and the effect it has on the children. There is a marked difference between what the working class children feel about the issue and the views expressed by the middle class children (schools E and F in particular). It is clear that policies of correction play a key role in forming negative attitudes towards school among the working class children. This is supported by the more positive view expressed by the children in School C where the teacher is not perceived to be as coercive as in other schools.

Choice and covert prestige

Throughout the conversation working class children expressed various levels of prestige and support for their own vernacular. This value on the vernacular limits the success of language altering policies and highlights the difference between home and school for the children (Montgomery 1995, Downes 1984, Milroy 1991). The implications for the children should they change their language variety are clearly articulated by them in the following comments.

Comments of working class children

Researcher	Could you say 'I'm going to buy a computer' (said in a very 'posh voice') on your road?
Child A	They'd say 'yeh w'a'?
Child A	They'd all say 'shu' up'.
Child A	Yer jeered for posh.
Child A	Yeh can't say posh words, yeh can't even wear Adidas runners, cause it means yeh can't afford Air Macs, that wha' it says.
Child A	Jus' say yer ou' an' yer walkin' past these young fellas an' yeh say somethin' posh they probably turn round an' hit yeh a box.
Child A	You wouldn't find us sayin words from school at home or anythin'.
Researcher	Why not?
Child A	We just don't like speakin like that, we'd rather jus' speak like we do.
Child B	When yer in school yeh have t' try an' be posh an all that', when yer out a school yeh can relax.
Child B	It's like two different lives.
Researcher	Is it really?
Researcher	Do you think your teacher's posh?
Children	Yeah … mad posh.
Child B	If the teacher wasn't posh we could talk our own way.
Child B	We'd only have one life.
Child B	Ye'd get on wi' the teachers better yeh would an' ye'd get higher marks 'cause they'd talk the way you do.
Child B	Yeh might come to school better 'cause yeh can talk the way yeh want to in school … yeh'd like school more.
Child B	Yeh'd be able to have a laugh with the teacher.

This home school difference in relation to language is developed further below.

Comments of middle class children

Child B	When you're in school you wouldn't be able to say words … words like the ones you say at home.
Child B	There's a lot of words you can't say at school.
Child B	You can't say 'can you', yeh have to say 'may I'.
Child B	The teachers can talk the way they want when they come into school … its like in the olden days when they whacked you on the arse when you were bold.

Child B	Why can't we just talk like we usually talk.
Child B	They are here to teach us – not to tell us what to say.
Child B	We should talk the way we want to … it's our language.
Child B	Why should we not be able to talk the way we want to talk … They're up in the staffroom talkin' the way they want to.
Child B	We want to talk the way our parents talk, not the way the teachers talk
Child B	They want us to talk … you know, the way our teacher says it, they want us to talk posh the way they do … they want us to be all goodie goodies an' all.
Child B	They're probably talking any way they want … they only talk like posh to us, they're probably sayin' curses an' all when they're in the staffroom
Child B	You know when a teacher asks you somethin' and yeh say yeah and she says 'is that the way to talk to a teacher?'
Child B	Yeah can say i' a' home.
Child B	They shouldn't force yeh.
Researcher	Does your teacher ever do that … explain things in your words?
Child B	She never uses any of the words we use.

Comments of upper middle class children

Child F	We don't use curses in school … or slang.
Child F	On the yard with your friends you can use slang but you wouldn't to the teachers.
Child F	She'd always think bad of you if you spoke bad.
Researcher	So when are you most happy speaking, if you get corrected at home and you have to be careful at school?
Child F	When you're with your friends … then you're relaxed.
Child F	I only use big words at school.
Researcher	Are you not encouraged to use them at home as well by your parents?
Child F	Yes we do … but its much quicker without big words … with big words you have to think what you're saying.

There is a sense of solidarity among the children for their own language variety in the comments above. The children often do not conform to the language demands of the school. This results in policies of correction in the school that are viewed unfavourably by the children. Attempts at correction are viewed by the children as attempts to change their language. It is here that the prestige and the sense of solidarity with the language variety of the environment is most evident. This issue of covert prestige among the working class children for their own vernacular exists despite the high level of awareness among all children of the social value of the different language varieties. This is consistent with the examination of covert prestige among the adult working classes (Montgomery 1995). The children seem to fully appreciate that, in correcting their language variety, the school system is not accepting or affirming their linguistic background. The comments of many of the children above indicate evidence to support Willis in saying that 'one of the most oppressive forces is the belittling and sarcastic attitude of some teachers' (Willis 1977: 77). In accordance with the notion of covert prestige, the children in the working class areas have made a choice not to use the language of the school outside the school. This decision is based on a high level of awareness among the children of linguistic difference and of the consequences of changing language varieties.

Comments of working class children

Child A	No one would understan' me.
Child A	They're long words.
Researcher	What would people think of you if you were using words like that?
Children	Stupi', big fool, poshie, wierdo, a muppe', a geek, a nerd.
Researcher	Do you think the words suit your voices?
Children	No!
Child A	No they don't, we're not posh.
Child A	We come from a mad area – junkie land – there's all drug free hunts an' everythin' around here.
Researcher	How does that stop you saying these big words?
Child A	Ye'd get bet up.
Child A	If yeh say it they bayet yeh up.
Researcher	Why wouldn't you use school words?
Child B	'Cause they're posh.
Child B	'Cause I think they're stupi'.
Child B	They're all big posh hard words … big mad words.
Researcher	If you tried to be posh what would your friends say to you?
Child B	They'd kick and push ye'.
Child B	They'd give ye dead arms … a deadner … they'd bayt you up.
Child B	I'd slag them if they were posh.
Child C	We're from ***** we don't use them words.
Child C	There's all junkies round here.
Child C	Everybody else talks common so we wanna say it too, 'cause you'd be sort' t' the odd one out.

Child C	Ye'd get bet up … ye'd ge' yer windows smashed.
Child C	Ye'd get kilt all the young one 'id think yer posh or sometin'.
Researcher	Who'd kill ya?
Child C	Everyone would for sayin' them words.

Conclusion

The data quoted in this chapter indicates that children have constructed the value of the prestige varieties of language and are clearly aware of the social and educational implications of the different language systems. There is a high level of resistance among many of the children to the language variety promoted by the school. There is, accordingly, a high level of covert prestige for vernacular language systems among many of the children researched. The data also indicates that, although the working class children support the notion of the correctness of the standard language variety and are clearly aware that adherence to this standard is necessary for success in education, they continue to exhibit a high level of solidarity in relation to their vernacular and are resistant to the linguistic change sought by the school. Notwithstanding this class specific pattern, a level of an anti 'school language' attitude is evident in all the children irrespective of their socio-economic class. Middle class children view the school language as too formal and would prefer to use a less formal register. Working class children, on the other hand, possess and want to use a different variety altogether. This results in different experiences for children of different social classes within the school system. The working class children in particular perceive the school, and the norms that the school enforces, as not reflecting their own cultural context. This is revealed by this research to be a prime source of home/school discontinuity. The children view the language of the school as 'posh' and 'goodie goodie' and of little relevance to their lives outside the school. As a result of this there is a high level of enforced compliance among these children with the linguistic demands of the school. This results in a specific 'school language' that is deliberately avoided outside the school environment.

The views of the children reveal how informed they are in relation to their own lives and their position within the hierarchy of linguistic codes and their clear understanding of the implication of this positioning. Research of this nature enable the lives of children to be made visible, however uncomfortable this may be for the dominant orthodoxy. The marginalisation of children from certain groups is evident and calls for a position within education that 'pushes history against the grain, by challenging those forces within existing configurations of power that sustain themselves by appeals to objectivity, science, truth, universality and the suppression of difference' (Giroux 1983: 147). In an education system that strives to eliminate disadvantage, the perceptions of children reported in this research strongly points to the fact that negative attitudes to school are created among many of the children, reinforcing the disadvantage experienced by the working classes in a very specific way.

Bibliography

Bernstein, B. (1971) *Class codes and control Volume I: theoretical studies towards a sociology of language*, London, Routledge and Kegan.

Bernstein, B. (ed.) (1973) *Class codes and control Volume II: applied studies toward a sociology of language*, London, Routledge and Kegan.

Bernstein, B. (1975) *Class codes and control Volume III: towards a theory of educational transmission*, London, Routledge and Kegan.

Bernstein, B. (1990) *The Structuring of Pedagogic Discourse*, London, Routledge and Kegan.

Bourdieu, P. and Passeron J. C. (1977) *Reproduction in Education, Society and Culture*, London, Sage.

Bourdieu, P. (1990) *In Other Words*, California, Stanford.

Bourdieu, P. (1991). *Language and Symbolic Power*, edited by J.B. Thompson, Cambridge University Press, Polity Press.

Burr, V. (1995) *An Introduction to Social Constructionism*, London, Routledge.

Burton, P. (1997) *Get a Grip,* Dublin, St Lawerence O'Toole Special School.

Chesire, J. (1991) 'Dialect features and Linguistic Conflict in Schools', in *Language and Education*, Vol 4, No 4, pp 261-292.

Corson, D. J. (1990) *Language Policy Across the Curriculum*, Clevedon, Multilingual Matters Ltd.

Corson, D. J. (1994) 'Minority Social Groups and Nonstandard Discourse: Towards a Just Language Policy', *The Canadian Modern Language Review*, Vol 50, No 2, pp 270-295.

Department of Education and Science (2000) *Learning Support Guidelines,* Dublin, Stationary Office.

Devine, D. (2003) *Children, Power and Schooling – How childhood is structured in the primary school,* Stoke-on-Trent, Trentham Books.

Downes, W. (1984) *Language and Society*, London, Fontana.

Drudy, S. and Lynch, K. (1993) *Schools and Society in Ireland*, Dublin, Gill and MacMillan.

Education Research Centre (1994) *Administration Manual and Technical* Manual, Drumcondra.

Primary Reading Test, Levels 3-6, Dublin, Education Research Centre (1994) Drumcondra.

Primary Reading Test, Level 6, Dublin, Education Research Centre.

Edwards and Allard (2000) 'A typology of parental involvement in education centring on children and young people: negotiating familiarisation, institutionalisation and individualisation' in *British Journal of Sociology of Education,* Vol 21, No 3, pp 435-454.

Edwards, T. (2002) 'A remarkable sociological imagination', *British Journal of Sociology of Education,* Vol 23, No 4, pp 528-535.

Edwards, A. (1989) *Language and Disadvantage* (2nd ed.), London, Edward Arnold Ltd.

Edwards, J. (1985) *Language, Society and Identity*, New York, Blackwell Ltd.

Foucault, M. (1979) *The History of Sexuality, Vol 1: An Introduction,* Translated by Robert Hurley, London, Penguin.

Garwood, A. (ed.) (1992) *Black Americans: A Statistical Handbook*, Boulder, Colorado, Numbers and Concepts.

Giroux, H. (1983) *Theory and Resistance in Education – A Pedagogy for the Opposition,* London, Heinemann.

Gordon, J. C. B. (1981) *Verbal Deficit*, Croom Helm, London.

Hasan, R. (2002) 'Ways of meaning, ways of learning: code as an explanatory concept', *British Journal of Sociology of Education,* Vol 23, No 4.

Labov, W. (1969) 'The logic of non-standard English', *Georgetown Monographs on Language and Linguistics* Vol 22, Washington DC, Georgetown University Press.

MacRuairc (1997) *Big Mad Words – Perceptions on Language Variation in Schools: A Sociological Analysis*, Unpublished MEd thesis, Education Department, UCD.

Milroy, L. and Milroy, J. (1992) 'Social Network and Social Class: Towards an Integrated Sociolinguistic Model', in *Language in Society,* Vol 21, pp 1-26.

Milroy, L. and Milroy, J. (1991) *Authority in Language* (2nd edition), London/New York, Routledge.

Montgomery, M. (1995) *An Introduction to Language and Society* (2nd edition), London, Routledge.

Pollard, A. (2000) *The Social World of Pupil Assessment: Processes and contexts of Primary School*, London, Continuum.

Richardson, P. (1991) 'Language as a Personal Resource and as a Social Construct: competing views of literacy pedagogy in

Australia', in *Educational Review,* Vol 43, No 2.
Trudgill, P. (1975) *Accent, Dialect and the School*, London, Edward Arnold Ltd.
Willis, P. (1977) *Learning to Labour*, Hampshire, Gower Ltd.

CHAPTER 10

Interviewing the vampire slayers: active media consumption, imagination and gendered identity

Anne Lodge[1]

Introduction

Alongside the family, education and peers, television has become a key socialising institution in modern western culture. It teaches children about life, about people, about their society (Signorielli 2001). Indeed, television and media culture are central to the lives of many children, many of whom regard school as peripheral in comparison. At the same time, education regards 'the popular as profane' and pays little heed to television and popular culture (Kenway and Bullen 2001:15). This chapter considers the active nature of children's consumption of a media product, an American television programme entitled *Buffy the Vampire Slayer* aimed primarily at the adolescent market but also appealing to the pre-adolescent market. The chapter reports on conversations held with two different groups of pre-adolescent girls in Irish primary schools with regard to their viewing experiences, focusing in particular on the ways in which they engage with the narrative.

The educational significance of popular culture

Walkerdine (1997) notes the dearth of research on pre-adolescents and popular culture. She questions why there has been so little written about something that has become a central element of the

1 I would like to express my thanks to Brian Donovan for sharing ideas and suggesting reading material during a number of conversations we had regarding this research. I would also like to thank Maeve O'Brien for her (unfailingly) insightful comments on an earlier draft of this chapter.

lives of children. Much, however, has been written or considered about popular culture,[2] and in particular, television viewing, and its impact on children. For example, 'common sense' connects watching television with a damaged attention span and the consequent negative impact on educational participation and attainment (Levine and Waite 2000). Popular culture (particularly television, video and computer games) has been accused of corrupting the innocence of childhood (Postman 1994) and even of inciting violence and murder in the aftermath of the Jamie Bulger murder case. Furthermore, popular culture itself has been regarded as being of little cultural significance and devoid of educated taste or value (Kenway and Bullen 2001). Such assumptions are based on classed hierarchies of taste (Bourdieu 1984, Buckingham 2000). In recent years, however, such cultural demarcations have been less a reflection of *what* is consumed rather than *the manner* of that consumption (Storey 2003).

Much of what has been researched and written about television (and other media through which young people experience popular culture) has been negative, focusing on the damaging impact of media on its apparently passive audience. Furthermore, little of this material has engaged actively with children as a television audience to seek their views and experiences (Gunning 1997). This reflected the low status of children within academic research generally (James et al 1998, Lynch 1999). However, there are some studies examining children's experiences as an active television and video audience (Buckingham 1993, Gunning 1997, Belton 2000, Messenger Davies and Machin 2000).

Some commentators address the need for educationalists to recognise that popular culture is one of the realms in which young people actively engage in order to make sense of themselves and their world (Giroux and Simon 1989). It is, as Giroux argues, 'the primary way in which youth learn about themselves, their relationship to others, and the larger world' (1999: 2). It has been argued that educators have a responsibility to engage young people in an active and critical analysis of the material that entertains them (Cortes 2000, Giroux and Simon 1989). Kenway and Bullen (2001) argue that political engagement by young people with media consumer culture should be a vital dimension of education.

Popular culture, and media such as television through which we experience it, occupy a central place in our culture, whether we are

---

2 'Popular culture' includes television, film, video, computer and other multimedia material, popular music, books and other print material. The focus in this paper is on television and video as this is the way in which viewers experience the television programme under analysis.

adults or young people. Denzin (1993) argues that contemporary life is cinematised. Our reality is filtered through, and transformed by, cinematic or televisual meanings and images. Perhaps the revolution will not be televised, but we have increasingly come to accept, and expect, that we will experience dramatic local and world events such as the destruction of the World Trade Centre in New York, the Gulf War, flooding in France or an earthquake in Iran through television. As Cohen (2001) argues, the media acts as a primary source of information about suffering and disaster in a way that promotes voyeurism rather than compassion.

We understand our world in part through the integration of the illusions created by film and television and the reality we personally experience. Thus, the media and popular culture have a pedagogical role (Gazetas 2000, Giroux and Simon 1989). The lessons presented through media such as television reflect particular values, particular interests (Giroux 1999). Television offers certain perspectives on the social world, giving the viewer access to categories with which to organise and make sense of experience (Bourdieu 1998). Such frames or categories are organised by age, by gender, by class, by race and so on (Giroux and Simon 1989, Seiter 1995). The images presented in popular culture are often characterised by stereotypical presentations of minorities (Foucault 1989) or of women (Signorielli 2001). Popular culture presents to young people specific social values and hierarchies of identity (Giroux 1999).

Imagination and identity

Television is the dominant technology implicated in identity production (Kenway and Bullen 2001). It is the foremost modern source of shared narratives (Signorielli 2001). Active engagement with the narrative of a television programme involves the projection of the imaginary self into that story (Gazetas 2000) and continued imaginative engagement with the story after the programme has ended (Sutton-Smith 1997). Imagination can be regarded as liminal, given that 'the imaginary occupies a space between the actual and the non-existent; it is prospective, contestable, yet informs social practices and discourse' (Dahlgren 1995: 133). Engagement with television or written narrative using the imagination allows the viewer to explore the characters, to manipulate plot, to re-play particular scenes.

The imagination is not only something that young people (and adults) engage while they are watching television or a film, or indeed, reading literature for educational or other purposes (Dart

2000). Imagination is an element of the complex way in which individuals understand their own experiences, feelings and realities (Sutton-Smith 1997), and how they explore and make sense of their own identities (Davies 1990, Davies and Harre 1990, Davies 1993, Davies 2003). The act of imagining is an intrinsic part of human subjectivity (Lemke 1995) and identity construction. Both adults and children make sense of their worlds by imaginatively positioning themselves in terms of personally or culturally known categories and narratives (Davies and Harre 1990). Identity is constructed with reference to the individual's personal stories that are, in turn, informed and permeated by cultural norms and narratives (Rosenthal 1992). Individuals' experiences of themselves as gendered beings, for example, have an imaginary dimension linked to personal and cultural narratives. Thus, there is an imagined self alongside the embodied, the historical, the social, the cultural, the emotional self (Lodge 1998).

'Buffy the Vampire Slayer'

Buffy the Vampire Slayer is an hour-long television programme (including advertising breaks). In total, seven series were produced. It first aired in 1997 (Holder 2000). It is set in the fictional town of Sunnydale, California. At the beginning of the first series, the central character, Buffy, a sixteen-year-old high school student, moved with her mother to Sunnydale. The first three series were set in high school and the action subsequently moved to college and the world of work. The character of Buffy occupies an ambivalent position, given that she is both an ordinary adolescent and young adult as well as being a supernatural being – a vampire slayer (Pender 2002). The slayer (always a young girl) must protect the world against demons and vampires. As such, she has superhuman powers to enable her to carry on a constant war against demons, vampires and other monsters threatening the world. The fictional town of Sunnydale is situated close to Los Angeles on a hellmouth, and is therefore particularly susceptible to attacks by these creatures that wish to take back control of the earth from humans.

The other central characters can be organised into three disparate groups. Her friends in high school (Willow and Xander) are the core of the informal support group assisting Buffy in the battle against evil and demons. Various vampires and demons also feature prominently (Angel and Spike), some playing a significant role across several series, while others are destroyed by Buffy. Finally, there are a number of supporting adult characters, most of whom have no idea either that Sunnydale is such a dangerous place or of the true nature of Buffy, including, for a long time, her mother. However, Rupert Giles, her watcher and the school librarian, is fully aware of the truth. Much of the action takes place at night, given the predilection of vampires for darkness. However, a good deal more of it occurs during the day, some of it using the school, college, or various characters' homes as a backdrop. While the ongoing battle between good and evil is a constant theme, many other issues are explored also. These include the evolving nature of friendships, romantic and other relationships, coping with life first in high school and then in college, and learning from mistakes and experiences.

Buffy cannot be categorised easily into one genre. Typically of post-modern television, it is characterised by what Strinati terms 'generic confusion' (2000: 241) and has elements of a number of different types of television programme. Traditionally, television programmes fitted into particular categories (Fiske 2001). The emergence of this postmodern style of television programming can be argued to have begun in particular with David Lynch's *Twin Peaks* (Strinati 2000). Like *The X Files, Buffy* combines elements of the television serial with horror, romance, comedy and action. It also includes features typical of programming aimed primarily at the adolescent and pre-adolescent market. Among the locations in which it is set is the school (and subsequently college). However, the institution is not the focus of the drama, but features primarily as a backdrop for the real action (Dalton 1999).

Like other media texts, *Buffy* does not exist purely as a complete entity but rather is characterised by a high level of intertextuality. The programme itself is a spin-off of a 1992 box office failure of the same name written by the series producer Joss Wheedon. In its turn, *Buffy* has launched its own spin-off series, *Angel*, featuring some of the characters that left Sunnydale. There has been notable cross-participation by several characters in both programmes. There are series of books on both Buffy and Angel aimed at the young adolescent market. There is also a wide range of other products: including figures of certain characters; stationery, bags and other accessories; videos and DVDs of all seven series; books of scripts, interviews and other information; calendars, posters and magazines. There is a myriad of websites devoted to *Buffy*. Television aimed at young people is characterised by this level of commodification (Buckingham 2000). Communications media such as television are inextricably linked with consumer culture (Lyon 1999, Sayer 2001).

Buffy is aimed primarily at the adolescent female market (Pecora and Mazzarella 1999). Its continued popularity is evidenced by its constant presence on a variety of television channels. Postmodern texts tend to be characterised by parody and deliberate drawing on, or reference to, other forms (Buckingham 2000). This appeals to a particular part of the audience, literally giving them the opportunity to enjoy their own cultural capital and textual literacy. This was the case with many of the devoted fans of *Twin Peaks* for example (Strinati 2000). *Buffy* appeals at that level to an audience of people aged between twenty and forty with its multiple references to pop culture from the 1970s, 1980s and 1990s as well as the way it occasionally uses highly sexually suggestive violence and humour. *Buffy's* appeal goes beyond the adolescent market at which it was primarily aimed. Like *South Park* it has a broad appeal to a 'youth' market that encompasses viewers aged between ten and forty years of age (Buckingham 2000). As Kaveney points out 'preteens buy posters of the show, middle-aged writers and intellectuals discuss it over dinner' (2001: 2). *Buffy* is also very popular with the primarily male science-fiction fans (Gauntlett 2002).

Joss Wheedon, the creator and producer of *Buffy,* wanted her to be a self-conscious feminist icon in a feminist story (Appleyard 2000). Daugherty (2001) argues that the programme itself deliberately plays with the teen horror genre by inverting the expected female (especially those who are blonde and stereotypically pretty and feminine) victimhood and powerlessness. Buffy is blonde, but instead of being the stereotypical victim of the monsters of traditional horror movies, she is the hero who saves everyone, female and male. She is a powerful and skilful fighter (using both weapons and martial arts) who can slay monsters twice her own size. Parks (2003) argues that *Buffy* gives viewers an opportunity to re-consider the relationship between gender and power. She is also a caregiver. She has been described by *Time* magazine as a product of 'Camille Paglia-style feminism' (Appleyard 2000: 5). She is beautiful, and dresses fashionably. Naturally, she is thin, since modern beauty (for both females and males) is defined by having a slender and controlled body shape (Bentley 1999, Bordo 2003). She is heterosexual, and her romantic involvements (particularly with Angel, the vampire with a soul) have been central elements in the unfolding storyline, in the first three series in particular.

Interviewing the vampire slayers: a study of young people's experiences of watching television

One of the purposes of this study was to examine the extent to which younger female viewers of *Buffy* accepted the show's eponymous character as a feminist hero. In order to do this it was necessary to engage in dialogue with pre-adolescent girls (aged between ten and twelve years). Two focus group[3] discussions took place with two groups of pre-adolescent girls,[4] the majority of whom were avid fans of the programme *Buffy the Vampire Slayer.* I also held a whole-class discussion in one of the schools in order to ascertain the views of young people who did not like, or had no particular interest in, *Buffy*. I wanted to understand the girls' experiences as viewers of a television programme and how they engaged with the material presented to them.[5] After all, as Mayall argues, 'good information about childhood must start from children's experience' (2000: 121). One of the ironic aspects of the critical and theoretical material written about *Buffy* over the last few years has been the failure of the cultural theorists and other commentators to engage with young people about their own perceptions of the programme. As Levine and Schneider (2003) argue, most of the critical literature examining *Buffy* focuses on adult interpretations of how children and young people might or should

---

3 Rather than interview individuals I organised the participants into two focus groups. Again, this partly contributed to the participants having a sense of ease as they were with classmates. Focus groups are also regarded as a data-gathering method that optimises self-disclosure (Wilson 1997). Establishing a respectful environment between researcher and participants is a key element in establishing trust. At the outset, I made it clear to the participating young people that the material discussed was confidential and that they had the right to take part or withdraw during the course of the discussions. I sought their permission to use a tape-recorder and gave them control over that machine (Grieg and Taylor 1999).

4 This research focused solely on the experiences of girls, and the classes targeted were located in two different single-sex girls' schools. There was a number of reasons for this. In the first place, the central character of *Buffy* is female and I was particularly interested in the ways in which female fans reacted to, and engaged imaginatively with, her. In the second place, I am aware from previous research I have done at both primary and second level (e.g. Lodge and Flynn 2001, Lynch and Lodge 2002) that mixed gender focus groups can be dominated by boys. As Reay (2001) reminds us, girls can position themselves, and act, quite differently depending on the gender makeup of a group.

5 I decided to engage actively in the process of watching and discussing *Buffy* myself as part of my preparation for the focus group discussions. This enabled me to engage in a dialogue about the programme with the participating young people and provided a means of challenging the power and status differentials between us based on our respective ages. Buckingham (2000) argues that, in terms of popular culture consumption, age is partly determined by tastes. Thus, by sharing tastes and interests in a particular aspect of popular culture with groups of pre-adolescent girls I was consciously attempting to create a certain degree of parity of status between us. Given the reality of the age differential, I was deliberate in ensuring that at no point during the discussions did I attempt to challenge the young people's interpretations or views or offer adult explanations for particular events or behaviours.

read this programme (without actually asking children or young people), and in so doing, misses the source of their enjoyment. There is no doubt that adult commentators with a background in feminist or cultural or critical theories can bring a particular understanding to bear in an analysis of a media text. However, I would argue that no adult can begin to know how children or young people experience any narrative unless they engage in purposeful conversation about that experience with them.

A number of key themes emerged from the two focus groups and the whole-class discussion. It was clear from the girls' conversations that certain aspects of the programme were particularly appealing from their perspective. These included the use of action and violence, the presence of anti-heroes alongside heroes, a certain sense of chaos and elements of the horror genre. It was clear from the way in which the girls talked about watching *Buffy* that they were engaged at times as narrative viewers and at other times as critical viewers (Lembo 2000). They enjoyed immersing themselves imaginatively within the narrative but were also capable of being critical of an over-reliance on formula or events they considered implausible. It emerged from our discussions that their engagement with *Buffy* also involved consumption of some related products including posters and videos or DVDs.

Among the facets of *Buffy* that appealed most to the young people who participated in this study were the action and horror dimensions. Indeed, as Kaveney (2001) points out, this is also part of the programme's appeal for its adult audience. Every episode of *Buffy* has a minimum of two fight scenes, generally involving the central character and various demons in a kick boxing encounter. During conversation with the whole class group in the first school, these two aspects of the programme emerged as the most popular – two-thirds of them selected the horror dimension as their favourite element, while over half opted for the action and fighting as the aspects they liked best. The same proportion found the programme exciting to watch. During focus group discussions, different girls became very excited as they talked about watching Buffy fight demons. One described how she loved those scenes and, as they happened, would be 'jumping up and down doing it [the martial arts moves]'. Another participant described how she and her older sister (aged thirteen) were watching *Buffy* together one evening and her sister was acting out the fight sequence as it happened. She accidentally knocked over and broke her mother's vase and they were both in trouble. Watching Buffy fight made some of them feel 'strong' and 'the best!' according to individual participants.

Neither horror nor action and fighting would be characteristics of a narrative traditionally associated with a female audience, which have been assumed to favour material with a focus on relationships, and romance in particular (Tepper 2000). One girl (who was not a *Buffy* fan) in the first focus group discussion claimed that fighting is 'real boys' stuff – girls don't fight' and '[*Buffy*] isn't a girls' programme. Only boys would watch it. Its got fighting and stuff'. She was met with a chorus of disagreement from the others in the group. In fact, one did martial arts herself. The differences in opinion between the fans of the programme and the girl who did not like or watch it were very interesting. Those who liked *Buffy* clearly accepted the notion that girls could be powerful, they could fight and be victorious. Whether their acceptance of this idea was partly as a result of having accepted the ideas in the narrative of *Buffy* is another matter.

Horror texts (books, videos, DVDs, films, television programmes, computer games) have become a common element of material aimed at young people, female and male, in recent years (Buckingham 2000). Since the 1950s, horror movies aimed at the adolescent market have been commonplace (Strinati 2000). With the advent of video, and subsequently DVD, it became much more difficult to ensure that age limits on access to such material could be imposed. Most of the young people who took part in this research had also seen horror films such as *The Crow*, *Nightmare on Elm Street* and *Scream*. The horror dimension of *Buffy* that the research participants enjoyed particularly was the element of surprise – 'demons can jump out – you're waiting for them and you never know when they'll jump out!' Different participants described it as 'exciting' and that it 'gives you a thrill!'

Some members of the first focus group made reference to the predictability of the outcome as something that could be annoying – 'after like ten episodes you wish she'd die for once – even when she got killed [at the end of Series 1] she came back to life'. Here, these girls were clearly demonstrating their ability to view a programme critically, making judgements about plausibility and recognising the use of formula (Lembo 2000). By the time the second focus group discussion had taken place, Series 5 had ended and Buffy had died, sacrificing herself to save her young sister Dawn. This had come as a huge surprise to the girls taking part in that discussion, one of them claiming that it was 'the saddest thing ever'.

Particular aspects of *Buffy* can be rather frightening, given that it has a strong horror dimension. The young people taking part in the focus groups coped with the 'scary' element in different ways.

One participant in the second focus group described how she would hide behind the sofa during very frightening parts. Another explained that she was 'scared and a bit nervous but only when I'm watching it, not afterwards'. Indeed, that sensation of fright and tension contributed to the young people's enjoyment of viewing, something that Buckingham (2000) also reported.

For some of the young people, fear or nervousness was something that they experienced after the programme was over and they continued to engage with the narrative in their imaginations. One of the participants in the second focus group explained how she had been at home due to illness and watched some of her *Buffy* videos to pass the time. Later on, she kept imagining demonic characters from the programme were sitting on the end of her bed. One girl in the first focus group explained that, after watching, 'in your imagination you're in it' and that she was able to control the narrative, resulting in different outcomes – 'you imagine you're the person [who gets killed] and go back in your imagination and fix what they did wrong and not get killed'. Belton (2000) describes similar strategies used by children with whom she worked.

Gunning (1997) found that one of the primary appeals of the characters on RTE 2's *Den TV* for the children with whom she worked had to do with some of their anti-authority behaviour and humour. *Den TV* was characterised by a certain element of chaos. Similarly, it was clear that one of the appeals of *Buffy* for the girls taking part in these discussions was the presence of characters who inspired chaos and who were not subject to the authority of adults, or anyone else. Several of the vampire characters (especially Spike and Angel when he was evil) were popular because, in part, of their power and strength but also because of the fear they inspired and the chaos they created. Indeed, part of the fascination that some of the young people had for Angel had to do with the fact that he was a vampire and was the subject both of day-dreams (because of his stereotypical good looks) and nightmares.

The other significant anti-hero whom several of the participants admired was Faith, also a Slayer. Unlike Buffy, she did not have a sense of moral limits in how she used her superpowers, nor did she feel ties or obligations to other people. In fact, Faith is a more stereotypically masculine character than is Buffy given her lack of dependence on others and the extent to which she despises Buffy for her dependence on, and care for, her friends. One of the girls in the first focus group expressed approval of Faith because 'she's independent like – she doesn't obey rules – she doesn't depend on anyone else'. Each of the participants in that group (with the exception of the girl who didn't like *Buffy*) enjoyed the character of Faith because of her ability to fight, her independence and her toughness.

As was outlined above, several of the participants in the focus group discussions described the way in which they actively engaged with aspects of the programme while watching, particularly, fighting scenes. Others described how they would play games based on Buffy (in which they generally wanted to be a Slayer themselves). During the course of the focus group discussions it emerged that the participants were highly knowledgeable about events in episodes from different series and, on several occasions during each discussion, excited conversation regarding various incidents on different programmes began.

All of the participants in both focus groups were avid fans of *Buffy*, with one exception. They were aware of the range of different products connected with the series that they could buy. Most of them owned posters, videos, books, stationery and two of them also owned figures based on different characters. One girl had a poster of Angel on the ceiling over the top bunk where she slept. Several of them owned videos or DVDs of the programme, the appeal of which was that they could re-visit favourite episodes whenever they wanted. Not only did the purchase of merchandise associated with the programme enable these young people to express personal taste; it also gave them control over when they engaged with particular aspects of the narrative.

Buffy: a femininst icon for pre-adolescent girls?

Feminist commentators on *Buffy the Vampire Slayer* disagree as to whether Joss Wheedon has been successful in producing a show with a feminist central character and a feminist message. As Pender (2002) outlines, feminist and cultural theorists are not collectively agreed on the feminist status of Buffy. For some she is a feminist role model because of her strength and power. For others, however, she can be accused of subscribing to (and thus reinforcing) patriarchal and commercial values given the character's interest in fashion and the blonde, petite prettiness of Sarah Michelle Gellar who played the role. Pender (2002) argues that the programme operates out of a more complex and contested notion of gender narratives. Hobbs describes *Buffy* as 'feminism in a different key' (2003: 53) – females are powerful, but there are limits to their power and barriers to its expression. Buffy is full of contradictions. She is pretty and petite, yet powerfully strong and heroic (the role usually reserved for males in stories with pretty, petite blonde heroines). She is the lone Slayer who has inherited the power to, as well as the burdensome task of, slaying demons and vampires but she needs her friends to support her in order to succeed in most of her missions. She is a strong, skilled fighter who is also keenly interested in fashion and shopping. The story is about horror, action and heroism, in which female characters play many of the more traditional male roles, but it is also a romance with a perpetual deferral of desire more typical of a television serial (Krimmer and Ravel 2002).

What emerges from the discussions with the girls in this research is that they liked *Buffy* for contradictory reasons. They reacted very positively to a powerful female central character. At the beginning of the discussion in the second focus group, the participants agreed that one of the best things about *Buffy* was that it was 'good that a girl can have all the power. Usually on programmes its just men, but women can be more powerful'. Buffy was a hugely appealing character to the girls in this research because of her strength and power, her ability to fight and to win – 'I like her fighting and winning!' and 'because she's better than boys!' They were also impressed by the more nurturing aspect of Buffy's power and commented on the fact that she defended others, her friends as well as people with whom she had more difficult relationships. Indeed, care and nurture are central aspects of Buffy's heroic qualities. She chose to die to save her younger sister who was in the process of being sacrificed in order to bring about Armageddon at the end of Series 5 and it could be argued that this act was firmly within the sacrificial, maternal tradition.

The most appealing thing of all for many of those who took part in the focus group discussions, however, was Buffy's relationship with Angel. The majority of them liked Angel (who is tall, dark, handsome, moody and a tortured soul – most of the time). In fact, discussion about Angel caused giggling among his fans. They admitted to liking him 'cos he's nice looking!' or 'he's gorgeous!' A central element of his appeal was his romantic attachment to Buffy – 'he always backs up for Buffy' and 'he kinda loves her'. Therefore the romantic element of the narrative, more typical of traditional storylines, about the doomed love between a tall, dark and handsome hero and a beautiful younger (in this case, much younger) girl was an intrinsic part of the appeal of the programme.

I asked the participants in the discussions whether they would like to be any of the characters in the programme. Most in the first focus group either wanted to be Buffy or to be another Slayer who fought alongside Buffy. For these girls, the appeal lay in Buffy's (or another Slayer's) strength, power and heroism. However, one specifically admitted that she wanted to be Buffy 'cos she goes with Angel', thus demonstrating again the appeal of the more traditional romantic narrative. It was different for the group in the second focus group, however. The appeal of the power and strength of the Slayer character had not diminished for them. At this point, Buffy had died in order to save her younger sister from being killed as a sacrifice and to prevent Armageddon. They discussed how they would not like being a Slayer because of the loneliness and the level of responsibility involved.

Concluding comments

The young people who took part in this research demonstrated in the course of the conversations we held that they engaged as active rather than passive viewers of *Buffy the Vampire Slayer*, a programme that the majority of them thoroughly enjoyed. They understood the formulaic nature of the narrative and were capable of being critical of this. They were sophisticated viewers, following the story at several different levels of development – when different series of *Buffy* were on more than one channel on a weekly basis, they watched the various programmes, juggling the narrative strands. Active imaginative engagement with the text was not confined to the time when they were watching the programme. One of the participants described how she used her imagination to cope with elements of the narrative that frightened her, revisiting and changing those scenes in her mind.

Was *Buffy* a successful feminist icon for the girls in these discussions? Part of the reason that they liked Buffy as a character was because of her power, her strength and the unusual nature of her role, traditionally more likely to be a male one. The fact that Buffy is an appealing character and that these viewers could imagine either being her, or being like her, also contributed to their acceptance of a narrative with a feminist message. It is worth noting that not only did they accept and admire Buffy as action hero – they also held Faith in high regard (despite, or perhaps because of the fact that she is more of an anti-hero) for the same reasons. Willow, Buffy's much more feminine friend, was not held in similarly high esteem. Indeed, several of the participants could not recall her name, referring to her as 'the girl with the red hair' even though she features in every episode. Unlike the powerful and strong Slayers, Willow was 'always coming out the bad end in fights'.

Clearly however, there were other, more conventional elements of the story that also had a huge appeal and contributed to the girls' imaginative involvement, particularly the ill-fated romance between Buffy and Angel. Davies (2000) warns that narratives operating in new or alternative discourses run the risk of being interpreted through older, familiar discourses. I would argue that the young people participating in this research accepted *Buffy* partly as a result of the fact that it operated simultaneously within feminist and traditional narrative gender discourses. It simultaneously tells a new (feminist) and an old (romance) story. It also tells it in such a way that engages the imaginations of these young people with both the narrative and the characters.

The girls who participated in this research shared with me the way in which they engaged imaginatively with a television programme, re-inventing themselves as slayers – strong, powerful, independent, female heroes. Friday (1993) argues that one reason women have begun to create for themselves more powerful roles in their sexual fantasies is that it reflects social and cultural change in female status and power. Certainly, the girls in this research enjoyed *Buffy* because it presented them with an image of femininity that is powerful. They in turn can imagine themselves as similarly powerful, thus being provided with the opportunity to explore different aspects of their gender identity, and push out the boundaries of what it means to be female.[6] Walker (2001) reminds us that we cannot simply expect people to endlessly re-invent themselves as gendered beings, but argues that the provision of alternative narratives helps in challenging gender boundaries and norms. As Davies (2000) explains, change results from our understanding of the clashes and contradictions that arise when old and new or different narratives co-exist.

The girls who took part in these conversations were aware of the contradictory gender messages embedded in the narrative of *Buffy*. However, their school curriculum was not providing them with an opportunity to engage with the different narratives arising out of different gender discourses, and in so doing to understand the appeal of the romantic narrative on the one hand and a different feminist story on the other. The development of such understanding requires time and space to think, to reflect and to discuss. At present, primary education is not sufficiently engaging young people in a critical way about their favoured media texts to allow them to develop this type of understanding.

---

6 Feminist scholars are critical of the understanding of gender identity in dualistic female-male terms (Davies 1989). A more useful way of understanding the complexity of gendered identity is to envisage it as a spectrum or range of possible traits and behaviours moving from highly stereotypical femininity at one end to highly stereotypical masculinity at the other end, passing through an androgynous centre. Rather than being located at one specific point along this spectrum all of the time, individuals can display a range of different aspects of gender identity at different times and in different situations (Lodge 1998). The imagination offers the possibility of exploring, and perhaps expanding, the boundaries of gendered identity without incurring disapproval.

A number of different commentators have argued convincingly that education should provide young people with the opportunity to engage politically with media cultures and texts (Giroux and Simon 1989, Seiter 1995, Kenway and Bullen 2001). The girls who took part in this research demonstrated that they were sophisticated viewers of a television programme on both narrative and critical levels. However, the only opportunity that these girls had to discuss this particular media text in an educational context was when they engaged in the research process with me. In fact, those who took part in the second focus group discussion did so when the rest of their class were on their annual summer picnic. They chose to miss a class treat in order to talk about *Buffy*.

Bibliography

Appleyard, B. (2000) 'A teenager to get your teeth into', *The Sunday Times Culture Supplement,* pp 4-5.

Belton, T. (2000) 'The "Face at the Window" study: a fresh approach to media influence and to investigating the influence of television and videos on children's imagination', *Media, Culture and Society* 22, 5, pp 629-643.

Bentley, M. K. (1999) 'The Body of Evidence: Dangerous Intersections between Development and Culture in the Lives of Adolescent Girls', in Mazzarella, S. R. and Pecora, N. O. (eds) *Growing Up Girls: Popular Culture and the Construction of Identity,* New York, Peter Lang.

Bordo, S. (2003) *Unbearable Weight: Feminism, Western Culture, and the Body,* Berkeley, University of California Press.

Bourdieu, P. (1984) *Distinction: A Social Critique of the Judgement of Taste,* Cambridge, Mass, Harvard University Press.

Bourdieu, P. (1998) *On Television,* New York, The New Press.

Buckingham, D. (1993) *Children Talking Television: The Making of Television Literacy,* London, Falmer Press.

Buckingham, D. (2000) *After the death of childhood: growing up in the age of electronic media,* Cambridge, Polity Press.

Cohen, S. (2001) *States of Denial. Knowing about Atrocities and Suffering,* Cambridge, Polity Press.

Cortes, C. (2000) *The children are watching: how the media teach about diversity,* New York, Teachers' College Press.

Dahlgren, P. (1995) *Television and the Public Sphere,* London, Sage Publications.

Dalton, M. M. (1999) *The Hollywood Curriculum: Teachers and Teaching in the Movies,* New York, Peter Lang.

Dart, L. (2000) 'Literacy and the lost world of the imagination', *Educational Research* 43, 1, pp 63-77.

Daugherty, A. M. (2001) 'Just a girl; Buffy as icon', in R. Kaveney (ed.) *Reading the Vampire Slayer: An Unofficial Critical Companion to Buffy and Angel,* London, Tauris Parke.

Davies, B. (1989) 'The Discursive Production of the Male/Female Dualism in School Settings', *Oxford Review of Education* 15, 3 pp 229-241.

Davies, B. (1990) 'Lived and Imaginary Narratives and Their Place in Taking Oneself up as a Gendered Being', *Australian Psychologist* 25, 3, pp 318-332.

Davies, B. and Harre, R. (1990) 'Positioning: The Discursive Production of Selves', *Journal for the Theory of Social Behaviour* 20, 1, pp 43-63.

Davies, B. (1993) *Shards of Glass,* Sydney, Allen and Unwin.

Davies, B. (2000) *A Body of Writing 1990-1999,* Walnut Creek, Altamira Press.

Davies, B. (2003) *Frogs and Snails and Feminist Tales. Preschool Children and Gender* (revised edition), Cresskill NJ, Hampton Press.

Denzin, N. K. (1993) *Images of Post-Modern Society: Social Theory and Contemporary Cinema,* London, Sage Publications.

Fiske, J. (2001) 'Intertextuality', in Harrington, C. L. and Bielby, D. D. (eds) *Popular Culture: Production and Consumption,* Oxford, Blackwell.

Foucault, M. (1989) *The Archaeology of Knowledge,* London, Routledge

Friday, N. (1993) *Women on Top: How Real Life has Changed Women's Sexual Fantasies,* New York, Mass Market Paperback.

Gauntlett, D. (2002) *Media, Gender and Identity, An Introduction,* London, Routledge.

Gazetas, A. (2000) *Imagining Selves: The Politics of Representation, Film Narratives, and Adult Education,* New York, Peter Lang.

Giroux, H. A. and Simon, R. I. (1989) *Popular Culture: Schooling and Everyday Life,* London, Bergin and Garvey.

Giroux, H. (1999) *The Mouse that Roared: Disney and the end of innocence,* New York, Rowman and Littlefield Publishers.

Grieg, A. and Taylor, J. (1999) *Doing Research with Children,* London, Sage.

Gunning, M. (1997) 'Children and Television Pleasure', in Kelly, M. J. and O'Connor, B. (eds) *Media Audiences in Ireland: Power and Cultural Identity,* Dublin, UCD Press, pp 249-268.

Hobbs, T. (2003) 'Buffy the Vampire Slayer as Feminist Noir', in J. B. South (ed.) *Buffy the Vampire Slayer and Philosophy: Fear and Trembling in Sunnydale,* Chicago, Open Court.

Holder, N. (2000) *Buffy the Vampire Slayer: The Watcher's Guide Volume 2,* London, Pocket Books.

James, A., Jenks, C. and Prout, A. (1998) *Theorizing Childhood,* Cambridge, Polity Press.

Kaveney, R. (2001) 'She saved the world. A lot', in R. Kaveney (ed.) *Reading the Vampire Slayer: An Unofficial Critical Companion to Buffy and Angel,* London, Tauris Parke.

Kenway, J. and Bullen, E. (2001) *Consuming Children: education-entertainment-advertising,* Buckingham, Open University Press.

Krimmer, E. and Raval, S. (2002) '"Digging the Undead": Death and Desire in *Buffy*', in R. V. Wilcox and C. Lavery (eds) *Fighting the Forces: What's at Stake in Buffy the Vampire Slayer,* Lanham, Rowman and Littlefield.

Lembo, R. (2000) *Thinking Through Television,* Cambridge, Cambridge University Press.

Lemke, J. L. (1995) *Textual Politics: Discourse and Social Dynamics*, London, Taylor and Francis.

Levine, L. E. and Waite, B. M. (2000) 'Television Viewing and Attentional Abilities in Fourth and Fifth Grade Children', *Journal of Applied Developmental Psychology* 21, 6, pp 667-679.

Levine, M. P. and Schneider, S. J. (2003) 'Feeling for Buffy: the girl next door', in J. B. South (ed.) *Buffy the Vampire Slayer and Philosophy: Fear and Trembling in Sunnydale,* Chicago, Open Court.

Lodge, A. (1998) *Gender Identity and Schooling: a two-year ethnographic study of the expression, exploration and development of gender identity in seven to nine year old children in their school environment*, Unpublished PhD thesis, Education Department, NUI Maynooth.

Lodge, A. and Flynn, M. (2001) 'Gender Identity in the Primary School Playground', in Cleary, A., Nic Ghiolla Phadraig, M., Quin, S. (eds) *Understanding Children Volume 1: State, Education and Economy,* Dublin, Oak Tree Press.

Lyon, D. (1999) *Postmodernity* (second edition), Buckingham, Open University Press.

Lynch, K. (1999) *Equality in Education,* Dublin, Gill and Macmillan.

Lynch, K. and Lodge, A. (2002) *Equality and Power in Schools,* London, Routledge Falmer.

Mayall, B. (2000) 'Conversations with Children: Working with Generational Issues', in Christensen, P. and James, A. (eds) *Research with Children: Perspectives and Practices,* London, Falmer Press.

Messenger Davies, M. and Machin, D. (2000) '"It helps people make their decisions": Dating games, public service broadcasting and the negotiation of identity in middle-childhood', *Childhood* 7, 2, pp 173-191.

Parks, L. (2003) 'Brave new *Buffy:* Rethinking TV Violence', in M. Jancovich and J. Lyons (eds) *Quality Popular Television: Cult TV, the Industry and Fans,* London, British Film Institute Publishing.

Pecora, N. and Mazzarella, S. P. (1999) 'Introduction', *Growing Up Girls: Popular Culture and the Construction of Identity,* New York, Peter Lang, pp 1-10.

Pender, P. (2002) '"I'm Buffy and You're ... History"; The Postmodern Politics of *Buffy*', in R. V. Wilcox and C. Lavery (eds) *Fighting the Forces: What's at Stake in Buffy the Vampire Slayer,* Lanham, Rowman and Littlefield.

Postman, N. (1994) *The Disappearance of Childhood,* New York, Vintage Books.

Reay, D. (2001) '"Spice Girls", "Nice Girls", "Girlies", and "Tomboys": gender discourses, girls' cultures and femininities in the primary classroom', *Gender and Education* 13, 2, pp 153-166.

Rosenthal, M. (1992) 'What was Postmodernism', in *Socialist Review,* 22, pp 85-99.

Sayer, K. (2001) 'It wasn't our world anymore. They made it theirs', in R. Kaveney (ed.) *Reading the Vampire Slayer: An Unofficial Critical Companion to Buffy and Angel,* London, Tauris Parke.

Seiter, E. (1995) *Sold Separately: Children and Parents as Consumers,* New Brunswick, NJ, Rutgers University Press.

Signorielli, N. (2001) 'Television's Gender Role Images and Contribution to Stereotyping. Past, present and future', in D. G. Singer and J. L. Singer (eds) *Handbook of Children and the Media,* London, Sage Publications.

Storey, J. (2003) *Inventing Popular Culture: from folklore to globalisation,* Oxford, Blackwell Publishing.

Strinati, D. (2000) *An Introduction to Studying Popular Culture,* London, Routledge.

Sutton-Smith, B. (1997) *The Ambiguity of Play,* Cambridge, Mass, Harvard University Press.

Tepper, S. J. (2000) 'Fiction reading in America: Explaining the gender gap', *Poetics* 27, pp 255-275.

Walker, M. (2001) 'Engineering Identities', *British Journal of Sociology of Education* 22, 1, pp 75-89.

Walkerdine, V. (1997) *Daddy's Girl: Young Girls and Popular Culture,* London, Macmillan Press.

Wilson, V. (1997) 'Focus Groups: a useful qualitative method for educational research?', in *British Educational Research Journal* 23, 2, pp 209-224.

CHAPTER 11

Experiencing racism in the primary school – children's perspectives[1]

Dympna Devine, Mairin Kenny and Eileen McNeela

Introduction

Irish society has undergone substantial change in the past thirty years, typified by a rapidly changing social and economic structure, urbanisation and competition within a global economy. Such change has been accompanied by changing demographic patterns, with massive emigration in the 1980s replaced by increasing immigration following the unprecedented economic growth in the mid-1990s. Attitudes toward this change have been mixed and recent research points to the prevalence of negative attitudes toward minority ethnic groups among the Irish public (Amnesty International 2001). Concern has also been expressed at the stereotyping of minority ethnic groups in the media in primarily negative and sensationalist terms (Casey and O'Connell 2000, Fanning et al 2001, Guerin 2002, Nozinic 2002, Sinha 2002) while particularly high levels of prejudice have been identified with respect to the Traveller community (MacGreil 1996, McDonagh 2002, Ní Shuinéar 2002, O'Connell 2002).

Children, like adults, are part of this changing social landscape. As their communities and schools become increasingly diverse, they face challenges and opportunities in adjusting to this change. This chapter is based on research (Devine et al 2002) conducted into the experience of ethnicity in a sample of primary and second-level schools. It explores how children's behaviour can be exclusionary and derogatory of minority ethnic groups as well as inclusive and respectful of ethnic difference. The analysis is organised into a number of overlapping themes related to:

[1] While all three named individuals were involved in the collection of data on which this chapter is based, both the analysis of the data and the writing of this chapter were carried out by Dympna Devine. Particular thanks to Dr Anne Lodge for her helpful comments on earlier drafts of this chapter.

– Children's awareness and understanding of racism
– Racism and name-calling in school

The chapter begins with a review of previous research in the area of children's experience of racism in schools.

Children, racism and schooling

Research into children's attitudes toward and experience of ethnic diversity paints a mixed picture, with some identifying racial prejudice in children from the age of five while others dispute such findings (Black-Gutman and Hickson 1996, Holmes 1995 Doyle and Aboud 1995, Ramsey 1991 and Katz 1983). In an Irish context, O'Keeffe and O'Connor (2001) highlight the prevalence of racist attitudes towards Travellers among children aged nine to eleven years. While there may be some dispute about the extent of prejudice among young children, prejudice itself is firmly linked to the experience of and attitude toward difference. Such difference can be central to the dynamics of power and control between children in their interaction with one another. In the general cut and thrust of children's interaction, differences (on the basis of ethnicity/ gender/ dis/ability, sexuality and social class) can be used by children to assert power and status with one another in their peer groups, often with negative consequences for those who are labelled as 'different' (Connolly 1998, Deegan 1996, Devine et al 2002, Kenny et al 2003, Troyna and Hatcher 1992). While much racism in schools remains hidden, taking place in the backstage regions of school life (corridors, toilets, school yard) its prevalence has been widely noted in the international literature (Codjoe 2001, Connolly 1998, ICIS 1996, Jones 1997, Henze et al 2000, Myers 2003, Pilkington 1999, Varma-Joshi et al 2004).

The most salient form of racism among children and young people appears to be in the form of racist name-calling (Connolly 1998, Mac An Ghaill 1994, Troyna and Hatcher 1992) which can take place both inside and outside of the school. Name-calling is an endemic feature of child culture – part of the repertoire of strategies employed by children in the negotiation of their status with peers (Devine 2003). Distinct social processes within child culture such as acting tough, conflict between older and younger children, exclusion from peer groups and the assertion of ethnic identity are all open to being racialised as children negotiate their status, belonging and position within the peer group (Troyna and Hatcher 1992). While there may be differences in the literature on the nature and extent of racism in children's interaction with one another, the research is clear on children's sensitivity to ethnic identity as a marker of social difference. Given the growth in minority ethnic representation in Ireland in the past ten years (CSO 2002) and the prevalence of racism in Irish society (Amnesty International 2001), it is pertinent to examine children's own perceptions and experience of race and racism in their school lives.

Methodology

Qualitative fieldwork over a period of eight months was conducted into the experience of ethnic diversity in a selected sample of primary and post-primary schools. The remainder of this chapter details findings drawn from the primary sample, with a specific focus on the children's experience and understanding of racism. It draws on data gathered from group interviews involving 132 children (of diverse ethnic identity) in three primary schools, as well as observations of classroom practice and schoolyard behaviour.

Table 1: Participating primary schools in the study

School	Location	Social Class	Gender	Total enrolment	Minority ethnic enrolment	Minority ethnic as % of enrolment
Oakleaf	Suburban	Designated disadvantaged	Co-Ed	300	73	24 %
Newdale	Rural	Mixed social class	Girls*	415	47	11%
Riverside	Suburban	Mixed social class	Co-Ed	268	25	9%

**Newdale primary was co-educational up to first class and single-sex, girls, from second to sixth. The classes presenting for interview were all girl classes.*

The data in this chapter is drawn from interviews with children at junior and senior levels across the three primary schools as follows.

Children were organised for interviews on a friendship group basis, with no interview group larger than five children. Children in second and fourth/fifth class were targeted, with the total cohort of children in each of the classes interviewed.[2] Observation of the children both in the classroom and in the schoolyard was also

[2] While interviewing all of the children in each targeted class was time consuming, nonetheless it was important in revealing the overall patterns of friendship within each of the classes, through socio-metric analyses. Keddies (2004) also notes the value of interviewing children in such groups.

conducted. The remainder of the chapter documents the findings in relation to one aspect of the research – namely the children's awareness and understanding of racism, as well as their experience of racism in school.

Table 2: Ethnic profile of interviewees[3]

Name of school	Junior class (2nd)		Senior class (4th/5th)	
	Minority ethnic	Majority ethnic[4]	Minority ethnic	Majority ethnic
Oakleaf primary	5	15	8*	33
Riverside primary	3	17	4	22
Newdale primary	2	13	3	17

**This group includes a selected sample of five Traveller children taken from a number of classes, as there were no Traveller children in the classes presenting for interview.*

Children's awareness and understanding of racism

The interviews were conducted in a very informal manner with a gradual lead in to issues that concerned ethnicity and schooling. While direct discussion on racism was only dealt with when it emerged as part of ongoing conversation, it was clear that the majority ethnic children had a limited understanding of what racism meant. Explanations of the term, where offered, consistently drew links between racism and negative/abusive behaviour toward black people:

Interviewer: Did you ever hear of racism?
Child 1: Yeah you really hate black people and you're sexist. (majority ethnic females, senior class, Oakleaf Primary)
Interviewer: What is a racist?
Child 3: You're white and there's coloured people and you don't like any colouredy people or your black and you don't like any white people.
Child 1: Michael Jackson is a racist.

3 The minority ethnic profile of those interviewed included five Traveller children and children from the following countries: Nigeria (5), Somalia (1), Pakistan (2), Bangladesh (1), India (1), Nepal (1), Libya (3), Romania (1), Lithuania (1), Latvia (1), Croatia (1), Kosovo (1), Armenia (1).

4 In this study, the white settled Irish population is referred to as 'majority ethnic'. The term 'Irish' denotes place of origin and a facet of ethnic identity and is not intended to carry normative tones.

Child 2: Because he changed his colour. He got all the surgery done because he doesn't like black people. (majority ethnic, seniors, Riverside Primary)

Children's interpretation of racism was also firmly rooted in their day to day interaction and, as Troyna and Hatcher (1992) noted, in the dynamics of power, control and status between peers. These dynamics are evident in the following excerpt from an interview with a mixed gender group of children in Riverside primary. Their focus of discussion was upon Ava,[5] a Nigerian girl, who was identified by both the teacher and pupils in the class as an excellent worker in school.

Child 1: There's a girl I sit beside called Ava
Child 2: And she's coloured … .
Child 1: And she tells me to shut up a lot of the time
Child 2: She's racist, Ava's a racist
Child 1: If I say I need a loan of your rubber she says no
Interviewer: I heard you saying there that Ava was a racist, what did you mean by that?
Child 2: She doesn't like white people
Child 3: She does get along with white people but sometimes she doesn't really like to be their friend
Child 2: She thinks she's all smart and all and great because she's from a different country. She knows her Irish the most. She thinks she's all popular.
Child 3: It's not fair at all to say she's a racist, because she's not, she does like white people. She doesn't get along with some of them, that doesn't mean she's a racist.

In this discussion there are a number of overlapping strands that give some sense of how these children interpret racism as well as some disagreement as to when the term should be applied. What some of the children describe is a form of inverse racism,[6] where as white children they feel themselves to have been the victim of racial abuse by a black child. This abuse is not in the form of name-calling (as we will see later) but rather in a black child not sharing with them and subjecting them to a form of one-up-man-ship in her interactions with them. These latter are important markers of friendship in child culture – where being the same as

---

5 Pseudonyms are used throughout the text.

6 This was something which also emerged consistently in the interviews with second-level students. Any discussions about racism with majority ethnic students invariably revolved around how they, as white students, were subject to discrimination.

others, not overstepping others in terms of ability etc signify a willingness to be included/excluded in the peer group (Devine 2003). That this interpretation of Ava's behaviour is not shared by all the children in the group highlights the children's own differing interpretations of what racism entails, as well as their differing loyalties to Ava as a friend in class.

The link the majority ethnic children continually made between racism and skin colour was reinforced by the general absence of naming Travellers as a group who were exposed to racial abuse in school. While children often condoned racial name-calling, name-calling of Travellers was never spoken of in critical terms. An example of this trend is evident in the following conversation with a group of senior boys in Oakleaf Primary:

Interviewer: One of you used the words earlier about being racist. What does that mean?
Child 1: It means you don't like black people
Child 2: People in this school are racist – most people
Child 1: I'd just stick up for them
Child 2: My nephew is black so how could I be racist?
Child 1: What's the difference with black people and white people, black people just their skin colour, there's no difference
Interviewer: What about Travellers, are there any here?
Child 2: Yeah and I slag Andy (a Traveller child)
Interviewer: Why do you slag him?
Child 2: Because he's a little knacker
Interviewer: What does that mean?
Child 2: It means your scum, scumbags. (majority ethnic, male, senior class, Oakleaf Primary)

By failing to attribute racist intentions to such abuse, these children drew distinctions between what they saw as the legitimate abuse of Travellers (by virtue of their lifestyle) in contrast to the unfair abuse of other minority ethnic children (by virtue of their skin colour). The children's conceptualisation of racism was evidently not located within a broader context of race relations and differences in power and status between ethnic groups in society. In relation to Travellers, their views signalled an absence of identifying Travellers as a minority ethnic group, with the right to be respected on their own terms. Traveller children, for their part, were aware of their lower standing among their peers and of how this was directly attributed to their culture and lifestyle:

Child 1: Girls in my class don't know I'm a Traveller … I'm ashamed, I don't want to tell them

Interviewer: Why do you say that – they wouldn't make friends with you?
Child 2: They don't even know we are Travellers
Interviewer: Maybe they know, they just don't care, they like you anyway
Child 2: They just don't want to tell you maybe?
Child 1: They don't want to insult you or anything. (Travellers, Oakleaf Primary)

Settled people, by and large, to this group of children viewed them with disdain, staring at them, calling them 'knackers' and refusing them entry to shops and pubs:

Child 1: Travellers when you are travelling round you get looked at all the time
Interviewer: So what would you say to settled people?
Child 2: We'd say: we are all the same people, but like only because we are Travellers you shouldn't put Travellers out for no reason at all. Like if you start fighting, they have to get put out. But if they've done nothing, they shouldn't be put out
Child 1: The mans in the shops put us out and if we do go in they are watching us every minute. (Travellers, Oakleaf Primary)

Listening to the children speak, it was clear they had a relatively defensive relationship with the settled community, conscious of their difference and of their lower status within the community generally. Indeed, while these children recognised that there was also some discrimination against other minority ethnic groups, they felt that they themselves were subject to greater levels of abuse:

Interviewer: So who do you think gets the rougher time, do you think [Travellers or foreign nationals] going down to the shops and that?
Child 1 Travellers mostly
Interviewer: And refugees? You don't think they get a hard time?
Child 2: The Afghanistan people they are getting a hard time too. (Travellers, Oakleaf Primary)

The analysis suggests differing perceptions and experiences of racism among minority and majority ethnic children. With respect to the latter, their interpretation of racism appears to be located predominantly within the domain of skin colour, that to be racist is to denigrade somebody on the basis of their black skin. Other differences, such as those derived from cultural or linquistic patterns, are located as deficiencies in the minority ethnic child and are therefore not as explicitly named as the basis for racial abuse. This is evident in the comments of the children below, who refer to the 'other' status of a group of Muslim children by virtue of their cultural difference. The children's sensitivity to this otherness, their perceptions of ethnic difference, emerged in the course of interviews and centred primarily on language and culture, as well as physical appearance:

> Child 1: Muslims are different
> Child 2: They go on fast
> Child 1: That means you are not allowed eat
> Child 3: The Muslims they do fasts
> Child 1: That's all that's wrong with them. (majority ethnic, females, junior class, Oakleaf Primary)

A Muslim girl recounted her experiences of racism thus:

> Sometimes I hear a boy in my class say: I don't like these girls because they've a different language. (5th class Somali girl, Oakleaf primary)

An anti-English bias was also prevalent in some children's comments, with children who had returned from England or who had parents who were English singled out for their difference, manifest primarily in their accents:

> Mark gets called English bastard 'cos his mother is from England. (majority ethnic, male, senior class, Riverside Primary)

This absence of understanding is not surprising in the light of teachers' own stated reluctance to name issues directly related to racism (focusing instead on the more general issue of bullying) in their classrooms, a finding noted across all schools in the study. An exception appeared to be in Oakleaf primary where a group of Muslim girls recounted a teacher talking to them about racism:

> Interviewer: Did you ever hear of racism? Do you know what it means?
> Child 1: In my school a teacher came to talk about it. Can't remember what they said.
> Child 2: Oh yeah. Everyone from a different country in this school, the racism of people calling you names and everything. She tells us not to do that. Like a girl in my street won't play with me 'cos I'm different. (Muslim, females, senior class, Oakleaf Primary)

In terms of the actual experience of racial abuse within the broader community, this was an issue that emerged predominantly in interviews with minority ethnic children. In each of these interviews, reference was made to experiences of being shouted at, called derogatory names and other forms of abuse as minority ethnic children went about their business in their out of school lives. This appeared to be as common for primary school children as for their older second-level peers and did not appear to apply to one minority group over and above another (including Traveller children). The experiences mentioned are typified in the follow excerpts from interview transcripts and indicate these children's sensitivity to racial abuse on the basis of cultural and linguistic differences:

> Child 1: When I go to Spar I wear my scarf. One day me and my baby sister were going to Spar together, and they started making fun of our language
> Interviewer: How did that feel?
> Child 1: Bad, my sister really felt bad because she was the one who was wearing the scarf
> Interviewer: Would that happen to you often?
> Child 2: It always happens when we go to shopping centres. (Muslim, females, senior class, Oakleaf Primary)
>
> We live down on the site and when we'd walk to the shop, people used to call us: Go away knackers and all. (Traveller, male, Oakleaf Primary)

While it was clear that majority ethnic children had not themselves been victims of such forms of abuse, some had witnessed scenes of racial abuse, reinforcing the views expressed by the minority ethnic children:

> I was in Londis and this boy came in and he was from Nigeria and his face was all bashed in because he was the colour. (majority ethnic, female, senior class, Oakleaf Primary)

What these findings suggest is that while majority ethnic children in the study were aware of racism and had some understanding of what racism entailed, their understanding was limited, and very much located in their day to day experience. This often yielded contradictory and confusing responses that the children were uncomfortable expressing. For their part, minority ethnic children had a deeper understanding of racial abuse that was rooted in the reality of their daily lives and many viewed such abuse as an unavoidable fact of life. Further analysis of the children's perspectives indicated the salience of name-calling to the experience of racism in school.

Racism and name-calling in school

In-depth probing into the dynamics of pupil interaction and child culture, especially name-calling, indicated that children in the study drew on a wide repertoire of racially abusive terms, which they had both used and experienced in their school lives. In order to tease through the children's experiences, they were encouraged to talk about the conflicts which took place in the course of their everyday interaction and the incidence of teasing and name-calling in the course of such conflict. Their talk revealed the prevalence of name-calling in their interaction with one another and how it was firmly located in the context of difference and/or perceived deficiency in a child. One fifth class girl in Oakleaf put this aptly when she said: *If you are tall, short, fat, thin you get called names.*[7]

In this sense children who are ethnically different are obvious targets for name-calling. Names that related to ethnicity revolved primarily around skin colour and the extent of such forms of name-calling can be gauged from the fact that examples were quoted in every interview in the primary level sample as follows:

Interviewer: What sorts of names are used calling someone who is a different colour?

Child 1: Chocolate face. Mongolian. Chalkies. If someone has really dark skin they call them Charcoal. (majority ethnic, female, senior class, Oakleaf Primary) There's a girl in my class and she keeps saying I'm a black monkey. (minority ethnic, female, junior class, Newdale Primary)

Some name-calling also related to country of origin, the latter more prevalent for Muslim children in the wake of the September 11th attacks in New York:

Child 1: If you were a Palestinian and you came over here you'd get slagged. Nobody here likes them. People here are starting to hate Muslims. Like the Americans. It was on the news it was. I wouldn't like to be a Muslim. They say they're bastards. (majority ethnic, male, senior, Riverside)

---

[7] During the course of the interviews a full repertoire of the type of name-calling that took place included name-calling related to: child's size (as in the given quote), sexual orientation/connotations (gay/queer, poof, whore, prick), hair type (ginger, curly head, skin head, carrot top), ability (dope, idiot, git, thick, spa, handicapped Nerd, weakazoid), family status (bastard, bitch), gender (boy being called a girl), wearing glasses (four eyes, jam jars, googley eyes), animal names (flea, dozy cow) as well as rules within childhood related to telling the teacher (tell-tale, ratbag).

For Traveller children, name-calling derived from the difference of their lifestyles, as well as modes of speech and dress. The following excerpt is taken from an interview where the children recounted the high degree of slagging that involved Traveller children:

> Interviewer: Why are Traveller children picked on so much?
> Child 1: Because they don't change their uniform. And they usually have scruffy nails and face and ears.
> Child 2: And they go around in track suit bottoms with hooker boots on and everything
> Interviewer: So it's because of the way they dress?
> Child 1: Yeah (majority ethnic, females, junior class, Oakleaf Primary)

Most of the name-calling that the children recounted took place in the yard during playtime. As documented elsewhere (e.g. Devine 2003) here backstage behaviour abounds, as teachers find it impossible to keep an eye on all that the children 'get up to'. However, children also recounted the incidence of name-calling and verbal abuse on the way to and from school, again locations where adult supervision was minimised and children generally enjoyed greater freedom in their interactions with one another. In relation to racially motivated forms of abuse, some minority ethnic children spoke of not walking to and from school for 'safety reasons' as illustrated in the following interview extracts:

> Interviewer: What about coming and going to school?
> Child: My mum drives me for safety
> Interviewer: Why for safety?
> Child: Just so as not to get bullied and called names and that I used to be called names on the way home from school … because I wear a scarf on my head and when I wear it they call me names. (Muslim, female, senior class, Oakleaf Primary)

Reasons given for name-calling

When asked to explain why children engaged in name-calling, references were typically made to being annoyed by a child or disliking them. In such instances the name-calling engaged in with minority ethnic children is typical of what Troyna and Hatcher (1992) refer to as 'hot name-calling': names called out in the heat of the moment, but which draw on racist terminology in their effort to bestow a put down:

Child 1: When they are being slagged [children from other countries] I might stick up for them. But usually they can be annoying and real rough like. That's why they get called black bastards and niggers and all that.

Child 2: I'm nice to them, it's not fair. We'd never call them names. If they did something mean we might let it slip out, but we wouldn't really mean it that much. (majority ethnic, males, senior class, Riverside Primary)

Child: If you lose your temper you might call Mac (a Traveller child) a knacker

Interviewer: Would you really mean it?

Child: It depends – I mean every curse I've ever called him. (majority ethnic, male, senior class, Oakleaf Primary)

In each of the classes interviewed it was also clear that some children engaged in name-calling more than others, suggesting that their abusive behaviour was rooted in the desire to dominate and control others. For example, Margaret was spoken of in fifth class in Newdale Primary as being mean to everyone, but especially new girls who came into the class.[8] This rendered immigrant and Traveller children especially vulnerable to her abuse. Joseph in fifth class in Oakleaf Primary, and David and Peter in Riverside Primary were identified as general bullies who constantly demeaned and slagged children, minority and majority ethnic included:

Child 1: Margaret is the only one in class that's a bully

Child 2: That's what happened to me

Child 1: She says names to you and stuff ... you know the 'b' word and the 'f' word and the 'n' word

Interviewer: Oh would she? The 'n' word, I see

Child 2: What's the 'n' word ... knacker is it?

Child 1: No, no it's Nig-ger ... she calls the little small lads that are like her (pointing) Niggers. (mixed ethnic group, females, senior class, Newdale Primary)

Child 1: They used to call Mathew nigger. It wasn't really fair on him he was really nice. He left this school because of David and Peter for always calling him a nigger. He's gone to a different school

---

8 Kelly (2003) notes in her research the tendency for new girls (regardless of ethnic origin) to be accorded high status in female peer groups on their arrival into a class. This may explain Margaret's tendency to feel threatened by any new girl's arrival, hence her efforts to displace the popularity of such girls as quickly as possible.

Child 2: They always said to him go to the shop and wrap yourself up in a mars bar, we are going to eat you because you are a very dark chocolate and I want to eat you. He was very tanned black. (majority ethnic, females, senior class, Riverside Primary)

The meanness of names and reactions to name-calling

While children draw on a considerable repertoire of names in the course of their more negative interaction with one another, and many of these are racialised, it was also clear the children perceived some names to be worse than others. A hierarchy of meanness existed in the use of names, with children especially sensitive to being called a name which referred to their physical appearance. While it is not surprising then that minority ethnic children, especially those who were black, would be affronted by names relating to their colour, children generally (i.e. both majority and minority ethnic children) expressed the view that derogatory names relating to skin colour were the most serious of all the affronts that could be made to a child:

Interviewer: Are there some names that people are called that hurt the most?
Child 1: Yeah, they calls us the black people, chocolate boys
Child 2: Yeah, chocolate boys
Interviewer: Is that sixth class boys?
Child 1: Yeah. And fifth class and second class too. (Nigerian, juniors, male. Oakleaf Primary)
Interviewer: Is there a difference between names like Nigger or Chocolate Head and say Fatty or Four eyes? Which would be the meanest?
Child: Something about the colour black. (majority ethnic, male, senior class, Riverside Primary)

The distinctions children draw between 'colour based' name-calling and other displays of verbal abuse may be an indication of the disciplinary codes within each primary school and the children's awareness that such forms of abuse would be severely reprimanded by teaching staff and principal alike. However, it may also be attributed to the perceived 'otherness' of minority ethnic children and the understanding that such otherness carries with it a threat to inclusion in school. This is evident in the discussion below:

Interviewer: Do people ever get slagged because they come from a different country?

Child 1: Yeah Ava is called the black girl and Peter slags Antonio as well
Child 2: He nearly got suspended, he called her a nigger
Interviewer: Give me another name – say four eyes, will the principal nearly suspend them?
Child 1: You get a report. You have five days and if he doesn't like your marks after that you get suspended.
Interviewer: Why, when Mathew was called a nigger, is it more serious than say four eyes
Child 1: More serious calling him a nigger, that's a more bad name
Child 2: *Because we are normal and they are black.* (majority ethnic, senior class, Riverside Primary)

In a number of instances, majority ethnic children also suggested that being called a knacker was the worst possible name a child could be called, highlighting again the 'otherness' and accompanying lower status of Travellers in these children's minds:

Interviewer: Is it different calling someone a knacker than Pig Face? Which is worse?
Child: Knacker
Interviewer: Why?
Child: 'Cos they start slagging you about nits and all when they call you a knacker. (majority ethnic, females, junior class, Oakleaf Primary)

The data suggests that children draw distinctions between the types of names they call one another, with some names, especially those identified with minority ethnic status, perceived as worse than others. Children's reactions to name-calling were not uniform, however. Younger children in the study were generally more reluctant to talk about the issue of name-calling and many stated that it was not a problem for them in their class. This may be due to a fear of admitting that such 'bold' behaviour was engaged in, or it may actually signal a lesser focus on this type of interaction between children of this age. The prevalence of 'telling' among younger children would also ensure that teachers were enabled to curtail and correct such behaviour, when it occurred. For older children, name-calling appears to be a normal part of their interaction with one another and reactions to being called names varied. For Traveller children, especially the boys, they emphasised the need to physically respond when called a name:

Interviewer: And in this school you are not called names and stuff?
Child 1: If you start arguing with them and all, start fighting they will

Child 2:	If they call me a name I'd have to fight. (Traveller, male, senior class, Oakleaf Primary)

A girl in this group however was clear that she would immediately tell the principal if she was called any derogatory names because of her Traveller status:

Child.	A girl in my class called me a knacker and I went up and told the principal and he gave out to her. She threatened me. We are still getting it sorted out. (Traveller, female, junior class, Oakleaf Primary)

For other children gaining the support of peers was an important device and in the following excerpt we can see how some majority ethnic children defend their minority ethnic friends in the face of racial abuse:

Child:	They were calling Mary names like Chocolate and poo and all
Child 2:	Yeah, but we stand up for each other[9]
Interviewer:	What did you say?
Child 2:	We told them to leave her alone and stop bossing her around. And it's not fair 'cos if you were that colour you wouldn't like it if they were saying that to you
Interviewer:	And was it some of the time they did that or all of the time or just once?
Child 1:	All of the time
Child 3:	They'd come up sometimes and go 'hey poo woman'
Child 2:	If I could get near them I'd try to beat them up if I could
Interviewer:	Could you not beat them up in school?
Child 2:	No you'd get a red card straight away. (majority ethnic, seniors, Riverside Primary)

These children's comments indicate their sense of outrage over the racial abuse of their friend and their willingness to take a stand on her behalf. In general, minority ethnic children in the school felt that teachers reacted swiftly to incidences of name-calling and that they would be supported by them in the event of such abuse. Children were aware of the seriousness with which verbal abuse, especially racially motivated verbal abuse was taken by school staff, and of the punishments which ensued if they persisted with this form of behaviour.

---

[9] These comments indicate the formation of friendships that cut across ethnic boundaries with these majority white children asserting their loyalty to Mary, a minority ethnic child.

Concluding discussion

Racist name calling is a feature of children's interaction with one another at school. However, it was not something experienced in the same way by all minority ethnic children, nor applied consistently in all instances where there was conflict between children of differing ethnic origin. There was evidence in the study for example of majority ethnic children 'sticking' up for their minority peers in the face of racial abuse, or of conflict between differing minority ethnic children themselves that also drew on racial stereotypes.

One way of analysing these dynamics is to consider them along a continuum of two inter-linking and contrasting dimensions, the first relating to the dynamics of inclusion and exclusion in friendship patterns, while the second focuses on the experience of difference ('otherness' versus 'sameness') in children's relations with one another in school. These contrasting dimensions are indicated in Figure 1 below as they apply to the experience of ethnicity:

Figure 1: Dimensions of pupil social interaction and ethnicity in schooll[10]

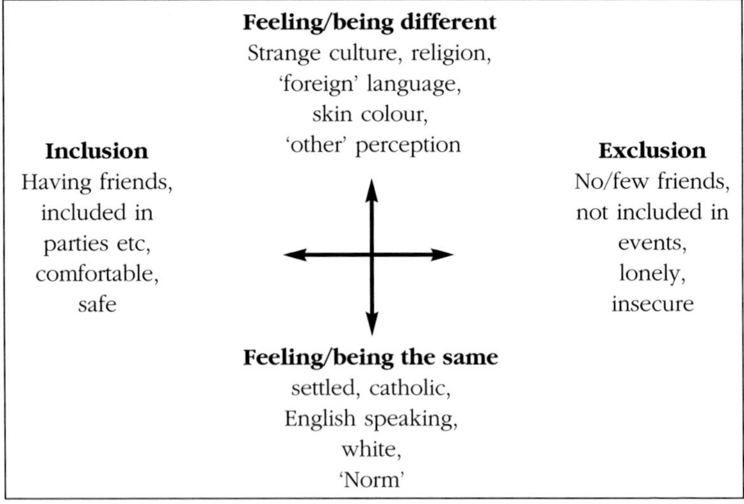

Taking the dimension of inclusion and exclusion firstly, interview data confirmed the centrality of children's social relationships to their school lives and of the sense of belonging and security which

[10] There are other status issues (related for example to gender, age, social class and dis/ability) which cut across these dynamics.

emerged as a result of their friendships in school. Such belonging overlapped with home lives in the invitations to birthday parties, sleepovers and general playing/interacting together in after-school hours. Being good at sport, sharing similar humour, not being favoured by teachers (teacher's pet) and sharing common interests were all identified in the course of interviews as facets of the dynamic interplay between inclusion and exclusion in the children's friendship formations, reinforcing findings identified in previous research in this area (e.g. Devine 2003, Lodge and Flynn 2001).

Cutting across such patterns however are also those relating to difference/sameness, with children who are perceived as being different often struggling to include themselves and be included in friendship groups. Perceptions of difference ('otherness') are intertwined with those of sameness ('the norm'), such perceptions governed in turn by discourses encountered in society through for example media, family and community influences (Foucault 1979, Devine 2003). Racism has its roots in discourse which defines those from differing ethnic groups as 'other', stereotyped according to a set of negative dispositions (lazy, dirty, aggressive etc) which appears to justify their exclusion from full participation in the society. Embedded within discourses of difference are also those of normality – to define someone else as 'other' is to have a clear sense of oneself as normal. With respect to ethnic identity, assertions of Irish identity may revolve around being white, Catholic and part of the settled community. Minority ethnic groups such as Travellers, Jews, or black Irish are often considered outside of this norm, with consequent implications for their status within Irish society as a whole. Children, no less than adults, draw on these discourses of difference, interpreting their interaction with others on their perceived normality or otherness with respect to dominant norms.

One aspect of sameness and difference repeatedly focused on by the children was that of skin colour, which in some instances was perceived as the basis for friendship formation. This particularly applied when a child was new to the school or classroom. In one interview for example, children spoke of the ease of a new child settling in if there were other 'coloured' children present:

Child 1:	Say one coloured person was in your class it would be really hard because it's just one coloured person. Say there's three coloured people in their class, 'cause they've got coloured people to play with them
Interviewer:	But Anthony plays with all people
Child 2:	Yeah but John and Luke only play with one person. They like playing with their own colour

Child 1: Sometimes we discuss this in our class during circle time
Interviewer: And what do you say?
Child 1: It's real hard for a new coloured person coming in as there's so many white
Interviewer: Would you like to be that child coming in?
Child 1: Mmm no
Interviewer: Why?
Child 1: Because you don't have as many friends as you do over here. (majority ethnic, females, junior class, Oakleaf Primary)

Likewise for a Nigerian boy in Riverside Primary the sense of security in having another Nigerian boy present was spoken of in the context of sameness of colour, a marker of ethnic similarity:

> I felt so shy, everybody was different to me. There was a boy who was there, his name was ... And he was a black boy as well, but now he left and I was the only one and I felt so shy. (Nigerian, male, senior class, Riverside Primary)

It is also worth noting, however, that friendships are not simply based on factors such as colour and that sensitivity to differences related to colour and/or ethnicity can be eliminated when common bonds are formed. In practice this was reflected in the level of inter-ethnic interaction which was visible in the school yards during playtime, as well as observations of children's interaction in the classroom, and borne out by the following comments made by a friend of the Somali girl mentioned above:

> It's all about fitting in like. When I look at Nicola, I don't see a black person from somewhere else. I just see my friend. I don't notice the colour of you. (majority ethnic, female, senior class, Oakleaf Primary)

The sensitivity that children displayed towards issues around skin colour must be located within the general context of peer relations and the desire by children to 'fit in' and be the same as their peers. It must also be understood however within a broader cultural context, in which Irishness is firmly linked with certain traits (to include being white, settled, Catholic etc) and those outside of this norm are clearly perceived as 'other'. Racist name-calling draws on discourses of difference or otherness and as such conveys the majority ethnic children's perceptions of what it is to be Irish and therefore the same:

Interviewer: Why do people call names because of colour?
Child 1: Maybe because they are Irish ... I'm not talking about you now Rachel (majority ethnic friend). Maybe because they are white and we are brown, we lived in another

religion. (minority ethnic girl, Junior class, Newdale primary)

Child: I wouldn't like to be a Muslim in any school
Interviewer: Why?
Child: I just don't want to get picked on by anybody. I wouldn't like to be a Protestant either. (majority ethnic, male, senior class, Oakleaf Primary)

While the children generally referred to differences in skin colour in negative terms, there were also incidences during interviews where children recounted positive black Irish role models, listing members of the Irish football team and singers such as Samantha Mumba. Such models in themselves were then important contra-indicators to the stereotypes children may have held regarding Irish identity and 'otherness'. The salience of colour to children's perceptions of ethnic difference however should not mask the impact of other factors, related to culture and lifestyle in children's exclusionary/inclusionary practices. For some minority ethnic children, while they integrated with their majority peers in school, they were sometimes reluctant to do so outside of school (in sleep-overs, having children to play in their house) precisely because of differences in culture and lifestyle.

Returning to our model, children may be located in any one of the four quadrants as the dynamics of difference/sameness and inclusion/exclusion are played out in their interaction with one another (Figure 1). Minority ethnic children may feel different to others but nonetheless be included in friendship groups (as in the case of Nicola, a Somali girl in Oakleaf) or they may feel different and be excluded (as in the case of a number of Traveller children). Similarly they may be the same and be included (as in the case for example of friendships within an ethnic grouping) or they may be the same ethnically and excluded. Racist name-calling is drawn upon in the negotiation of these friendship dynamics – as children are drawn together or move apart on the basis of shared/disparate interests that also incorporate factors related to the children's gender, ability, social class and personality. While for the purpose of this chapter the model prioritises the ethnic dimension in children's interaction, this is but one of a number of status identifiers which (others include gender, dis/ability, social class, age) influence children's friendship patterns and interaction.

The data clearly signals the need for teachers to tackle issues related to racism directly in schools. This should involve enabling children to name and explore their behaviour with one another and to consider the consequences of such behaviour for children who are racially abused. This needs to move beyond the language of bullying to a consideration of how people are bullied because of their ethnic background and identity. Children also need to recognise that racism does not stem merely from the abuse of children who are a different skin colour, but must be linked to respect for and tolerance of those who are also culturally different. Naming abusive behaviour for what it is – as racist – and locating it in the context of our experience of and attitudes towards difference challenges children to think of how they perceive themselves as well as others. It also challenges teachers to explore their own perceptions of difference and sameness, normality and otherness, so that they can bring to their interactions with children an openness to confronting and discussing racism issues when they arise. This can only be empowering for children, both minority and majority ethnic in their interactions with one another.

Bibliography

Amnesty international (2001) *Racism in Ireland – the views of black and ethnic minorities*, Amnesty Campaign for Leadership Against Racism in Ireland, Dublin, Amnesty International.

Black-Gutman Hickson, F. (1996) 'The relationship between racial attitudes and social cognitive development in Children', *Developmental Psychology*, Vol 32, No 3, p. 449.

Casey, S. and O'Connell, M. (2000) 'Pain and Prejudice: Assessing the Experience of Racism in Ireland', in MacLachlann, M. and O'Connell, M. (eds) *Cultivating Pluralism*, Dublin, Oak Tree Press.

Central Statistics Office (2002) *Census 2002: Usual Residence, Migration, Birthplace and Nationality*, http://www.cso.ie/census/Vol4_index.htm.

Codjoe, H. (2001) 'Fighting a Public Enemy of Black Academic Underachievement – the persistence of racism and the schooling experience of black students in Canada', *Race Ethnicity and Education*, Vol 4, No 4, pp 343-377.

Connolly, P. (1998*) Racism, Gender Identities and Young Children*, London, Routledge.

Connolly, P. (2000) 'What now for the Contact Hypothesis? Towards a New Research Agenda', in *Race, Ethnicity and Education*, Vol 3, No 2.

Connolly, P. with Maginn, P. (1999) *Sectarianism, Children and Community Relations in Northern Ireland,* Coleraine, Centre for the Study of Conflict, University of Ulster.

Deegan, J. (1996) *Children's Friendships in Culturally Diverse Classrooms*, London, Falmer.

Devine, D. (2003) *Children, Power and Schooling – How*

Childhood is structured in the primary school, Trentham Books, Stoke-on-Trent.

Devine, D., Kenny, M. with MacNeela, E. (2002) *Ethnicity and Schooling: A study of ethnic diversity in a selected sample of primary and post-primary schools*, Education Dept, UCD.

Doyle, A. and Aboud, F. (1995) A longitudinal study of white children's racial prejudice as a social-cognitive development, *Merrill-Palmer Quarterly*, Vol 41, No 2, pp 209-228.

Fanning, B., Veale, A. and O'Connor, D. (2001) *Beyond the Pale: Asylum Seeking Children and Social Exclusion in Ireland,* Dublin, Combat Poverty Agency.

Foucault, M. (1980) *Michel Foucault: Power Knowledge*, Hertfordshire, Harvester Wheatsheaf.

Guerin, P. (2002) 'Racism and the media in Ireland: Setting the anti-immigration agenda', in Lentin, R. and McVeigh, R. (eds) *Racism and Anti-Racism in Ireland*, Dublin, Beyond the Pale Publications.

Holmes, R. (1995) *How Young Children Perceive Race*, London, Sage.

Henze, R., Katz, A. and Norte, E. (2000) 'Rethinking the Concept of Racial or Ethnic Conflict in Schools: a leadership perspective', in *Race, Ethnicity and Education,* Vol 3, No 2, pp 195-206.

ICIS (International Centre for Intercultural Studies) (1996) *Routes of Racism: the Social Basis of Racist Action*, Stoke-on-Trent, Trentham Books.

Jones, C. (1997) 'Educational Contradictions: The Education of Stateless and State-denied Groups', in Jones, C. (ed.) 'Nation, State and Diversity', in Coulby, D., Gundara, J. and Jones. C. (eds) *Intercultural Education: World Yearbook of Education*, London, Kogan Page.

Katz, P. (1983) 'Developmental Foundations of gender and racial attitudes', in Leahy, R. (ed.) *The Child's Construction of Social Inequality,* London, Academic Press.

Keddie, A (2004) 'Research with young children: the use of an affinity group approach to explore the dynamics of peer culture', in *British Journal of Sociology of Education,* Vol 25, No 1, Feb 2004.

Kelly, M (2003) *A Study of Children's Perceptions and Experiences of Ethnic Diversity in an Irish Primary School*, Unpublished MEd thesis, Education Dept, UCD.

Kenny, M., McNeela, E. and Shevlin, M. (2003) 'Living and learning: the school experience of some young people with disabilities', in Shevlin, M. and Rose, R. (eds) *Encouraging Voices: Respecting the Insights of Young People who have been Marginalised*, Dublin, NDA.

Lodge, A. and Flynn, M. (2001) 'Gender Identity in the primary school playground', in Cleary, A., Nic Giolla Phádraig, M. and Quin, S. (eds) *Understanding Children, Volume 1: State, Education and Economy*, Dublin, Oak Tree Press.

Mac Gréil, M. (1996) *Prejudice in Ireland Revisited*, Survey and Research Unit, Maynooth, St Patrick's College.

Mac An Ghaill, M. (1994) *The Making of Men, Sexualities and Schooling*, Buckingham, Open University Press.

McDonagh, R. (2002) 'The Web of Self Identity: Racism, Sexism and Disablism', in Lentin, R. and McVeigh, R. (eds) *Racism and Anti-Racism in Ireland*, Dublin, Beyond the Pale Publications.

Myers, K. (2003) 'Critical Voices: refugees, exclusion and schooling', in Shevlin, M., and Rose, R. (eds) *Encouraging Voices: Respecting the Insights of Young People who have been Marginalised*, Dublin, NDA.

Ní Shuinéar, S. (2002) 'Othering the Irish (Travellers)', in Lentin, R. and McVeigh, R. (eds) *Racism and Anti-Racism in Ireland*, Dublin, Beyond the Pale Publications.

Nozinic, D. (2002) 'One Refugee Experience in Ireland', in Lentin, R. and McVeigh, R. (eds) *Racism and Anti-Racism in Ireland*, Dublin, Beyond the Pale Publications.

O'Keefe, B. and O'Connor, P. (2001) 'Out of the mouths of babes and Innocents: Children's Attitudes towards Travellers', in Cleary, A., Nic Giolla Phádraig, M. and Quin, S. (eds) *Understanding Children – Changing Experiences and Family Forms,* Dublin, Oak Tree Press.

Pilkington, A. (1999) 'Racism in Schools and Ethnic Differentials in Educational Achievement: a brief comment on a recent debate', *British Journal of Sociology of Education*, Vol 20, No 3, pp 411- 417.

O'Connell, J. (2002) 'Travellers in Ireland: An examination of discrimination and racism', in Lentin, R. and McVeigh, R. (eds) *Racism and Anti-Racism in Ireland*, Dublin, Beyond the Pale Publications.

Ramsey, P. (1991) 'The salience of race in young children growing up in an all white community', *Journal of Educational Psychology,* Vol 83, pp 28-34.

Sinha, S. (2002) 'Generating awareness for the experiences of women of colour in Ireland', in Lentin, R. and McVeigh, R. (eds) *Racism and Anti-Racism in Ireland*, Dublin, Beyond the Pale Publications.

Troyna, B. and Hatcher, R. (1992) *Racism in Children's Lives – A Study of mainly-white primary schools,* London, Routledge.

Varma-Joshi, M., Baker, C.J., Tanaka, C. (2004) 'Names will never hurt me?', *Harvard Educational Review*, Vol 74, No 2, 175-208.

Chapter 12

Children's perceptions of other cultures

Hugh Gash and Elizabeth Murphy-Lejeune

Introduction

Two major demographic and political changes are forcing the issue of intercultural communication and, as a consequence, that of social representations of otherness, in Ireland. The first one is the construction of Europe and the necessity couched in official texts since the 1992 treaty of Maastricht to develop a sense of European citizenship among schoolchildren. The European dimension in education implies being open to others who are outside one's own national context. The second change is the present more diverse context prevailing in Irish society, and more particularly in Irish classrooms, as a result of immigration since 1993. The presence of different others within one's own borders prompts more questioning than has been the case about cultural and ethnic diversity. Irish government policy identifies the European dimension and both tolerance and respect for diversity as key issues in primary education (Ireland 1999).

In this chapter, we will present various research projects dealing with children's perceptions of other cultures, the word 'culture' referring primarily in this instance to other national or ethnic entities. The issue of perceptions of other cultures is important in that it is linked with children's constructions of their identity and may eventually determine their attitudes and behaviour to many others. Children construct social images of the groups they belong to and of other groups at an early stage of their socialisation (Lambert and Klineberg 1967, Tajfel et al 1970, Aboud 1988). These early representations are acquired without them being aware of the processes at work. This is why representations often resist modification. This issue is difficult to deal with in schools and the tendency is for teachers to keep away from it. Outlining the nature, characteristics and role of social perceptions and representations of otherness in cross-cultural communication is a first step towards a fuller understanding of this area. We agree, however, with Goldstone (2000) who warns that researchers who identify difference merely reify it. We suggest strategies in line with the constructivist philosophy of the Primary Curriculum (Ireland 1999) to promote pluralism (MacLachlan and O'Connell 2000).

Social representations and racial or ethnic differences

As research reminds us (Zarate 1993, Cain and Briane 1994, UNESCO 1996), social representations play a crucial role in our encounters with different others. However, this role is often little discussed in education programmes. The sociologist Durkheim was one of the first to study social categorisation, a process acknowledged as the 'first step in the treatment of the perception of a given person' (Moscovici 1994: 182). Later on, in his study of prejudice, Allport (1954) analysed what he called 'preferential thinking' in the formation of in-groups and referred to 'the normality of prejudgment'. He maintains that individuals have 'a propensity to prejudice', which lies in their 'normal and natural tendency to form generalisations, concepts, categories, whose content represents an oversimplification of (their) world of experience' (Allport 1954: 26). As a result, categories and the personal values they convey frequently conflict with evidence. Indeed, there is often little correlation between the qualities alleged to mark a group as a whole and the complex realities of people's lives. Group differences are mostly ascribed and tell more about the originators than about their targets: 'the features that are taken into account are not the sum of "objective" differences, but only those which the actors themselves regard as significant' (Barth 1969: 299). In brief, the process of social categorisation is aptly described as a highly subjective constructivist process. At a more general level, Aboud (1988: 4) defined racial prejudice as 'an organized pre-disposition to respond in an unfavourable manner toward people from an ethnic group because of their ethnic affiliation'. While prejudice involves cognitive and affective components, stereotyping is often studied as a cognitive phenomenon and is defined as a generalised attribution of personal characteristics to a group.

Stereotypic racial and ethnic differences are studied because they represent 'the core for the categorisation of ideas about human differences' (Allport 1954: 106). Simmel (1971: 143-144), in his seminal essay on the stranger, was the first to draw attention to the social position of strangers as natural group members, highlighting their ambivalent position as elements 'whose membership within the group involves both being outside it and confronting it'.

In spite of their being in the group, there is a tendency on the part of other members to evaluate strangers on the basis of the categories to which they are assigned (Wood 1934). Thus, at first, strangers are not perceived as individuals, but typified as representative of their group. In this case, group traits predominate, while individual traits become invisible and the perceiver tends to apply similar traits to all group members. This process of initial over-generalisation followed by differentiation through experience is a general one in developmental psychology and serves as a model to understand how children's stereotypes change. It is important to remember, however, that stereotypes can be difficult to change once they form part of the child's identity (Gash 1992, Gash 1993a). This, therefore, is a crucial time for Irish society: will we be able to avoid the move from old-fashioned to systematic racism? (MacLachlan and O'Connell 2000).

Children learn racial stereotypes by the beginning of primary school (Bigler and Liben 1993, Aboud 1988). In their major study of children's views of foreign people, Lambert and Klineberg (1967) began with children's self-perceptions, and their conceptions of their own national group. The dimensions of foreign children they investigated included similarity-dissimilarity and desirability-undesirability. They argued that stereotypes emerge as children construct their own identity as contrasted with different others and, further, that the affective components of these early constructions tend to be maintained throughout life. While stereotyping appears early and, we would argue, serves to provide children with ways of understanding difference, it also clearly filters experience by focusing on what is expected (Bigler and Liben 1993). During the primary school age range, children's knowledge of other countries increases (Barrett 2000). Their views of others differentiate (Doyle, Beaudet and Aboud 1988) and become somewhat less stereotyped.

Cross-cultural communication and perceptions of other people: images, judgements, opinions and stereotypes

Cross-cultural communication implies that individuals from different cultures are interacting either directly, in face-to-face interactions, or indirectly, through mediated forms of communication, e.g. media (television, radio and newpapers), art and literature. Since direct interactions between strangers occur less frequently, there is usually a tendency to 'imagine' others or form a mental picture of them on the basis of partial information prior to any personal contact. In other words, socially-constructed representations constitute a prism through which intercultural communication is effected. In this context, the tension between distance and proximity is particularly forceful. In a relation of spatial proximity, such as a live intercultural encounter, mutual representations are constantly put to the test and reinvented. Personal and social identities are necessarily strained in this interplay between reality, perceptions and individuals. So how do people think when they think of other cultures?

We could sum up the process saying that four types of images coexist at two levels. The first level consists of self-images: as I see myself and as the other sees her/himself. The second level consists of hetero-images or images of others: as the other sees me and as I see the other. If group identities are involved, pronouns can be interchanged for we/us and they/them. It can be assumed that the link or prism between self-perceptions and perceptions of others colours or distorts all perceptions. As Robert Burns (1786) wrote, 'oh, would some power the gift give us to see ourselves as others see us'.

If the term 'images' was favoured in a study of young people's representations of other Europeans, it is because foreign places and their inhabitants are usually perceived as distant images before any real-life contact takes place (Murphy-Lejeune 1995a). In any case, physical proximity does not guarantee that the outcome of the contact will be positive (Amir 1969). Use of the term 'images' emphasises the mental distance between perceiver and object of perception, as well as the cognitive deficit at play. Schoolchildren are notoriously misinformed about other cultures, and confusions abound in their descriptions of others. In the twelve-year-olds' texts in the study reported here, Ireland is confused with Iceland, Holland or Scotland, 'somewhere in the North of England' with 'haunted castles' or alternatively as a place about which many 'don't know anything'. The term 'images' also captures the affective component present in these descriptions. Some children indicate their wish to become more knowledgeable about neighbouring countries and their desire to visit them. Others state that they cannot write about a country they have not visited. More rarely, a few display either a natural antagonism or closeness towards the unknown. The perception process is indeed multifaceted. Cognitive, affective, behavioural and symbolic elements are interconnected. As a result, merely correcting misinformation is not in itself sufficient to alter attitudes to different others.

The terms 'representation' and 'perception', which are quasi-interchangeable, are neutral generic terms. They designate the product and the process of mediation between reality and an individual's ideas. The terms 'judgement', 'opinion' and 'prejudice' emphasise the subjective nature of these perceptive products.

Judgements and opinions indicate a given intellectual or affective orientation which, once formed, affects subsequent perceptions. Other terms impart the often irrational and unreflective character of some perceptions. In prejudices, the attitude, positive or negative, precedes and predetermines contact with reality. The term 'stereotype' highlights the simplistic character of the response. Stereotypes are economical, standardised and rigid reactions sparing the perceiver the effort of having to cope with evidence. They are perceptive shortcuts humans avail of naturally. Indeed, one of the main results of research in the area is that the stereotyping tendency is pretty universal and inevitable. In this light, the issue is not so much how to prevent stereotyping, but how to deconstruct it and show it for what it is; an incomplete representation revealing the perceiver's impoverished knowledge and myopic attitude towards others.

Social representations, of national, ethnic or other groups, fulfil a powerful function. They express a certain worldview, assigning group members their 'right' place while providing their owners with the sense of security coming from keeping everyone 'in their place'. Perceptions of foreign cultures, maybe because they enter the realm of various curriculum subjects, constitute a rather hazy area in compulsory education. Yet, paradoxically, they represent a major stake in the construction of a more diverse and open Europe, not to mention in our understanding of global issues. Discourses about other cultures are more often orchestrated by the media than by teachers. The role of the latter in this context would be to offer alternatives to this kind of public discourse, allowing children first to express their views or to gather predominant views and, secondly, to analyse them so as to become aware of their main characteristics and content.

Data collection: from questionnaires to texts

Various research designs have been used over the years to investigate children's perceptions of otherness. Among the methods used, one could draw a line from documents with a predominantly quantitative approach, such as questionnaires or attitude scales, to those with a qualitative approach, e.g. open texts or interviews. The choice of technique will have an impact on the questions asked, more or less open or closed, on the quality of the answer, from a 'yes/no' choice to a page-long text, on the number of participants involved, small to large population, and on the subsequent analysis of the data, statistical or content-based.

Quantitative research methods ask questions which focus strictly on the research area. Answers must be sufficiently brief to allow for statistical treatment of a large sample. The earliest studies typically used checklists of adjectives attributed to diverse ethnic or national groups (Katz and Braly 1933). Frenkel-Brunswick's (1948) questionnaire on ethnocentrism represents a historical example of this type of approach. Its aim is to assess the degree of suspicion towards foreigners and people outside the child's in-group. The results are presented in the form of a prejudice scale and each child is assigned an ethnocentric score. The researcher usually then tries to correlate the results with variables such as age, socio-economic or personality groups or to bring to light dominant stereotypes among those suggested.

Gash, beginning in 1992, undertook a series of studies on children's perceptions of different others using questionnaires that included checklists of adjectives. Initially, the studies concerned perceptions of children with special needs (Gash 1993b, 1996, Gash and Coffey 1995). Later, a series of studies was undertaken about children from different countries and cultures (Gash 1995, 1999). Feerick (1993) developed the initial model questionnaire on Irish primary children. The questionnaires asked each child to imagine that another child was coming to his or her school and assessed attitudes and representations. The procedures used were similar in each study. In the studies described in the present chapter, the participants were asked to imagine that a child from 'another country' was going to come to their school. The questions measuring attitude gave respondents an opportunity to express how sociable they felt towards this child and how like oneself this child dressed or seemed. There were a number of questions also about inclusive schooling arrangements and the child's experience of children from this country, whether in school or outside school. Sociability scores, for example, were created by summing answers to the questions concerned with smiling at the child from the other country (1), asking him/her to sit beside you (2), chatting to him/her (3), telling him/her secrets (4), making him/her your best friend (5), inviting him/her to your house to play (6) or for a birthday party (7), picking him/her on your team (8), asking personal questions (9) and teasing (10). Class teachers read these questions and children noted 'yes' or 'no' on an answer form.

Another part of the questionnaire measuring different representations provided fifteen bipolar Likert-scale descriptors they might use to describe the child from another country. In each case the respondent was asked to circle one option: (The first one was) 'fights – sometimes fights – does not fight'; (the second was) 'shares – sometimes shares – greedy'; (and the third was) 'strong – a bit of both – weak'. Additional dichotomies used to capture prejudice included: good-bad, poor-rich, hard life-easy life, clever-stupid, happy-sad, clean-dirty, healthy-unhealthy, works hard-lazy, tells truth-lies, not nice.

Studies based on suggested lexical items obtain data in an experimental setting. They provide relatively simple answers, which can be quantitatively interpreted. But pre-selected answers somewhat limit the subject's freedom of expression. It could even be said that, in many instances, the stereotypical effect is built in the research instrument. This is why open-ended texts and/or interviews are sometimes preferred as a way of obtaining more personal data. The content of the questions does not necessarily differ between the two types of instruments, but the answers do. The techniques used to obtain textual data range from a list of key-words to a continuous text. In these cases, the outcome is a spontaneous answer eloquent about a child's attitudes and mental images. Such techniques have been widely used in research on identity, on cognitive and affective development and on representations of self and others.

Key-words were used by Cain and Briane (1994) to bring to light the kind of erroneous information and representations which lead to the construction of stereotypes among schoolchildren learning a foreign language. The children were asked to write down within a two-minute period of time the words they associated with a country whose language they were learning. A similar technique, with open-ended answers, was used to obtain longer texts exploring the representations which schoolchildren have constructed either of a foreign country, in this case Germany and France (OFAJ 1979, 1980), or of their own country, i.e. Ireland (Egan 1977, Egan and Nugent 1983). Murphy's research (1985, 1988) combined auto-images and hetero-images by asking children first to write about their own country and secondly about a given foreign country, Ireland or France in most cases, but also the United States. In all these instances, the brief given was: 'What do you think of when you think of your/another country? Write anything that comes to mind as freely as possible'. The data-gathering instrument used is easy to manage, efficient and provides rich insights into individuals' perceptions. The wealth of material allows for a diversity of classroom work based on the data collected.

The specific aims of these research projects, which use a similar data collection instrument, were quite close, but somewhat different in their perspective. The OFAJ research showed the richness of data collected with open texts where more or less accurate knowledge, images, stereotypes, attitudes to others and feelings derived from personal experience coexist in an idiosyncratic production. Egan's objective was to study the development of the conception of nationhood among schoolchildren and, more particularly, their affective development. To this end, he paid attention to what children think *and* feel and examined children's affective development in the light of Bloom's model and Dabrowski's (1966) four stages of development of the concept of nationhood. In this context, the texts illustrate the theory rather than the theory emerging from the data.

Murphy was interested in exploring the relationship between self and other, in-group and out-group, in children's descriptions of national groups. It was assumed that the native prism conditions perceptions of others and that the other culture functions as a mirror to the native culture. In this case, the aim was neither to assess the children's degree of knowledge nor to examine the extent to which their perceptions are founded on evidence. The presiding logic was to collect data so as to engage participants in a reflective process about how perceptions of self and others are constructed and about the kind of language people use when they think about identity issues. The data collected are usually extremely rich. However, the focus being on national descriptions, the risk is to reinforce a binary vision of cultural contacts, predicated on the contrast between 'us' and 'them'. Another risk is that the texts attract the very kind of generalisations inherent to group descriptions (*the* Irish *are* …). Finally, if the data collection instrument is close to that of the interviews, in that participants can freely express their thoughts, the activity is one way and the relationship to others exists only in the children's imagination. Adopting a different brief, as Cain and Briane did (1994, p. 18), restores the interactive dimension because a foreign interlocutor is posited as the addressee: 'If you had to present your country/a foreign country to someone of your own age who does not know it, what would you say?'

Children's texts involve their authors in some form of introspection. The data collection phase sets the scene for a process of reflection, ideally leading to greater awareness of identity and diversity issues. This is why this first phase should be followed by a close analysis of the texts collected, allowing for discussion of these issues.

Analysing children's perceptions of other cultures: what do we learn?

According to the objectives one pursues, the data collected may lend themselves to different analyses or uses by the teacher or the researcher. Some will focus on demographic results, others more on content or language analysis.

Demographic analysis

Two types of results occur repeatedly in Gash's questionnaire studies (Gash and Gash 1999). One is that Irish boys and girls differ on some dimensions, with boys appearing to be more negative. Second, there are some differences between rural and urban children, in which rural children appear more accepting. For example, Irish boys were significantly more racist about French children (greedy, bad, stupid, dirty, unhealthy, lazy, lies, not nice, don't like them) and inclined to see them as different (sad, does not look like me, does not dress like me) than Irish girls. In a study on Greek children, Irish boys were more likely than Irish girls to think about Greeks in terms of a negative image 'Slob' (doesn't fight, rich and unhealthy). In a study on Third World children, Irish boys were again more racist than Irish girls (bad, dirty, does not fight, greedy, lazy, tells lies, sad, and stupid). There was a greater tendency also for Irish boys than Irish girls to think about Third World children with a 'famine image' (poor, dirty and hungry).

In some studies, Irish rural children were friendlier and more accepting than Irish urban children. Girls were more sociable and socially concerned than boys in the study on Third World children. Older children who were in second class in this study were more sociable and more inclusive than first class children. Interestingly, more rural children than urban children knew children from the Third World, had contact with them in their schools and were less inclined to see Third World children in terms of the unhealthy famine image.

Urban children's representations of Third World children emphasised difference more than did those of rural children (does not look like me, and does not dress like me), and saw them as having access to the idyllic life (rich, easy life and happy). We suspect this was due to difference in access.

In a comparative Comenius study of French and Irish schools, boys were less sociable than girls, only in Ireland (Gash 1999). Detailed analysis showed there was an interaction between gender and country due to a greater difference between girls and boys in Ireland than in France. This arose because the Irish girls were the most sociable group and the Irish boys were the least sociable group. Irish children used negative prejudiced words (see above) more than did the French children, and analysis of boys and girls in each country showed again that the Irish girls used these words least and the Irish boys used them a lot more, as did the French girls. In regard to perception of difference, while there was neither a difference between Irish and French pupils, nor between boys and girls, Irish girls were inclined to see French children as less different in comparison with Irish boys and French girls saw Irish children with a similar level of difference as Irish boys.

The most recent data set using these questionnaires was collected in two Dublin schools (Gash, 2001). One school was an all boys' school in a middle class area and the other was a mixed (boys' and girls') school in West Dublin. The idea was to collect some contemporary pilot data since there has been a dramatic upsurge in refugees in Ireland since the early 1990s when the other data were collected. One additional feature was added to this study. The questionnaire was given to each child once with the target as a 'child from Africa' and once as a 'child from Ireland' in order to examine differences in responses (switched answers) to the different target children.

Questions for which there were significant differences in switched answers were concerned with: inviting him/her to your house to play; and the questions about the ability of the child to do the same maths and reading as the other children, and whether the new child would have the same hobbies as the other children. A small number (5%) of the children who said they would invite the African child to their house said they would not extend this invitation to the Irish child; whereas a significantly ($p<0.01$) greater proportion (15%) of the children who said they would invite the Irish child to their house said they would not invite the African child home. Only 3% of the children who said the new African child in the school could use the same books as the other children said that the new Irish child couldn't, and 36% of the children who said the new Irish child could use the same books said that the new African child could not ($p<0.001$). In the cases of maths and hobbies, the picture was the same: estimations that a new African child in the school would be superior to an Irish child were (6%) for maths and (7%) for hobbies, whereas significantly larger numbers (27% and 40% respectively) said the new Irish child would be superior to the new African child ($p<0.001$).

There were some differences in sociability in these data. Girls were excluded from these comparisons as one school was boys' only and, as we have seen, girls tend to be more sociable. Pupils in the more racially integrated school were more sociable towards the hypothetical African child, and third class boys were more sociable than fifth class boys ($p<0.05$). The general picture of racism that emerges in these data is consistent with findings elsewhere in contemporary Ireland (e.g. Casey and O'Connell 2000, MacLachlan and O'Connell 2000).

Analysis of open texts

Being open, the texts collected come in many forms. Some contain lists of words-images, rather similar to unconscious thoughts. Others present a mixture of facts and opinions, sometimes in the form of stereotypes or clichés. In most cases, the texts demonstrate that thinking about national identity, one's own or others', is an emotional, frequently non-rational process. Some texts reveal that their authors are aware of their own subjective standpoint and of the limits of their knowledge. A few, among the older ones, are capable of distancing themselves from the collective discourse inherited from their early socialisation.

The texts can be analysed and used for pedagogical purposes in several different ways. To analyse here means to observe from various perspectives what has been written. The language used, by children or adults alike, reveals the way the participants categorise reality and organise their perception of the world on the basis of their experience.

Lexical analysis represents a first approach focusing on the language used. It consists in dividing the texts into thematic units, e.g. key words or recurring themes, and grouping them into semantic categories such as 'environment', 'people', 'politics/history', 'national economy', and 'traditions/culture'. Language analysis is another approach which focuses on specific linguistic elements in the texts, e.g. verbal tenses (the present tense indicating permanence, static immutability), articles and qualifiers (the all-embracing 'the' or the more cautious 'some'), pronouns (I/we, they/them), modals ('may' expresses some degree of circumspection about one's discourse rather than certainty), generic/specific terms (e.g. 'eat'-'sleep' or 'Eiffel Tower'-'*baguette*'). Close linguistic analysis of the texts brings forth the characteristics of discourse in relation to identity issues, i.e. perennial visions, generalisations, binary oppositions, and general lack of regard for complexity, change and objective knowledge.

A semantic content analysis would focus on the meanings or what is expressed, rather than on how it is expressed, and would address the following questions:

- what kind of mental images or representations emerge from the descriptions?
- what are the predominant images about self and about others?
- any stereotypes?
- are these representations shared by most or are there marked individual differences or contradictions?
- how can the similarities and differences in views be accounted for?

- do they reflect the beholder's personal perspective, a social point of view, a national vision?
- what is the value (positive, neutral, ambivalent, negative) attached to these images and perceptions? what do they reveal about attitudes towards the countries mentioned and about the students' affective development?
- when comparing descriptions from individual to individual, can correlations be observed between the two descriptions?
- what role does knowledge play? is lack of knowledge recognised or not? are the sources of information identified?
- what can we learn about group perceptions, their function, social transmission, limits, from these descriptions?

Lexical or thematic analysis involves identifying the choice of topics mentioned by the children and the frequency of these topics. The choice of topics may be construed as an indication of the dominant national self-image. For example, images in Irish self-descriptions are predominantly psychological (Murphy 1985): the Irish saw themselves primarily as a people with specific character traits embodying a certain way of being. By contrast, pupils surveyed mainly express the predominant French self-image in terms of the economy (agriculture, food) and the political values the country seems to represent, i.e. freedom and democracy. In brief, the concept of the nation varies from country to country according to historical and geopolitical factors. The choice of topics also highlights an age factor. Conceptions of one's country tend to evolve over time, younger pupils focusing on the physical environment rather than on more abstract aspects of their country. The tone of the descriptions reflects the affective development of the child according to Dabrowski (1966) from unquestioned attachment, ambivalence, moral evaluation to personal identification, as well as the individual's affective maturity.

A cursory look at the choice of topics and a lexical comparison between self- and other-descriptions from individual to individual validates the hypothesis of the perceptual link or filter: the two descriptions are usually a reflection of one another, a result which underlines their subjective nature. Further analysis of the descriptions corroborates that we usually perceive other cultures through the lenses of our own native glasses. In other words, when we describe other cultures and people, we do so from a culturally grounded perspective saying a lot about ourselves. For example, the Irish tend to see France as a large country where the weather is nice by comparison to their own. A Nigerian student described France as cold. Indeed, the contradictions observed throughout the descriptions of any given country highlight the non-rational and affective nature of representations. Their factual basis is slim, but their imaginary content is high.

Generally, attitudes towards the two cultures differ in cognitive terms. While knowledge about one's own country is assumed to be extensive and well-grounded, the texts manifest more modesty concerning foreign countries. Ignorance is frequently mentioned as an obstacle to describing another place. This lack of knowledge about other cultures may sometimes act as an incentive to learn foreign languages. In Murphy's research, few students showed that they were aware that national identity is usually an accident of birth. In other words, awareness of one's own enculturation and socialisation does not come naturally (Berry 2000).

The results emerging from the analysis can be discussed usefully in class. To voice one's own mental representations and to hear others voicing theirs, to confront one's own images with other images, to listen to voices coming from different social, ethnic or national settings, to apprehend them in their own singular time and place, to distance oneself from the immediacy of social, and more narrowly national, enculturation, these are some of the aims of a pedagogy of otherness which remains to be invented (Murphy-Lejeune 1995b). The notion of socio-cultural distance or proximity is central to the issue of our representations of others and of ourselves. What constitutes the distance between two individuals, between one culture and another, or between two individuals from the same culture and from different cultures? What is a stranger? When are we strangers? These are some of the questions to engage in when dealing with perceptions of other cultures.

Conclusion

The data that we have presented show that Irish children are often quite prejudiced about other children who are different from themselves, particularly when these others are not well known. It seems as though it is part of the human condition to be willing to project those parts of ourselves that we do not want to accept and with which we have not come to terms. In this case, it is very important for teachers to be ready to prepare children for all newcomers to class who may elicit prejudice, and, in particular, to monitor their entry conditions so that newcomers to classrooms from different countries are not treated in exclusionary ways. This is a whole-school issue and needs to be part of any school's policy so that all teachers and workers in the school are aware of the policy and are proactive in preventing racist abuse of children who are different. The advantages of moving early and definitely are clear.

One strategy advocated is the use of a constructivist approach in classrooms to promote tolerance and interpersonal mutual respect (Gash and Gash 1997, 1999). This strategy arises from ethical implications of the constructivist approach to learning, an emergent form of Piaget's theory underlying the 1999 Curriculum (Gash 1993c, 2000). Theoretical principles underlying this approach include the self-directed and developmental nature of learning (Ireland 1999). A constructivist approach (1) invites learners to accept responsibility for their constructed knowledge and feelings because these arise as results of their own directed action: and, in addition (2), to be sensitive to possible limitations in their constructions because learning is not only directed or focused but also developmental. Knowledge is often at the boundary of the unknown; at any moment conditions may change and what was certain may no longer be viable. This acceptance of limitations and responsibility for the processing of what is known, invites discussions of the origins of differences between people in their points of view. So each of us has our own view, but no one view is necessarily the only view. In this deep way, the constructivist model of knowing invites a pluralist multicultural approach. Teachers and educators may on the one hand be constructivists without knowing it, or, alternatively, they may need experiences to allow this approach to knowing to emerge.

Bibliography

Aboud, F. E. (1988) *Children and Prejudice*, New York, Basil Blackwell.

Allport, G. (1954) *The Nature of Prejudice*, Reading, MA, Addison Wesley.

Amir, Y. (1969) 'Contact Hypothesis in ethnic relations', *Psychological Bulletin*, 71, pp 319-342.

Barrett, M. (2000) http://www.surrey.ac.uk/Psychology/staff/papers/mb-litrev.html

Barth, F. (1969) *Ethnic Groups and Boundaries. The Social Organisation of Culture Difference*, Boston: Little, Brown and Co.

Berry, J. (2000) 'The Sojourn Experience: An International Commentary', in MacLachlan, M. and O'Connell, M. (eds) *Cultivating Pluralism: Psychological and Cultural Perspectives on a Changing Ireland*, Dublin: Oak Tree Press, pp 297-301.

Bigler, R. S. and Liben, L. S. (1993) 'A cognitive developmental approach to racial stereotyping and reconstructive memory in Euro-American children', *Child Development,* 64, pp 1507-1518.

Burns, R. (1786) *To A Louse On Seeing One On A Lady's Bonnet At Church.*

Casey, S. and O'Connell, M. (2000) 'Pain and prejudice: Assessing the experience of racism in Ireland', in MacLachlan, M. and O'Connell, L (eds) *Cultivating Pluralism: Psychological and Cultural Perspectives on a Changing Ireland*, Dublin, Oak Tree Press, pp 19-48.

Cain, A. and Briane, C. (1994) *Comment collégiens et lycéens voient les pays dont ils apprennent la langue. Représentations et stéréotypes*, Paris, INRP.

Dabrowski, K. (1966) *Mental Growth Through Positive Disintegration*, London, Gryf Publications.

Doyle, A., Beaudet, J. and Aboud, F. (1988) 'Developmental patterns in the flexibility of children's ethnic attitudes', *Journal of Cross Cultural Psychology,* 19, pp 3-18.

Durkheim, E. (1902) 'De quelques formes primitives de classification. Contribution à l'étude des représentations collectives', *Année sociologique*, 6, pp 1-72.

Egan, O. and Nugent, K. (1983) 'Adolescent conceptions of the homeland: a conflict of ideals and realities', *Journal of Youth and Adolescence*, 12 (3), pp 185-201.

Egan, O. (1977) 'Affective development in adolescent conceptions of the homeland', *Irish Journal of Education*, 11 (1-2), pp 61-73.

Feerick, A. (1993) *Integration: Attitudes of regular education children towards their special class peers*, Unpublished MEd thesis, University College Galway.

Frenkel-Brunswick, E. (1948) 'A study of prejudice in children', *Human Relations*, Vol 1, pp 295-306.

Gash, H. (1992) 'Reducing prejudice: constructivist considerations for special education', *European Journal of Special Needs Education*, 7, pp 146-155.

Gash, H. (1993a) 'Stereotyping and constructivism: Learning to be men and women', *Cybernetics and Human Knowing*, Vol 1 (4), pp 43-50.

Gash, H. (1993b) 'A constructivist attempt to promote positive attitudes towards children with special needs', *European Journal of Special Needs Education,* Vol 8, pp 106-125.

Gash, H. (1993c) 'The status of Piaget today in mathematics education', *Compass*, Vol 22, pp 65-75.

Gash, H. (1995) 'Attitudes of Irish primary school children to European and Third World children', in Hackett, M. (ed.), *Intercultural Education. Celebrating Diversity Conference Proceedings*, Dublin: Drumcondra Education Centre, pp 44-65.

Gash, H. (1996) 'Changing attitudes towards children with special needs', *European Journal of Special Needs Education*, Vol 11, pp 286-297.

Gash, H. (1999) *Prejudices of Irish and French Pupils*, Unpublished paper presented at the Troisième Congres International d'Actualité de la Recherche en Education et Formation, Bordeaux France, June.

Gash, H. (2000) 'Epistemological origins of ethics', in Steffe, L. P. and Thompson, P. W. (eds) *Radical Constructivism in Action: Building on the Pioneering Work of Ernst von Glasersfeld*, Falmer, London, pp 80-90.

Gash, H. (2001) *Prejudice in Dublin primary schools*, Unpublished work in progress.

Gash, H. (2004) 'Attitudes Towards African Children in Some Irish Primary Schools', paper presented at the Conference on Globalisation and Inclusion, University College Cork, 1 June.

Gash, H. and Coffey, D. (1995) 'Influences on attitudes towards children with mental handicap', *European Journal of Special Needs Education*, Vol 10, pp 1-16.

Gash, H. and Gash, V. (1997) 'Constructivism and tolerance of difference', in Lasker, G. E. (ed.) *Advances in Education,* International Institute for Advanced Studies, Windsor, Ontario, pp 141-146.

Gash, H. and Gash V. (1999) 'Constructivism and the ethics of mutual respect', in Lasker, G. and Lomeiko, V. (eds) *Culture of peace: Survival strategy and action programme for the third millennium,* International Institute for Advanced Studies: Windsor Ontario, pp 51-58.

Gash, H., Guardia Gonzales, S., Pires, M. and Rault, C. (2000) 'Attitudes Towards Down Syndrome: A National Comparative Study: France, Ireland, Portugal and Spain', *Irish Journal of Psychology*, Vol 21, pp 203-214.

Goldstone, K. (2000) '"Rewriting You": Researching and writing about ethnic minorities', in MacLachlan, M. and O'Connell, M. (eds) *Cultivating Pluralism: Psychological and Cultural Perspectives on a Changing Ireland,* Dublin, Oak Tree Press, pp 305-314 .

Ireland, Department of Education and Science (1999) *Primary School Curriculum: Introduction*, Dublin, Stationery Office.

Katz, D. and Braly, K. (1933) 'Racial stereotypes of one hundred college students', *Journal of Abnormal Social Psychology*, Vol 28, pp 280-290.

Lambert, W. E. and Klineberg, O. (1967) *Children's views of foreign peoples: A cross national study,* Appleton Century Crofts, New York.

MacLachlan, M. and O'Connell, M. (2000) 'A State of Diversity?', in MacLachlan, M. and O'Connell, M. (eds) *Cultivating Pluralism:*

Psychological and Cultural Perspectives on a Changing Ireland, Dublin, Oak Tree Press, pp 1-16.

MacLachlan, M. and O'Connell, M. (2000) (eds) *Cultivating Pluralism: Psychological and Cultural Perspectives on a Changing Ireland,* Dublin: Oak Tree Press.

Moscovici, S. (dir.) (1994) *Psychologie sociale des relations à autrui*, Paris, Nathan Université.

Murphy-Lejeune, E. (1995a) 'Images of other cultures in Europe', in Hackett, M. (ed.) *Intercultural Education. Celebrating Difference Conference Proceedings*, Dublin, Drumcondra Education Centre, pp 66-80.

Murphy-Lejeune, E. (1995b) *A Picture Book/Un livre d'images*, Dublin, French Department, Saint Patrick's College.

Murphy, E. (1988) 'Images de l'Irlande et de la France', *Teangeolas*, Vol 25, pp 9-13.

Murphy, E. (1985) 'Identités nationales en cultures maternelle et étrangère', *Dialogues et Cultures*, Vol 27, pp 79-90.

Office Franco-Allemand de la Jeunesse (OFAJ) (1980) *Ce que je sais de la France. Images que se font des élèves allemands de leur voisin d'Outre-Rhin*, Paris: OFAJ.

Office Franco-Allemand de la Jeunesse (OFAJ) (1979) *Ce que je sais de l'Allemagne. Images que se font des élèves francais de leur voisin d'Outre-Rhin*, Paris: OFAJ.

Simmel, G. (1971/1908) *On Individuality and Social Forms*, Chicago, University of Chicago Press.

Tajfel, H., Jahoda, G., Nemeth, C., Campbell, J. and Johnson, N. (1970) 'The Development of children's preference for their own country: a cross-national study', *International Journal of Psychology*, Vol 5, pp 245-253.

UNESCO (collectif) (1986) *L'étranger vu par l'enfant*, Paris, Flammarion Médecines-Sciences.

Wood, M. (1934) *The Stranger. A Study in Social Relationships*, New York, Columbia University Press.

Zarate, G. (1993) *Représentations de l'étranger et didactique des langues*, Paris, Didier.

SECTION 3

In conclusion

Chapter 13

'Intentionally or otherwise:' children and diversity in statutory and policy discourses in Ireland

Jim Deegan

> We have come a long way since the 1960s, 70s and 80s when the outcome of policy, intentionally or otherwise, was to make minority ethnic groups as invisible as possible (Watt 2000: 1).

> Rather the concern is with the cognitive and ideological repertoire of concepts, ideas, propositions, issues, and forms of discourse employed to mentally engage the phenomenon of Irish education and to inform the process and content of policy making. The adequacy of this repertoire, its establishment and legitimation, content and exclusions, maintenance and modifications as well as its social and ideological base is considered (Mulcahy and O' Sullivan 1989: 4).

Introduction

This chapter explores the changing landscape of recent statutory and policy discourses on children and diversity in Ireland. It draws attention to the ways that 'official discourse' has intentionally or otherwise used a particular formula of words to deny culturally diverse realities in contemporary Ireland. This denial has been particularly acute concerning children and diversity in some recent statutory and policy frameworks. Unravelling the denial of children and diversity in official discourse is a complex task. It involves matters of substance and style. While matters of substance have been a common focus of policy critiques in Ireland (O'Buachalla 1988), those of style have been conspicuously rare.

The spark for this chapter derives from the seminal work of Mulcahy and O'Sullivan (1989) on substance and processes in Irish educational policy. These writers claimed that Irish educational thought was 'conceptually and analytically weak, paradigmatically insulated and ideologically domesticated' (p. 4). Few would argue that the decade following this claim was not a memorable one for the generation and diffusion of a slew of significant governmental publications on children's welfare (Devine 2000). These publications helped to redress the gradual incrementalism in policy production that had lasted for almost a century. Given that educational policies have a limited life in practice, it now seems timely to begin the work of taking stock of the accomplishments of recent years.

In this chapter, I provide a critical and postmodern exploration of some recent statutory and policy discourses on children and diversity. Given that the critical traditions have not featured significantly in Irish educational discourse, the terms and concepts used will be strange on first reading but hopefully they will help readers to see things differently and in a revealing light. Mindful of the wariness that often follows the mention of the word postmodern, I begin with a simple and declarative definition. After Popkewitz (1991: 2), I define postmodern as a 'mix' of corresponding ideas in sociological, educational, political and economic literatures. My aim is to provoke thinking 'against the grain' of recent statutory and policy discourses. Foucault (1991) described this kind of thinking as 'shaking up commonplace beliefs and taking a new measure of rules and institutions' (cited in Popkewitz and Fendler 1999: 2).

Research on children's lives related to race, ethnic, gender, class, ability, belief and community variables, among others, remains largely ambiguous, distributed and undertheorised in Ireland. In line with the critical traditions in the social and political sciences (Foucault 1972, Giroux 1983, Kincheloe and McLaren 1994, Popkewitz and Fendler 1999), I define critical as confronting 'official discourses' that privilege, secure, and normalise the status quo. As Watt (2000: 1) reminds us, there was a time not so long ago 'when the outcome of policy, intentionally or otherwise, was to make minority ethnic groups as invisible as possible'. Examining the connections between knowledge and power in these circumstances is conceptually problematic. It is compounded by the fact that the twin themes of children and diversity are not stable and bounded and subject to the vagaries and uneven flow of time.

Representing a new measure of children and diversity

Given the theoretical and conceptual shortcomings in the discourse on children and diversity, it is more appropriate, at this juncture, to speak of a discourse *on* as opposed to a discourse *of* children and diversity. But just how much has been revealed and what kinds of things are still not spoken about is a moot question.

Put simply, what has been accomplished intentionally or otherwise? Using a critical and postmodern stance, however, can potentially yield meaningful and useful perspectives on the largely unseen, unheard and unimagined place of children and diversity in recent statutory and policy discourse.

The strangling of voice is a recurring theme in the chapters in the present volume. Gowran describes how issues of gay and lesbian sexualities have not been seen, heard or spoken about under a blanket of silence in the dominant culture of heterosexism. The power of the 'eye' is also present in MacRuairc's chapter when he exhorts readers to make the lives of working class children visible however uncomfortable this may be for the dominant orthodoxy. And again, Egan writes of the significance of presences and absences of peers in the lives of children who are Down's syndrome. Perhaps the most powerful statement on seeing and not being heard comes from the girl in fifth class in Churchfield Primary School in Devine's chapter on children's views of school, who is admonished when she listens and when she doesn't listen to the teacher. It speaks volumes for what Delpit (1995) has described as the challenge of raising the 'silenced dialogue' in diverse contexts.

A critical grammar of children and diversity in 'official discourses'

One of the most prolific sites of recent discourse production and reproduction has been statutory and policy discourses on children's welfare. Examples of this discourse include the following:

- *Report of the National Commission on the Family: Strengthening Families for Life* (1996)
- *Report of the National Forum on Early Childhood Education* (1998)
- *White Paper on Early Childhood Education: Ready to Learn* (1999)
- *Primary School Curriculum* (1999)
- *National Children's Strategy: Our Children, Their Lives* (2000).

The following recent governmental publications are selectively culled from the broader discourse on children's welfare for review:

1) *White Paper on Early Childhood Education: Ready to Learn* (1999)
2) *National Children's Strategy: Our Children, Their Lives* (2000).

These publications are indicative of a particular seam in the discourse that fails to articulate a 'position' (Ferguson 1990, Nakayama and Krizek 1999) on children and diversity as central and visible. My focus is limited primarily to the above selected publications and those that specifically address constitutional, family and welfare do not fall within the scope of the present study (Lynch 1998, Kennedy 2001, Richardson 2001).

Theoretical and conceptual lacunae

There has been an outgrowth of legal and constitutional discourses about asylum-seeking children, immigration policies and increasing cultural and linguistic diversity in the last five years in Ireland (Cullen 2000, Faughnan and Woods 2000, MacLachlan and O'Connell 2000, Fanning 2002). We know little, paradoxically, about the everyday realities of race, ethnic, gender, class, beliefs, ability and community variables in children's lives. A specific lacuna is the near absence of research on refugee and asylum-seeking children's own perspectives on day-to-day realities, with a few notable exceptions (McGovern 1990, Little and Lazenby Simpson 1996, Lodge 1995, O'Regan 1998, Fanning et al 2001, O'Connor, 2001, Nolan, 2001). Influenced by Popkewitz and Fendler's (1999) reworking of Michel Foucault's (1972) critical theories on knowledge/power and bell hooks' [1] (1994) postmodern feminist writings, I draw attention to the ways understandings of children and diversity have changed and been represented in recent policy discourses. After O'Sullivan (1989), I believe there is a need to theoretically and conceptually break with existing indigenous intellectual traditions and empirical discourses, and in terms of an enduring anthropological maxim, 'make the familiar strange and the strange familiar'.

Discourse as 'bourgeois decorum'

Scholars who describe policy as discourse are motivated, as Bacchi (2000: 46) writes, 'to illustrate that change is difficult, not only because reform efforts are opposed, but because the ways in which issues get represented have a number of effects that limit the impact of reform gestures'. A focus on the ways things are represented produces a focus on language and the conceptual frameworks used to describe social and political processes. The theoretical and conceptual framework here is influenced, in part, by Foucault's (1972) idea of an 'episteme' as circulating and authorised ideas that become self-evident for thinking, mapping and acting about certain subjects. In similar vein, Macdonnell (1986: 87) defined the temporal dimensions of an episteme as 'the ground of

---

[1] This author, bell hooks, does not use initial captials in her name.

thought on which at a particular time some statements – and not others –will count as knowledge'.

I suggest what hooks (1994: 183) describes as 'bourgeois decorum' could be used as a heuristic device or *camera lucida* for helping to bring into sharper focus what is rendered visible and invisible in contemporary discourse on children and diversity. In her book, *Outlaw Culture*, hooks (1994: 183) uses the description of 'bourgeois decorum' as a sardonic couplet to refer to 'a repertoire of strategies that censor rigorous opposition and resistance to party lines by silencing dissenters.' She draws our attention to the euphemistic, disembodied and hyperpolite discursive strategies used to belie a slew of invisible and unimagined culturally diverse realities in contemporary discourse. Similarly, as Eagleton (1991: 194) maintains, 'bourgeois' has less to do with the 'kind' of languages 'than the effects they produce: effects, for example, of closure whereby certain forms of signification are silently excluded, and certain signifiers fixed in a commanding position'.

Children as marginal and invisible

In December 1999, Micheál Martin, Minister for Education and Science launched what he described as the 'first ever' *White Paper on Early Childhood Education: Ready to Learn* (1999), with the following principal objective of government policy in regard to early childhood education:

> To support the development and educational achievement of children through high quality early education, with particular focus on the target groups of the disadvantaged and those with special needs (p. 1).

In the press release for the launch of the *White Paper*, the minister explained that to date Ireland's policy in early childhood education had been 'piecemeal and incomplete' (1999: 1). In general, he stated that 'the focus has been on creating places for children rather than on the quality of the education provided' (1999: 1). The minister announced that the *White Paper* represented an attempt to 'shift the debate' (1991: 1). Included in the set of governing principles is a commitment to target resources on the children most in need, build on provision within the existing regulatory framework, and implement change on a phased and consultative basis.

The statutory context for the operational definition of the discourse of educational disadvantage used in the *White Paper* derives from the [Irish] Education Act (1998) of the previous year. The Education Act defines educational disadvantage as: 'the impediments to education arising from social or economic disadvantage which prevents students from deriving appropriate benefit from education in schools' (cited in *White Paper* 1999: 97). It borrows this definition as a legitimating statement for the focal section entitled 'Children who are disadvantaged'. The arguments presented in this section owe much to a model of social pathology and subjective discrimination (Mac an Ghaill 1999). They support essentialist and reductionistic notions of what happens in 'bell-wether' or highly developed instances of social and economic disadvantage (Kelleghan et al. 1995). What is remarkable is that the prevailing discourse has endured as the 'commonsense' of reform and renewal since the landmark Rutland Street Project some thirty years ago. Whether the debate has meaningfully shifted or simply shuffled has received little attention in the hiatus since the publication of the *White Paper*.

Logics of sameness and difference

A distinguished lineage of discursive practices on 'difference' abounds in literary and social domains in Ireland. In contrast, 'sameness' has generally remained undertheorised in social critiques, despite its deep-seated connections to cultural nationalism and majority religions for most of the last century (O'Buachalla 1988). Variants of sameness and difference have gradually and incrementally insinuated themselves into official discourse, most notably in the US where the concept of diversity is a contested feature of policy discourses. What is remarkable is the largely uncritical use of a clutch of 'double logics' (Popkewitz and Lindblad 2000: 41), for example, same/different, equal/unequal, advantaged/disadvantaged, included/excluded and targeted/untargeted. The conflation of the logics of disadvantage without reference to advantage and exclusion without reference to inclusion generates considerable conceptual confusion. Until the recent publication of research on asylum-seeking children and social exclusion, for example, there was a tendency to conflate and relegate asylum-seeking children's issues and concerns with those of their parents (Fanning et al. 2001). Indeed this matter of seeing children as extensions of their parents continues to be a contentious one in popular and academic contexts.

The benign juxtaposing of 'double logics' (Popkewitz and Lindblad 2000: 41) has been glossed over in a range of official discourses. In counterpoint to restricted expressions of disadvantage, exclusion has been expressed not only in terms of national and ideological contexts, but also in relation to discussions about the new poverty and inequality (for example, single-parent families), discrimination, marginality, foreignness, alterity, affiliation, dispossession, deprivation and destitution (Silver 1994/1995). Popkewitz and Lindblad (2000) argue that empiricist stances on methods and results alone cannot confront the wide slew of issues implicated in the inclusion/exclusion debate. Alternative conceptualisations that might potentially 'unlock' prevailing double logics are needed, if we are to make sense of the complexities of diversity in contemporary cultures.

Cells of populational reasoning

Popkewitz and Fendler (1999: 23) wrote 'we can think of populational reasoning as securing identities through assigning individuals to particular groups associated with probability statistics'. Their writings on the etiology of statistics as a political arithmetic used in social administration are resonant in the *White Paper*. Specifically, the political arithmetic employed uses 'measured and measurable' indices of location and hardship to derive a percentage for resourcing the needs of the most vulnerable in society. The arbitrary and convenient operational variable is sixteen per cent.

The calcified cells for social administration are described as 'designated disadvantaged schools' (*White Paper* 1999, p. 97). Power and Tormey (2000) have advanced useful challenges to the reliability and validity of the operational variable. The *White Paper* significantly negates any kind of broad-based commitment to confronting social injustices and oppression related to diversity. What is remarkable is that the *White Paper* eschews any reference to race or ethnicity, other than a two-paragraph nominal reference to Traveller children and families. What is truly perplexing is that the variable has remained a constant throughout the virtues and vicissitudes of unprecedented social, educational, economic and scientific development in Ireland.

A threefold series of state interventions described as *Early Start*, *Breaking the Cycle*, and *Home School Community Liaison* are chronically implicated in the network of 'designated disadvantaged schools'. While these initiatives have been well received by teachers and parents at a popular level, it is noteworthy that we do not have a holistic rubric for calibrating their success. Their success has been generally dimensionalised across a set of behavioural and cognitive indices.

Indices of becoming an adult

Chapter 1 of the *White Paper* (1999: 3) argues that the 'essential starting point' is to define what we mean by early childhood education. While ostensibly a logical starting point, the *White Paper* leaves the anterior question about what we mean when we talk and write about children and childhood at a tacit- or taken-for-granted level throughout the remainder of the document. The singularity of 'the psychological child' is not evident in the text, however the implicit binarism of classic socialisation theory, which casts the child in a perpetual state of becoming an adult, is present. It is revealed in an excess of psychologising – what Harré (1986) in his critique of developmentalism described as an over-emphasis on the individualistic, abstract and outcome indices of development. Indices such as 'behaviour,' 'motivation' and 'problem-solving' are the circulating and authoritative conceptual 'epistemes' in the *White Paper*.

While there is generally a significant importation of apposite ideas from the *Background Paper* to the *National Forum on Early Childhood Education*, and, in turn, the *White Paper*, the following imbalances are evident:

- disproportionate emphasis on IQ and the near-absence of a wide range of sociocultural variables related to race, ethnicity, gender, ability, community, or indeed any sense of sociocultural variables that might exist in particular milieu
- over-representation of data on educational achievement, as opposed to social processes in children's schooling and lives
- reliance on aggregate analyses of stereotypical processes in young children's lives to the neglect of individual and small group differences.

What are missing are the sustained calls for greater attention to issues of agency and representation expressed by those in a diversity of faith, cultural and vested interest groups, including Pavee Point, Barnardos and the National Children's Alliance, among other groups. Many of these clarion calls for greater attention to issues of agency and representation are echoed in earlier chapters in the present volume.

While the *White Paper* abounds with statistical data related to cognitive, language and motor behaviours, 'due recognition' for social and personal development is left at a tacit- and taken-for-granted level. There is clearly a tension between text and context (Apple 1992). While few would argue about the lasting effects of literacy and numeracy for young children advocated in the *White Paper*, the absence of any reference to the social constructions of reality is a grievous neglect. Priorities on literacy and numeracy, notwithstanding, more than cursory and benign references to culturally neutral and jaundiced notions of self, other and society will be needed, if we are ever to come close to the reality of diversity on the ground. On the credit side, the White Paper resists essentialising early childhood education in unequivocal terms as follows:

> The inextricable linkage between education and care means that early education comprises just one element in an all-encompassing policy concerning the rights and needs of young children (p. 5).

These are noble aspirations: however the discontinuity between this particular piece of legislation and the attempts to reconcile international and national discourses on children's rights is particularly acute. As will be indicated in the next section of the chapter, it is possible to have an 'all-encompassing policy' that doesn't necessarily include 'all' children.

Children as central and visible

In November 2000, An Taoiseach, Bertie Ahern TD launched *The National Children's Strategy: Our Children, Their Lives* with the following *vision*:

> An Ireland where children are respected as young citizens with a valued contribution to make and a voice of their own; where all children are cherished and supported by family and the wider society; where they enjoy a fulfilling childhood and realise their potential (*Strategy*, p. 4).

In the preamble, he sealed a clutch of ideological linkages between a 'positive vision' of The *United Nations Convention on the Rights of the Child* (UNCRC) (1989) and the *Strategy*. He welcomed the *Strategy* as the harbinger of a 'society which fully values and respects its children' (2000: Foreword) and described it as 'a major initiative to progress the implementation of the Convention in Ireland' (2000: 6). Recent constitutional, statutory and policy themes, for example children's rights, voice and decision-making are affirmed under the Convention. The Convention's guiding principles on children's basic rights without discrimination, best interests of the child as a primary concern in decision-making, children's right to life, survival and development, and the imperative for views of children in matters affecting them are presented as touchstones for progress and implementation. In essence, the *Strategy* heralded what Lee (2001: 91) has described as a 'global place' for a 'global child citizen' in Ireland.

The *Strategy* is contextualised in terms of the following changing contexts of children's lives:

1) demographic trends and diversity in family life
2) economic progress and labour market restructuring

3) changing lifestyles
4) poverty and social inclusion indices.

It sets out an ambitious series of objectives to guide children's policy over the next decade. The *Strategy* identifies a common vision and proposes a set of principles focused on a holistic way of thinking about children, families, and communities. 'It represents a different way of doing business, which will, if we all work together' (2000: Foreword), according to An Taoiseach, 'help us become a society which fully values and respects its children' (2000: Foreword). Few could find fault with these noble aspirations. Some of the challenges arising from the *Strategy* relate more to the tacit nature of things – what is elusive and invisible – as opposed to what is declared and visible. One of the noteworthy omissions is asylum-seeking children who are not mentioned directly in the central theme of 'whole child' perspective nor recognised in the discussion of diversity.

'Whole child' perspective

The *Strategy* is theoretically rooted in a 'whole child' perspective (2000: 10). This perspective is operationalised and systematically layered throughout the *Strategy* as a 'means for identifying the range of children's needs that will help to identify how best to meet those needs by empowering families and communities' (2000: 10). Nine key dimensions of development are advanced 'if a child is to enjoy a satisfying childhood and make a successful transition into adulthood' (2000: 10). These are:

- physical and mental well-being
- emotional and behavioural well-being
- intellectual capacity
- spiritual and moral well-being
- identity
- self-care
- family relationships
- social and peer relationships
- social presentation.

Embedded in these actions are the principles of child-centred, family oriented, equitable inclusive, action-orientated and integrated operational principles.

In their research on asylum-seeking children and social exclusion, Fanning et al (2001) translated these six operational principles into a corresponding set of six actions. In short, these writers maintained that the *Strategy* provides an 'excellent basis as an organising framework in which to situate thinking about and responses to the well-being of asylum-seeking children' (2001: 18). They recommend proofing welfare measures and reception policies from a children's rights perspective, making asylum-seeking children a focus of intercultural and social inclusion policies and programmes, and a multi-sectorial and integrated services system.

Whole is greater than sum?

The 'whole child' (*Strategy*, 2001: 10) perspective is a variant on a principle that has a long and enduring history in educational discourse internationally, and a comparatively more recent history in Ireland. It represents a variant on the long-standing theme of the 'full and harmonious development of the child' (*The Primary Curriculum Handbooks* 1971: 13) in primary education. In his critique of child-centred curriculum perspectives, Sugrue (1997: 8) eschews any churlishness regarding the principle, but judiciously avoids sentiment with the interrogative: 'What would such provision look like in practice?' Interestingly, Sugrue's inclusion of subjects under a whole curriculum umbrella closely aligns with the dimensionalised elements of the 'whole child' perspective in the *Strategy*.

Drawing on the literature of progressivism in North America, Sugrue (1997) posits that liberal and broadly-based curricula do little for the socially disadvantaged or marginalised. At the root of this contention is the view that any broad-based approach can, ironically, be selective and restrictive when there is a neglect of the critical variable of systemic power relationships and individual experiences. Sugrue (1997) concluded that without direct reference to practice, the rhetoric of 'full and harmonious development' is a weak guide to action. It is a weak guide that is particularly acute in the discussion of the individual, interactional and power dynamics of diversity as everyday reality.

As Goodenough (1987:76) cautioned, aggregate analyses that treat minorities as homogenous and undifferentiated 'should not lure us into the false expedient of forgetting to look for individual and small group differences'. The focus on the individual child is foregrounded throughout the *Strategy*. The 'false expedient' lies with the absence of focus on small groups. More specifically, there is a lack of focus on social categories. Indeed, the annotated sections on the 'whole child' perspective, sub-headed 'Dimensions of child development' (*Strategy* 2000: 27) are framed around the singularity of the individual child making sense of identity, peers and friendships, with little sense of the interactive and group dimensions of these phenomena in contemporary context.

To paraphrase Hart, Burts, and Charlesworth (1997) in their

critique of 'whole child' perspectives and implications for practice, the *Strategy* (2001: xvi) provides important pieces of the 'whole' to be integrated but more information is needed. Sugrue's (1997) view serves as a cautionary reminder of the sentiment, on the one hand, and remoteness, on the other, that often lies behind sloganising in official discourses. Fanning et al (2001: 18) bridge aspirational and practice dimensions with their definition of 'inclusive' as meaning the *Strategy* 'is for all children, including those who sometimes get left out'(2001:18). The plight of asylum-seeking children is neither visible nor accorded a space in the *Strategy*. Quite simply, they are excluded and 'left out'.

Recognition and expressions of diversity

Recognition and expressions of diversity are foregrounded throughout the *Strategy*. The rationale section uses apposite language from the Convention. Children's entitlement to basic human rights without discrimination and concerns regarding issues of racism are enunciated in the rationale for the *Strategy*. Significantly the change in the cultural make-up of our society is acknowledged as a source of racism and discrimination. The *Strategy* (Section K:70-71) represents the particular challenges of educating and supporting children to value social and cultural diversity so that all children including Travellers and other marginalised groups achieve their full potential. In addition to a reference to the swing from emigration to immigration, there is a set of statements regarding tensions between some communities and the provision of halting sites for Travellers and accommodation for refugees and persons seeking asylum.

Welcome inclusions

The *Strategy* contains a key promissory note that tackling racism and promoting respect for socially and culturally diverse communities will continue to be a key social policy issue. While these official recognitions have featured in earlier official discourses such as the *White Paper on Education* (1995), perhaps, most significantly, there is a realisation in the *Strategy* (2002: 70) that 'there remain considerable barriers to the participation in Irish society of children from ethnic minority groups, including Travellers'. Taken together, the discursive pattern is tantamount to a set of 'impact statements' designed to represent diversity as 'optically central'. The obverse of this outcome is that some children have not been given recognition or expression. They have been rendered as invisible as possible in the *Strategy*.

On the credit side, the further actions proposed in the *Strategy* include support for whole school approaches and the incorporation of intercultural strategies into school plans, and the use of schools as key sites for an anti-racism public awareness campaign. Specific actions directed at refugee children include recognition and resourcing of the special needs of non-English-speaking children, incorporation of the specific needs of children from social, ethnic, cultural and linguistic minority groups in public services decisions. Other proposed actions are the treatment of unaccompanied children seeking refugee status in accordance with best international practice, including the provision of a designated social worker and *Guardian-Ad-Litem*.

Unwelcome exclusions

On the debit side, there are specific barriers relating to income poverty and social exclusion that underlie the goodwill of the *Strategy*. Fanning et al (2001) point to a number of tensions between the *Strategy* and the Convention, and the following governmental programmes:

- *Partnership 2000* (1997)
- *Programme for Prosperity and Fairness* (2000)
- *National Anti-Poverty Strategy* (1997).

They assert that 'the welfare discriminations experienced by asylum-seeking children on direct provision (a form of modified welfare) are unambiguously contrary to Ireland's obligations under the UN CRC' (2001: 4). Compounding income poverty is the social exclusion that arises from what *Partnership 2000* described as cumulative marginalisation 'from production (employment), from consumption (income poverty), from social networks (community, family, and neighbours), from decision making and from an adequate quality of life.' (cited in Fanning et al 2001: 13).

The outcome of these contradictions is that children are experiencing the effects of income poverty as a consequence of a provision that is in direct contradiction of a national *Strategy* purporting to champion the rights of 'all' children. While the *Strategy* makes clear the particular needs of Traveller children and children from ethnic minority communities, such as refugees, it fails as Fanning et al (2001:13) state to 'identify asylum-seeking children specifically.' Omissions of this kind have proven insidious in the past. As Fanning (2002:50) reminds us, 'the extent of ideological and social marginality of Travellers within the emerging nation can be seen from the near total lack of references to them in mainstream histories and studies of nineteenth- and twentieth-century Ireland'.

The *Strategy* conveniently and arbitrarily ignores historical precedent in this regard by subsuming the challenges of asylum-seeking children as 'generalised others' in the social and political stakes of diversity discourse.

Principle of subsidiarity

One of the significant breaks with previous discourse is that the *Strategy* not only recognises the centrality of children's own needs and the support services required to actualise these needs but also the irreducible and interrelated roles of their parents, brothers and sisters, wider family circle, and friends and neighbours. The importance of family is foregrounded in the rationale section with distinct resonances to the Convention. Children's entitlement to basic human rights without discrimination and concerns regarding issues of racism are enunciated in the rationale for the *Strategy*. The touchstone for the *Strategy* (Objective L: 72) is that 'children will have the opportunity to experience the qualities of family life'. The challenges are conceptually split into a set of actions supporting families locally, alternatives to family care and families in conflict. One of the proposed actions for supporting families locally is quality parenting programme provision, 'with a special emphasis on the needs of fathers, lone parents, ethnic minority groups, including Travellers and marginalised groups' (p. 72).

Family autonomy versus children's rights

While these actions are commendable, the hoary chestnut regarding the status of the constitutional principle of subsidiarity remains unclear. In the Irish Constitution (*Bunreacht na hÉireann* 1937), there is no specific declaration of the rights of the child, although this can be inferred from the rights of all individuals. Ireland has traditionally maintained the principle of family autonomy, which assumes that children are best left to the care and protection of their own parents and extended family, except where they seriously fail in their duty towards them.

Lynch (1998: 324) argued that official discourse on children revealed that historically 'our treatment of children is welfarist and patronising; at worst, it is indifferent, condescending and lacking in respect'. One of the outcomes of the principle of 'family autonomy' is that vulnerable children often fall victim to a non-interventionist official response. As Lynch (1998) pointed out, the situation is not that children are omitted from the formula of words used to indicate relativities of interest between children and parents but that there is not a simple and declarative requirement that recognises the rights of children in times of conflict.

Conclusion

The ways in which we think about children and diversity in contemporary society have undergone profound change in the last decade. The way children understand diversity and embed these understandings in their "own" everyday lives has not been the focus of the same sustained attention. This neglect goes to the heart of the rationale for the present volume in raising the silenced voices of children on diversity. It also has significance for the role of teachers, principals, parents, and policy makers, among others, in creating learning environments in which all children can learn, work and live together, free of social, sexual, religious, racial, and ethnic prejudice.

Now there is an emergent corpus of research grounded in empirical data on diversity, equality and childhood, which could potentially be used in future policy development and implementation on children's welfare and education in Ireland. Still much more research that assesses the substance of educational policy and analyses the processes by which policy is formulated in Ireland is urgently needed. The research findings reported in the present volume indicate that inquiring into the tensions and harmonies that exist when majority and minority dynamics exist in Irish primary schools needs to be comparatively located, conceptually robust, and paradigmatically cosmopolitan. It involves not only challenging the status quo regarding matters of substance and process but also confronting the discursive strategies that often lie hidden in the underbrush of policy presentation. This challenge is especially problematic when discourse is presented as a tightly-braided and seamless set of national/international principles and practices.

Moving the discourse of children and diversity forward requires a 'triangulation' of questions of structure, agency and globalisation, if the inclusionary aspects of the *Strategy* are to be fulfilled and the exclusionary aspects corrected. Geertz (1983) captures the challenge as 'a continuous dialectical tacking between the most local of local detail and the most global of global structure in such a way as to bring them into simultaneous view' (cited in James, Jencks and Prout 1998: 145).

Specifically, I suggest that we need to go about this work of relating local and global matters by building on the theoretical observations of children and diversity in the present volume. We need to complement and counterpoint the single site and setting investigations in the present volume with sustained and focused research on multiple sites and settings. Research of this kind could create new spaces and opportunities for much needed programmatic, comparative and longitudinal perspectives on children's lives in Irish primary schools.

Studies of the *hybridity* of race, ethnic, gender, class, belief, and ability, or indeed any other variable of social analysis need to be critically conceptualised against a backcloth of the social, economic, cultural and political stakes of educational policy (Apple and Weiss 1983, McCarthy 1990, Troyna and Hatcher 1992). After Popkewitz and Lindblad (2000) what I understand as hybridity is the interrelation of discourses of race, ethnicity, gender, and class not as arbitrary and convenient divisions but overlapping discourses of no singular origin as they enter into the problem-solving of policy and educational practices.

I suggest the following set of questions that range across theory, practice, curriculum and policy as ways of developing and elaborating the emergent literature on children and diversity in Irish primary schools:

- How, and to what extent does diversity emerge as an appealing and plausible mode of reasoning in children's routines, rituals, activities and values across school, home and community contexts?
- Why, and under what circumstances, do children operationalise diversity as an organising framework for their everyday experiences in sharing and social participation, attempts to deal with adult confusions, fears, and conflicts, and resistance to adult rules and authority?
- What are the implications of children's own perspectives on diversity for developing culturally relevant teaching, learning, curricula, and resources in educational contexts?
- What are the policy implications of programmatic, comparative and longitudinal research on children and diversity for policy development and implementation?

Whether the progression from *White Paper* to *Strategy* traced in the present chapter is an educational and cultural sea-change will be a matter of critical significance in rendering a truer picture of discourses on children and diversity today. The *Strategy* is by no means the only marking on the children's discourse map. It is, however, likely to serve as the compass for children, parents, teachers and policy makers in helping to navigate a trajectory on discourse on children and diversity into the future. It marks a new set of signposts on the changing landscape of educational discourse on children and diversity—the emergence of 'a global child space' for some but not all children in Ireland. Should we continue to pursue a discernible line of policy and practice for children and diversity without equality for *all*, then we will continue to produce and reproduce silence and invisibility—intentionally and not otherwise.

Bibliography

Apple, M. (1992) 'The Text and Cultural Politics', *Educational Researcher*, Vol 21, pp 4-11

Apple, M. and Weiss, L. (1983) *Ideology and Practice in Schooling*, Philadelphia, Temple University Press.

Bacchi, C. (2000) 'Policy as Discourse: What Does It Mean? Where Does It Get Us?', *Discourse: Studies in the Cultural Politics of Education*, Vol 21, pp 45-57.

Bhabha, H. (2003) 'On Writing Rights', in M. Gibney (ed.) *Globalizing Rights*, Oxford, Oxford University Press, pp 162-183.

Corsaro, W. and Eder, D. (1990) 'Children's Peer Cultures', *Annual Review of Sociology*, Vol 16, pp 197-220.

Cullen, P. (2000) *Refugees and Asylum Seekers in Ireland,* Cork, Cork University Press.

Delpit, L. (1995) *Other People's Children,* New York, New Press.

Department of Education and Science (1999) 'White Paper on Early Childhood Education: Ready to Learn', Press Release, Dublin, Department of Education and Science.

Devine, D. (2000) 'Constructions of Childhood in School: Power, Policy and Practice', in Irish Education, *International Studies in Sociology of Education*, Vol 10, pp 23-41.

Eagleton, T. (1991) *Ideology: An Introduction,* London, Verso.

Fanning, B. (2002) *Racism and Social Change in the Republic of Ireland,* Manchester, Manchester University Press.

Fanning, B., Veale, A. and O'Connor, D. (2001) *Beyond the Pale: Asylum-seeking Children and Social Exclusion in Ireland,* Dublin, Irish Refugee Council and Combat Poverty Agency.

Faughnan, P. and Woods, M. (2000) *Lives on Hold: Seeking Asylum in Ireland,* Dublin, Applied Social Science Research Programme.

Ferguson, R. (1990) 'Introduction: Invisible Centre', in R. Ferguson, M. Gever, T. Trinh and C. West (eds) *Out There: Marginalisation and Contemporary Cultures,* New York, New Museum of Contemporary Art and MIT Press, pp 9-14.

Foucault, M. (1972) *The Archaeology of Knowledge,* London, Tavistock.

Foucault, M. (1991) *Remarks on Marx: Conversations with Duccio Trombadori,* translated by R. Goldstein and J. Cascaito, New York, Semiotext(e), Columbia University.

Geertz, C. (1983) *Local Knowledge: Further Essays in Interpretive Anthropology,* New York, Basic Books.

Giroux, H. (1983) *Theory and Resistance in Education,* South Hadley, MA, Bergin and Garvey Publishers.

Goodenough, W. (1987) 'Multiculturalism as the Normal Experience', in E. Eddy and W. Partridge (eds) *Applied Anthropology in America,* New York, Columbia University Press.

Government of Ireland (1937) *Bunreacht na hÉireann (Irish Constitution),* Dublin, Government Publications.

Government of Ireland (1971) *The Primary Teacher's Handbooks Volume 1 and 2,* Dublin, Government Publications.

Government of Ireland (1996) *Report of the National Commission on the Family: Strengthening Families for Life,* Dublin, Government Publications.

Government of Ireland (1997) *The National Anti-Poverty Strategy: Sharing in Progress*, Dublin, Government Publications.

Government of Ireland (1997) *Partnership 2000 for Inclusion, Employment and Competitiveness,* Dublin, Government Publications.

Government of Ireland (1998) *Education Act,* Dublin, Government Publications.

Government of Ireland (1998) *Report of the National Forum for Early Childhood Education,* Dublin, Government Publications.

Government of Ireland (1999) *White Paper on Early Childhood Education: Ready to Learn,* Dublin, Government Publications.

Government of Ireland (1999) *Primary School Curriculum,* Dublin, Government Publications.

Government of Ireland (2000) *National Children's Strategy: Our Children, Their Lives*, Dublin, Government Publications.

Government of Ireland (2000) *A Programme for Prosperity and Fairness,* Dublin, Government Publications.

Hart, C., Burts, D. and Charlesworth, R. (eds) (1997) *Integrated Curriculum and Developmentally Appropriate Practice: Birth to Age Eight,* New York, SUNY.

Harré, R. (1986) 'The Step to Social Constructionism', in M. Light (ed.) *Children of Social Worlds: Development in a Social Context*, Cambridge, Harvard University Press.

hooks, b. (1994) *Outlaw Culture: Resisting Representations,* New York, Routledge.

James, A., Jencks, C. and Prout, A. (1998) *Theorizing Childhood,* Cambridge, Polity Press.

Kelleghan, T., Weir, S., Ó hUallacháin, S. and Morgan, M. (1995) *Educational Disadvantage in Ireland,* Dublin, Department of Education and Combat Poverty Agency.

Kennedy, F. (2001) *Cottage to Crèche: Family Change in Ireland,* Dublin, Institute of Public Administration.

Kincheloe, J. and McLaren, P. (1994) 'Rethinking Critical Theory and Qualitative Research', in N. Denzin and Y. Lincoln (eds) *Handbook of Qualitative Research*, London, Sage.

Lee, N. (2001) *Childhood and Society: Growing Up in an Age of Uncertainty*, Philadelphia, PA, The Open University Press.

Lentin, R. (ed.) (2000) *Emerging Irish Identities*, Dublin, Trinity College, University of Dublin.

Little, D. and Lazenby Simpson, B. (1996) 'Meeting the Language Needs of Refugees', *Centre for Language and Communication Studies,* Dublin, Trinity College.

Lodge, C. (1995) 'Working with Refugees in Schools', *Pastoral Care in Education*, Vol 13, Dublin, NAPCE.

Lynch, K. (1998) 'The Status of Children and Young Persons: Educational and Related Issues', in S. Healy and B. Reynolds (eds) *Social Policy in Ireland: Principles, Practices and Problems,* Dublin, Oak Tree Press, pp 321-353.

Mac an Ghaill, M. (1999) 'Coming of Age in 1980s England: Reconceptualising Black Students' Experience', *British Journal of Sociology of Education*, Vol 2, pp 273-286.

Macdonnell, D. (1986) *Theories of Discourse,* Oxford, Blackwell.

MacLachlan, M. and O'Connell, M. (eds) (2000) *Cultivating Pluralism: Psychological, Social and Cultural Perspectives on a Changing Ireland,* Dublin, Oak Tree Press.

McCarthy, C. (1990) *Race and Curriculum: Social Inequality and the Theories and Politics of Difference in Contemporary Research and Schooling,* London, Falmer Press.

McGovern, F. (1990) *Vietnamese Refugees in Ireland, 1979-1989: A Case Study in Education and Resettlement*, Unpublished MEd thesis, Dublin, Trinity College.

Martin, M. (December 1999), Press Release, *White Paper on Early Childhood Education: Ready to Learn,* Dublin, Department of Education and Science.

Mulcahy, D. and O'Sullivan, D. (eds) (1989) *Irish Educational Policy: Processes and Substance*, Dublin, Institute of Public Administration.

Nakayama, T. and Krizek, R. (1999) 'Whiteness as a Strategic Rhetoric', in T. Nakayama and J. Martin (eds) *Whiteness: The Communication of Social Identity*, Thousand Oaks, CA, Sage, pp 87-106.

Nolan, G. (2001) 'A Foreshortened Childhood: Refugee and Asylum-Seeking Children in Ireland', in A. Cleary, M. Nic Ghiolla Phádraig and S. Quin (eds) *Understanding Children Volume 2: Changing Experiences and Family Forms,* Cork, Oak Tree Press.

O'Buachalla, S. (1988) *Educational Policy in Twentieth Century Ireland,* Dublin, Wolfhound Press.

O'Sullivan, D. (1989) 'The Ideational Base of Irish Educational Policy', in D. Mulcahy and D. O'Sullivan (eds) *Irish Educational Policy: Processes and Substance,* Dublin, Institute of Public Administration, pp 219-274.

O'Regan, C. (1998) *Report of a Survey of the Vietnamese and Bosnian Refugee Communities in Ireland,* Dublin, Refugee Agency.

O'Toole, J. (2000) 'Early Childhood Education and Care in Ireland and the Challenge to Educational Disadvantage', *Irish Journal of Applied Social Studies,* Vol 2, pp 125-148.

Popkewitz, T. (1991) *A Political Sociology of Educational Reform: Power/Knowledge in Teaching, Teacher Education and Research,* New York, Teachers College Press.

Popkewitz, T. and Fendler, L. (1999) (eds) *Critical Theories in Education: Changing Terrains of Knowledge and Politics,* New York, Routledge.

Popkewitz, T. and Lindblad, S. (2000) 'Educational Governance and Social Inclusion Exclusion: Some conceptual difficulties and problematics in policy and research', *Discourse: Studies in the Cultural Politics of Education*, Vol 21, pp 5-44.

Power, C. and Tormey, R. (2000) 'Refocusing the Debate: An Examination of the Interplay between Measurement and Intervention in Educational Disadvantage', Limerick, CEDR and CDU, Mary Immaculate College, Limerick.

Richardson, V. (2001) 'Legal and Constitutional Rights of Children in Ireland', in A. Cleary, M. Nic Ghiolla Phádraig and S. Quin (eds) *Understanding Children Volume 1: Children and the State,* Cork, Oak Tree Press, pp 21-44.

Silver, H. (1994/1995) Social Exclusion and Social Solidarity: Three Paradigms, *International Labour Review*, Vol 133, pp 531-577.

Sugrue, C. (1997) *Complexities of Teaching: Child-centred Perspectives,* London, Falmer Press.

Troyna, B. and Hatcher, R. (1992) *Racism in Children's Lives: A Study of Mainly-White Primary Schools,* London, Routledge.

United Nations (1989) Convention on the Rights of the Child, Geneva, United Nations.

Watt, P. (2000) 'Opening Remarks', in R. Lentin (ed.) *Emerging Irish Identities*, Dublin, Trinity College, p. 1.

Chapter 14

Activating voices through practice: democracy, care and consultation in the primary school

Dympna Devine, Anne Lodge and Jim Deegan

Introduction

In highlighting primary voices, this book has concerned itself with minority voices, many of which are excluded from full participation in the primary school system. Key among these have been the voices of children and others who are marginalised because of their dis/ability, sexual orientation, ethnic or cultural background. This chapter draws together many of the arguments that emerged as central to the preceding chapters. The discussion is framed in terms of key principles that we have identified as central to an inclusive vision of primary education – democracy in education, activating subordinate voices and the caring/emotional dynamic within educational relationships. These principles, it is argued, should underpin core educational practice including pedagogical and curricular practice in schools. The interrelated and irreducible connections between teaching and teacher education are also considered.

Democracy in primary education

Traditional accounts of democracy are typically equated in the first place with citizenship education and, in the second place, with representative engagement by interest groups. While citizenship education represents a welcome development in the Irish school system (e.g. through SPHE and CSPE programmes), we would argue strongly that education *about* citizenship is insufficient – children are not citizens-in-the-making but are actual citizens (Devine 2001, 2003) who have a right both to exercise their voices and to be heard in schools. Drawing on the work of Dewey (1916), our vision of democracy in schools involves the full recognition and inclusion of *all* diverse groups in society. Like Dewey, we conceptualise schools as communities, and education as active participation in the life of the community. Fundamental to this concept of democracy is the notion that a shared set of principles arrived at through negotiation by all parties underpins practice in all aspects of the life of the school.

The Education Act (1998) names and sanctions the voices of certain key groups. This representative democratic model enables the voices of recognised key players to contribute to policy formulation and development and to comment on educational issues in the public domain. However, we regard this as a limited model of democracy and one that silences the voices of marginalised others, both children and adults. As presently structured, Boards of Management preclude the realisation of this form of democracy. Given the majority representation of the Trustee, as enshrined in the Education Act, the discordant voices of others can be silenced if it is perceived that they threaten the dominant ethos of the school.[1] Furthermore, these others do not represent the full range of the school community. Only teachers as a group and parents as a group are currently entitled to elect members to their school's Board of Management. This is untenable given the increasing diversity and complexity of Irish society, and the growing awareness by certain subordinate groups of their right to be afforded respect and recognition.

Activating subordinate voices

Irish society has tended to envisage and structure itself as homogeneous with negative implications for those who are outside of the norm. We have seen, for example, how the primary system has been structured around assumptions about cultural homogeneity, thereby rendering invisible those of other beliefs. A mindset that presumes homogeneity has negative implications for all participants in education (teachers, parents and children) whether majority or

---

1 The problem in this instance is that, for those who differ from the norm – for example, those who are of different belief or religious and cultural origin – there is little or no opportunity to choose a faith-appropriate or multi-denominational primary school given the widespread lack of such alternatives. The Education Act 1998 obliges the Board of Management of a denominational school to uphold that school's (religious) ethos. Because of the legislative protection for a specific religious point of view and life-world in the great majority of primary schools and because of the lack of alternatives, the minority of parents and children whose beliefs, cultures and life-worlds differ cannot be given equal representation in the current context.

minority. A consistent theme that emerged across all of the chapters concerned the silencing of the voices of those of subordinate status in Irish primary education. When given the chance to speak, those whose life-worlds have been rendered invisible told their own stories of powerlessness and hurt at not being heard. As Lodge outlined in Chapter 2, some parents of minority beliefs were deeply angered by the failure of individual teachers or schools to address their rights and concerns. They also expressed an overarching sense of frustration at the inadequacies of the current denominational structuring of the primary education system. Similarly, the children in Chapter 7 expressed negative feelings arising out of the exclusion of their voice in the organisation of school and classroom life. The positive impact of listening to subordinate voices was also outlined, however. Children spoke positively of teachers who listened to them and treated them with respect and fairness. The families in the ESL initiative outlined by Ryan in Chapter 5 were appreciative of the efforts made by individuals and institutions to recognise their particular needs with regard to educational engagement.

The invisibility and silencing of certain groups cannot be separated from the power and dominance of others. Key players in Irish primary education include institutions such as the main Churches, the state Department of Education and Science and teacher unions. Their voices, perspectives and agendas have been central to defining policy and practice in Irish primary education over a lengthy period. More recently, other interest groups such as parent bodies have begun to emerge, asserting their perspectives and interests. However, such bodies or groups have not necessarily empowered or represented the interests of those who are marginalised in primary education. The current laissez faire approach to inclusion cannot work because it fails to challenge the dominant/subordinate dynamic in existing power structures. Real inclusion challenges traditional hierarchies and norms by threatening the pre-eminent position of the powerful. Young (1990) identifies the exclusion of the voices of marginalised groups from decision-making as one of the five faces of oppression. Those whose identities are lower status (e.g. working class, minority ethnicity or sexuality) often internalise their socially ascribed positions in the social world from an early age. Thus, those of lower status can come to denigrate themselves (Plummer 2000). The colonisation of the life-worlds and voices of the marginalised by powerful interest groups (Lynch and O'Neill 1994) compounds their subordination. As Lukes (1977) argued, those who are not afforded the right to self-determination and expression are being rendered powerless and invisible and are not granted equal status with their fellow human beings.

Activating voices is not simply about being given an opportunity to speak however. Rather it is a more proactive process that is concerned with the facilitation and support of the powerless, who have the right to have their voices heard. It is unreasonable to expect members of any marginalised group to articulate their viewpoint proficiently in the absence of structured support. The establishment of a student council in a primary school as outlined in Chapter 8 highlighted how both children and teachers were positively challenged by the greater involvement of the children in decision-making in school. This process evolved over the period of a school year and involved the active participation of a committed facilitator to ensure its success. However, without this, it is difficult to imagine how either the teachers or the children could have benefited so positively from the establishment of more democratic structures in their school.

Caring and emotional work of engagement in education

Implied in the concept of democracy we have outlined is an expectation of respect, care and concern for all in the educational community. This notion of care should automatically imply respect for, and recognition of difference, a commitment to inclusion, and a sensitivity to the whole person of the individual. Fundamental to the notion of care, therefore, as we define it is the recognition of the individual in social context. Education fails to embrace the whole child when the curriculum negates a part of that individual's life-world and culture. The primary reward for teachers emerges out of this social dimension of their working lives (Lortie 1975, Hargreaves 2002) and remains central to the way in which Irish primary teachers define themselves (Ryan, 2003). It is not only what teachers know and do that underpins what happens in classrooms and schools but also the influence of their emotional lives on their practice as teachers. Hargreaves (2002) discussed this dimension of classroom and school life as *emotional geographies* – the closeness and distance that characterises our social and emotional lives, contributing to and deriving from our own sense of self and our manner of interaction with others. However, despite growing awareness of the importance of the emotional life in the teaching and teacher education literature, the focus of policy and governmental publications has been elsewhere. Recent debates about education and schooling both in the academic and popular domains have been dominated by a focus on outcomes, accountability and efficiency (Reed 1998) to the detriment of a focus on the caring and emotional dimension of the teaching role. Yet, as Ryan noted in Chapter 5, it was this very aspect of the personal engagement of teachers with students under the ESLI that was positively commented upon by participants. Furthermore, as Devine (2003) argued, children's identification of a good teacher is one that embraces these notions of care, concern and respect.

Primary schooling is, in many ways, structured to facilitate the development of strong, interpersonal relationships between teachers and pupils, and children and their peers. Children tend to have, typically, one teacher for at least a school year and they remain with the same peer group throughout their eight years in the primary school, a substantial proportion of their childhood. As a result, it is often assumed that primary education is child-centred. However, primary education is underpinned by a paternalistic framework which assumes that adults will always act in the best interests of children and that existing institutional structures are equally suited to all. We would argue that the competitive, individualistic, meritocratic model of achievement that characterises Irish education at all levels (Devine 2003, Lynch 1989) undermines the potential for a caring climate. The resultant emphasis on authority and control can compromise the caring and emotional aspect of teacher-pupil relationships, with negative implications for both children's and teachers' experiences of school.

Planning for and promoting change through consultation

Having emphasised the centrality of democracy, voice and care in primary education, we now turn to a discussion of how this can be realised in practice. If we are to change what is happening in primary schools, to give greater voice to those who are currently excluded or marginalised, how can this be realised? Research into improving school practice identifies four distinct yet interrelated levels in which change can be made (Swan and Devine 2002, Teddlie and Reynolds 2000): these are national, school, class and individual level factors. At the level of national policy, consideration must be given to government policy and initiatives in this area and how the notion of partnership in education that currently prevails is one which matches both the needs and rights of more marginalised groups. With respect to parents, for example, assuming that the National Parent's body is the best mechanism through which representation can be made by minority or marginalised parent groups is not entirely appropriate, given the current absence of the voices of these groups in policy development. With respect to children, their voices have to date been clearly absent from policy development at national level (Devine 2003), although the manner of their input into the *National Children's Strategy* (2000) and the inclusion of their perspectives at a recent forum on education disadvantage (Zappone 2002) points a way forward.

Consultation with those who are marginalised should be mandatory in the development of all policy initiatives at primary level, such groups having the right to structured representation on policy-making bodies, having their voices heard in an inclusive and respectful manner. In practice, this means that policy-making and other bodies must actively seek to engage with the marginalised. This type of engagement needs to facilitate the expression of views and experiences, it needs to develop understandings of the education system and needs to be open to listening to critique and to personal or group stories of difficulty and disappointment. Such engagement requires time, expertise and sensitivity – the kinds of skills and approaches that are typically associated with adult and community education. Mechanisms must be developed that allow for continuing dialogue with different marginalised (and other) groups[2] as a policy or curriculum or other change is being developed. This ongoing dialogue should inform the development process. Minority groups should be given a role in dissemination of changed policy or curriculum, both in bringing an understanding of the process and the outcome back to other members of their community or organisation and also in dissemination to teachers and other education bodies. It is crucial that the process of consultation and dialogue allows for the establishment and support of formal and informal networks between the marginalised and other bodies[3] in order to increase mutual understanding and inclusion.

At the level of the individual, all stakeholders in education must recognise that consultation requires commitment, taking responsibility, and a willingness to listen to the voices of others. This requires skill and also a gradual induction into the process of

---

2 We are not advocating a consultative process that only heeds the voices of the marginalised. Rather, we are arguing that the views of the marginalised need to be acknowledged and considered *alongside* the majority voices, whether or not the perspectives and concerns of the former are discordant from those of the majority. True interculturalism and social inclusion rather than assimilation is only possible when dialogue between different groups is fostered and becomes commonplace, when all members of society accept that no one group has a monopoly on truth or goodness, that the life-worlds and cultures of *all* groups have something positive to offer to others and can also learn and benefit from one another.

3 Connell (1993) reports that one of the major benefits of the Disadvantaged Schools Programme in Australia was the fact that it led to the establishment of formal and informal networks between teachers, parents and community activists.

consultation and collaboration with the school. For those who have been traditionally marginalised, part of that marginalisation can often be a fear of exercising their voice, a reluctance to name their concerns. In such instances, the nature of school culture and the sensitivity and awareness of educational professionals is paramount as it is they who can initiate support structures within the school through which these individuals' voices can be heard. Articulating one's voice is not something that comes easily and to be effective requires training and support. With respect to children for example, Devine (2003) notes the importance of gradually inducting them into a system of inclusion and partnership in the organisation of the school.

The translation of national policy into practice at local level takes place primarily through the activities of teachers and principals in schools. At the school level, national and international research in the area of school improvement points to the significance of school culture in effecting real change (Hargreaves 1995, Harris et al 2003, Tuohy 1999). A school culture that is traditional and hierarchical in type will preclude consideration of difference and accommodation in its practices and effects. Diversity and inclusion within such a culture is interpreted as a challenge and dealt with in terms of hostility, resistance and suppression. The corollary, a culture that is open, transparent and dynamic, views inclusion and diversity as an opportunity, no less great in its challenge, but one which is worked through in an open and constructive manner.

The development of a Whole School Plan provides an important framework within which the voices of all those involved in and touched by the work of the school can make their voices heard. This requires organisation and initiative by professionals within the school, providing both the spaces and opportunities for others to exercise their voice in a manner that is listened to and valued. At its core is recognition of the school as a community, in which all actors have an important role to play. While the enactment of an inclusive culture in schools rests on the commitment of teachers and school principals as the primary mediators of educational policy, the importance of accountability, through Whole School Evaluation, should not be underestimated. In this sense, the state, through the inspectorate system, has a primary responsibility to ensure that schools are inclusive of marginalised groups in their practice. This role cannot be fully undertaken without the inspectorate itself being fully briefed and aware of issues centred on voice and equality in our schools. One of the most significant outcomes of the Whole School Evaluation Pilot Project Report (1999) was the underscoring of the centrality of the principle of ownership. Implicit in the report is a realisation that the renewal and development of teaching and learning must be rooted in the reality of what is actually happening in classrooms and schools.

Practice at the school level filters into practice at class level, by providing the support for and indicating the vision of the school. If the prevailing ethos within the school is one of inclusion, respect for and accommodation to difference, then teachers in their classroom practice, both with pupils and parents, must reflect this. Creating a welcoming environment for all parents, providing a space for children to air their views, recognising diversity in the classroom as a positive element of classroom culture are all significant elements in translating the goals of effective inclusion into classroom practice. While the area of social relations (between pupils and teachers, teachers and parents) has been identified as a key area of potential transformation and change (Devine 2003), teachers also have considerable flexibility as indicated in the *Primary School Curriculum* (1999) in both their pedagogical and curricular practice. While recognising that teachers are not curtailed either in terms of their pedagogical or their curricular approaches, it is important to appreciate that bringing about change in one's practice involves risk-taking and that many teachers require support and encouragement in order to do this. Formal and informal teacher networks can offer opportunities for peer mentoring and dissemination of good practice. Recent research for example demonstrates the value of such networks and the contribution they make to teacher professional development in attempting to work through the challenges posed by increasing ethnic diversity in our primary schools (Devine et al 2002). We would also stress however, the benefit to teachers of engaging directly with marginalised groups. Through such contact deeper understandings of the particular concerns of, and issues facing, such groups emerge and can contribute to profound changes in teacher outlooks and practice.

Inscribing diversity as a core curriculum area

The *Primary School Curriculum* (1999) provides us with a useful and important framework within which to explore and develop understandings of diversity and inclusivity. Rooted in the integrity of the child's life as a child and as a member of society, the Curriculum acknowledges the dynamic and interactive relationship between education and society. Themes that lie at the intersections of children's sense of belonging, relationships with other children and adults, and their place in the wider world are discussed here.

Social, Personal, and Health Education (SPHE) is a new curriculum area that is conceptualised and organised to help prepare children for active and responsible citizenship. It aims to develop a respect for cultural and human diversity in the world and an appreciation for the democratic way of life. In this sense, it is an important mechanism for promoting inclusion. However, there is a danger that the key principles we have outlined in this chapter will become confined to one curricular area rather than being seen to be at the core of all curricular practice in primary schools. Issues to do with democracy, voice and respect/care should not be confined to SPHE alone but should inform the full scope and sequence of the curriculum in action. For example, Haran and Tormey (2002) argue that the work of integrating intercultural education is not about doing more but about doing things differently. Within our framework this involves teachers developing a belief and commitment to these principles and bringing this into their practice and engagement with teaching, learning, curriculum and assessment. Neither can we settle for additive extra status in a supplementary curriculum guide. The history of curricular additives is a long and desultory one. Any diminution in the status of diversity as a consequence of reduced resources for school development planning and curriculum support will only serve to pincer a fledgling diversity agenda between a full curriculum, on the one hand, and a limited timetable, on the other. Without core curriculum status, there is a real threat that diversity will be treated sporadically and strewn across the broad sweep of the curriculum in fractured bits and pieces.

A curriculum for diversity and equality needs to avoid the trap of exclusive reliance on 'soft' issues, which can induce benign support but fall short on meaningful change and action. For example, 'we are all friends in this school', while promoting a notion of community and positive interrelationships can overlook the more invidious patterns of inclusion/exclusion in children's peer cultures that are rooted in hierarchies arising out of racism, sexism, classism, and so on. These need to be dealt with in a caring and sensitive manner, acknowledging the lived realities of the families and communities in which children live.

Responding to caring in schools and classrooms

Deegan (1996) derived a set of starting points for organising classrooms around themes of caring. Influenced by Noddings (1992) who underpinned an 'ethic of caring' with respect for the equality of relationships, he suggested key themes for teachers attempting to foster a caring ethic in their schools and classroom. First, is the centrality of the child evidenced in giving voice to different children and talking with children about differences, actively listening to more than one side of a story and avoiding grouping that defines children as 'inferior' or reflects stereotyping. Second, encourage ways of embedding caring in action-based classroom conversations by devoting part of the day to children's interests and concerns, affirming caring and helping actions, and helping children to understand that individuals and groups can be by turns harmonious and conflictual. Third, promote the idea that caring can be an expression of moral strength and courage by recognising qualities of loyalty and trust, honouring situations when children stand up for each other and just causes, and judiciously acknowledging the efforts of those who discourage other children from behaving in uncaring ways. Fourth, relax the impulse to control children by making the things that matter most to them the substance of curriculum themes and strands, and developing positive management approaches that are conducive to active social responsibility towards self and others. Finally, collaborate with children to confront negative stereotypes including classism, racism, sexism, dis/ablism and sectarianism through challenging the status quo and modelling respect for difference. Creating an inclusive culture in schools, which an ethic of caring implies, is a challenging task, and can only be realised in practice when teachers are supported in this process. As a first step Teacher Education has a key role to play.

Teacher education for diversity and equality

There are currently more than 3,500 student teachers[4] registered on primary teacher education programmes in this country, coupled with an increasing number of teachers engaging in post-graduate Masters and Doctoral education studies (Sugrue et al 2001). Into the future it is impossible to say where the influences of these teachers will end for children of particular races, ethnicities, genders, classes, faiths, abilities, sexualities and communities. What we do know, however, is that those countries that have deflected and deferred from significant investment in curriculum, pedagogy, and teacher education for inclusion in the past have paid dearly in terms of negative social, cultural and academic outcomes.

There is an old maxim that 'you cannot teach what you don't know and you can't lead where you won't go'. Herein lies the

---

4 The term student teacher is used to refer to student teachers during their entire teacher education experience, including but not limited to micro-teaching, teaching practice, and visits to a range of educational settings.

kernel of the challenge facing all those engaged in teaching and teacher education – making connections between the twin themes of knowledge and leadership in deliberative and democratic contexts. The challenge begs the following question: how, and in what ways can we develop new knowledge and kindle visionary leadership in teachers and teacher educators? In Apple's (1992) terms we need to reconcile the text and context when linking curriculum, pedagogy, and teacher education. Failure to reckon with these challenges will induce a wide gap between aspirations and realities. The reality is that diversity is not only about finding ways of celebrating difference but also of confronting social injustice and inequality. In order to build new curriculum knowledge and kindle visionary leadership, principles/ practices will need to be operationally defined. The following are a set of starting points for linking curriculum, pedagogy, and teacher education for diversity across classrooms, schools, homes and communities.

A key principle/practice is that learning about diversity is a pre-requisite for teaching about diversity and that there can be no teaching without prior learning. Teachers need to understand and personally value the goals and philosophies of pluralism and inclusion as a basic tenet of diversity learning and teaching. This implies that teachers need to be prepared to understand and reject the manifestations and consequences of prejudice, racism, sexism, classism, and all other social and cultural debilitating forces (Gollinick 1992). In the spirit of the curriculum, teachers must develop a willingness to confront their own cultural biographies and engage in dialogical encounters with each other about their own knowledge, attitudes and skills in learning about and teaching for diversity (Ladson-Billings, 1991). Such deep-seated beliefs and fears have an emotional dimension and are experienced as real by the individuals. They cannot be challenged and confronted quickly or easily and require generous time, space and opportunity for reflection and moving beyond socially constructed and accepted stereotypes.

The second principle/practice is that 'good teaching requires knowledge of both subject-matter and students' and the 'contextual fabric within which they meet' (Larkin and Sleeter 1995: 7). Knowledge of culture requires an anthropological mind-set that can potentially help students to 'see' themselves and 'others' recursively and avoid the pitfalls of what has been described as 'othering' (Epstein, O'Flynn and Telford 2001: 127). Teachers will need to be acutely aware of the importance of providing a range of experiences directed at helping students move beyond individual differences to a consideration of the power differentials between groups based on race, ethnicity, gender, class, ability, and beliefs, among other social and cultural variables (Deegan and Allexsaht-Snider 1999). In this regard it is important to remember that teachers will need to be resilient and not give up easily, developing interrogative skills for separately and interactively confronting the dilemmas of race, culture, and language diversity (Cochran-Smith 1995).

And this brings us to a net point. Teaching and learning for diversity and equality is a choice. A central question underpinning one of the choices facing all of us is how, and in what ways, we confront engrained approaches for doing things – what we might describe as the comfortable and safe practices of 'business-as-usual' – that typically lie deep and hidden in institutional structures such as primary schools. Investing time, space, and resources in helping children, teachers, and parents make choices for diversity is not only a different kind of educational investment but a prerequisite for helping to secure culturally relevant teaching and learning in an ever-changing society (Deegan 2003).

Concluding discussion

In this chapter we have identified key principles that should underpin practice in primary education and we have considered how these principles apply at national, local and classroom level. Integrated throughout our analyses have been themes of curriculum, pedagogy and teacher education. This discussion is framed within a sociological context and has particular relevance in the light of the rapid social and economic changes in Irish society in the last thirty years. Our argument derives from Irish legislative and policy contexts which, in turn, have been influenced by developments in the European and global spheres. Fundamental to such change has been the guaranteeing of rights of inclusion and recognition for all participants in state institutions. Therefore there is an onus of responsibility on both the service providers and the key stakeholders within the education system to ensure that the rights of all are vindicated.

Our notion of rights derives from a commitment to social justice and a belief that all persons are entitled to access and participate in state services such as education. This notion challenges paternalistic and welfarist approaches in the light of their reproduction of hierarchical social relationships and unequal power processes and structures. We are questioning the traditional constructs of pupils, parents and teachers that have resulted in the exclusion of those who differ from the norm. As a consequence of such practice the voices of the marginalised have been silenced (Shevlin and Rose 2003), a segregated education system has been justified, differential educational outcomes have been neglected and access to employment by some of those who wish to teach in the primary school system has been denied. While there have been many positive, targeted interventions directed at specific groups, the absence of a rights focus underpinning policy has resulted in an ad-hoc system of provision.

The recognised education partners have a crucial role to play in enabling human rights, equality and diversity issues to be successfully addressed in primary schools and in the primary education system as a whole. As Lodge and Lynch (2004) point out, effective change only takes place in Irish education when the major stakeholders both support and promote it. Key among the stakeholders is the state itself. Accountability is bound up with the responsibility of the state to provide adequate support to professionals on the ground, in their commitment to improving practice in our primary schools. This support takes a number of forms. In its broadest sense it involves prioritising the funding of primary education, bringing it at a minimum to levels currently available at second and third level. The regressive funding of the education system (Tussing 1978) can no longer be sustained, signalling as it does an under-valuation of the status of young children, hence their education, and an overly narrow focus on investment in those levels of the education system which tie directly with the labour market (Devine 2003).

While there has rightly been considerable controversy in recent years over the inadequate funding of the schools' refurbishment programme, mean pupil teacher ratios and average class size are still among the highest in the OECD countries. This is untenable in a society which has recently enjoyed an economic boom, and which posits itself as at the forefront of modernisation and development among its European partners. In the absence of sufficient state funding, schools are left to subvent their educational activities by appeals to the broader community, typically parents, to contribute to school funds. While 'voluntary' in name, these contributions are such an ingrained feature of the primary school funding system that in essence they act as a form of indirect taxation of parents who can afford to pay. Gross inequalities are thus perpetuated between primary schools, with those located in economically advantaged communities best placed to provide for the resources required by the school (Walsh 2002).

In spite of some of the challenges outlined in this chapter, which have both derived from, and contributed to, change, we have entered into a dynamic period of development in Irish primary education. We wish this book to signal the centrality of *voice* (both of children and of marginalised adults) to this process of change. Drawing on the evident commitment of many of those involved in Irish primary education, there is every reason to hope that the experiences of children and other marginalised groups can be framed in a respectful, inclusive and democratic manner. This book has highlighted some of these voices.

Bibliography

Apple, M. (1992) 'The Text and Cultural Politics', *Educational researcher*, Vol 21, pp 4-11.

Cochran-Smith, M. (1995) 'Color Blindness and Basket Making are not the Answers: Confronting the Dilemmas of Race, Culture, and Language Diversity in Teacher Education', *American Educational Research Journal*, Vol 32, pp 493-522.

Cochran-Smith, M. and Little, S. (1992) (eds) 'Communities for Teacher Research: Fringe or Forefront?', *American Journal of Education*, Vol 100, pp 298-324.

Connell, R. W. (1993) *Schools and Social Justice*. Philadelphia, Temple University Press.

Corsaro, W. and Eder, D. (1990) 'Children's Peer Cultures', *Annual Review of Sociology*, Vol 16, pp 197-220.

Deegan, J. (1996) *Children's Friendships in Culturally Diverse Classrooms*, London, Falmer Press.

Deegan, J. (2003) 'Roots and Wings: Teacher Education for Diversity in a Changing Ireland', in *Mosaic or Melting Pot? Proceedings of a Conference on Cultural Diversity*, Dublin, Irish National Committee of the European Cultural Foundation and the Royal Irish Academy, pp 63-71.

Deegan, J. and Allexsaht-Snider, M. (1999) 'Becoming Culturally Responsive: Self-Critical Inquiry in Preservice Teacher Education', *Irish Educational Studies*, Vol 18, pp 155-164.

Devine, D. (2001) 'Children's Citizenship and the Structuring of Adult/Child Relations in the Primary School', in Childhood, Vol 9, No 3, pp 303-321.

Devine, D. (2003) Children, *Power and Schooling – How Childhood is Structured in the Primary School*, Stoke on Trent, Trentham.

Devine, D., Kenny, M. with MacNeela, E. (2002) 'Ethnicity and Schooling – A study of ethnic diversity in selected Irish primary and post primary schools', Education Department, University College Dublin.

Dewey, J. (1916) *Democracy and Education,* New York, Macmillan.

Doherty, D. et al (2002) *Celebrating Difference, Promoting Equality: Intercultural Education in the Irish Primary Classroom*, Mary Immaculate College, Limerick, Centre for Educational Disadvantage Research and Curriculum Development Unit.

Epstein, D., O'Flynn, S. and Telford, D. (2001) 'Othering' Education: Sexuality, Silences and Schooling, *Review of Research in Education*, Vol 25, pp 127-180.

Gollinick, D. (1992) 'Understanding the Dynamics of Race, Class, and Gender', in Dilworth, M. (ed.) *Diversity in Teacher Education*, San Francisco, Jossey-Bass.

Government of Ireland (1998) *The Education Act,* Dublin, Stationery Office.

Government of Ireland (1999) *Primary School Curriculum*, Dublin, Government Publications.

Government of Ireland (1999) *Whole School Evaluation – Report on the 1998/1999 Pilot Project*, Dublin, Government Publications.

Government of Ireland (2000) *The National Children's Strategy: Our Children, Their Lives*, Dublin, Stationery Office.

Haran, N. and Tormey, R. (2002) *Celebrating Difference, Promoting Equality: Towards a Framework for Intercultural Education in Irish Classrooms*, Limerick, Centre for Educational Disadvantage Research and Curriculum Development Unit, Mary Immaculate College.

Hargreaves, D. (1995) 'School Culture, School Effectiveness and School Improvement', in *International Journal of School Effectiveness and Improvement*, Vol 6, No 1, pp 23-46.

Hargreaves, A. (2002) 'Teaching in a box: Emotional Geographies of Teaching, in Sugrue, C. and Day, C. (eds) *Developing Teachers and Developing Practice*, London, Routledge Falmer.

Harris, A. et al (2003) *Effective Leadership for School Improvement*, London, Routledge Falmer.

Ladson-Billings, G. (1991) Coping with Multicultural Illiteracy: A Teacher Education Response, *Social Education*, Vol 55, pp 186-194.

Larkin, J. and Sleeter, C. (eds) (1995) *Developing Multicultural Teacher Education Curricula*, New York, SUNY.

Lodge, A. and Lynch, K. (2004) (eds) *Diversity at School,* Dublin, IPA in association with The Equality Authority.

Lortie, D. (1975) *The School Teacher,* Chicago, Chicago University Press.

Lukes, S. (1977) 'Socialism and Equality', in L. Kolakowski and S. Hampshire (eds) *The Socialist Idea (Quartet),* reproduced in S. Lukes, *Essays in Social Theory*, London, Macmillan.

Lynch, K. and O'Neill, C. (1994) 'The colonisation of social class in education,' *British Journal of Sociology of Education*, Vol 15, pp 307-324.

Lynch, K. (1989) *The Hidden Curriculum*, London, Falmer Press.

McGrath, D. J. and Kuriloff, P. J. (1999) '"They're going to tear the doors off this place": upper-middle-class parent school involvement and the opportunities of other people's children', *Educational Policy,* Vol 13, No 5, pp 603-629.

Noddings, N. (1992) *The Challenge to Care in Schools: An Alternative Approach to Education,* New York, Teachers College, Columbia University.

Plummer, G. (2000) *Failing Working Class Girls,* Stoke-on-Trent, Trentham Books.

Reed, L. R. (1998) 'Zero Tolerance: gender performance and school failure', in D. Epstein, et al (eds) *Failing Boys? Issues in Gender and Achievement,* Buckingham, Open University Press.

Ruane, B., Horgan, K. and Cremin, P. (1999) *The World in the Classroom: Development Education in the Primary Curriculum,* Limerick, Curriculum Development Unit, Mary Immaculate College.

Ryan, A (2003) *Teacher Development and Educational Change: Empowerment Through Structured Reflection*, Unpublished Doctoral thesis, Education Department, UCD.

Shevlin, M. and Rose, R. (2003) (eds) *Encouraging Voices,* Dublin, National Disability Authority.

Sugrue, C., Morgan, M., Devine, D. and Raftery, D. (2001) *Policy and Practice of Professional Development for Primary and Post-Primary Teachers in Ireland: A critical analysis,* Commissioned Report by the Research and Development Committee, Department of Education and Science.

Swan, T. D. and Devine, D. (2002) 'Case Studies of more effective and less effective schools in the Republic of Ireland', in Reynolds, D., Creemers, B., Stringfield, S., Teddlie, C. and Schaffer, G. (eds) *World Class Schools: International Perspectives on School Effectiveness*, London, Routledge Falmer.

Teddle, C. and Reynolds, D. (2001) *International Handbook of School Effectiveness and Improvement,* London, Falmer.

Tuohy, D. (1999) *The Inner World of Teaching – Exploring Assumptions*, London, Falmer Press.

Tussing, A. (1978) *Irish Educational Expenditure: Past, Present and Future*, Dublin, Economic and Social Research Institute.

Walsh, T. (2002) 'Educational Disadvantage: Policy and Practice in Ireland', paper presented to the Annual Conference of the Educational Studies Association of Ireland, Trinity College Dublin, 21-23 March.

York, S. (1991) *Roots and Wings: Affirming Culture in Early Childhood Programmes*, Mt Rainier, Maryland, Redleaf Press.

Young, I. M. (1990) *Justice and the Politics of Difference,* Princeton University Press.

Zappone, K. (2002) 'Achieving Equality in Children's Education', in *Primary Education: Ending Disadvantage – Proceedings and Action Plan of National Forum*, St Patrick's College, Drumcondra.

Index

ability/disability 1, 4, 6, 240
  education of those with 5, 56-8, 60, 62-3
    teachers and 254, 256
  learning disability 57-8, 68, 71
  legal rights of those with 57, 58*n*
  prejudice and exclusion 52, 192, 245, 254
  research on 226, 228, 232
  and social interaction 184, 198*n*, 201
  see also Down Syndrome children
Aboud, F.E. 206
Academic Attainment Index 68-9
adolescent market 164, 168-9
adult and community education 250
Afghanistan 189
Africa 95, 214
age 5*n*, 196
  and children's rights 110-11, 114, 129
  and citizenship 113, 129
  and having a say in school 116, 120-2
  and perceptions of other cultures 210, 216
  and popular culture 166, 170*n*, 172
  and social interaction 198*n*, 201
Ahern, Bertie 233, 234
Akenson, D.H. 21
Allport, G. 206
America, North 235
Angel 168, 169
Anglicans *see* Church of Ireland
Apple, M. 255
Armenia 186
Asian people 100
assessments 59, 118, 148, 253
  psychological 60-1
  see also tests, standardised
Association of Secondary Teachers in Ireland (ASTI) 52*n*
asylum-seekers 228, 234-5, 236, 237-8
Australia 250

Bacchi, C. 228
Bahá'í community 18, 19*n*, 22, 28
  views on primary schools 22, 23, 26
    choice of school 23-4, 27, 29-30, 33
    religion in school 25, 29-30, 31
Baker, J. et al 33
Bangladesh 186
Barnardos 232
  Traveller education project 97
beliefs 19, 198, 240, 246-7
  attitudes to difference of 5, 232, 239, 254
    research on 226, 228
  see also minority beliefs; Protestantism; Roman Catholicism
Belton, T. 173
Bernstein, B. 83, 145-6
Board of Commissioners for National Education 3, 20
Boards of Management 3, 27, 79, 114, 246
  as employers 41-2
  and religious ethos of schools 20, 246*n*
  and student councils 131, 135, 141
books 166, 172
'Breaking the Cycle' programme 231
Brennan, A. 132, 136

Briane, C. 211, 212
Britain *see* United Kingdom
Buckingham, D. 170, 173
Buddhists and Buddhism 18, 19*n*, 22, 22*n*, 28, 30
  views on primary schools 22, 23, 26 7, 29
    choice of school 27, 28, 29, 30, 31
    religion in school 24, 25, 26, 28, 29-30
Buffy the Vampire Slayer 164, 167-8, 170-1, 178
  genres 168
    action and violence 168, 169, 171-2, 174-5, 176
    chaos 171, 173
    comedy 168, 169
    hero 169, 171, 174, 175, 176, 177
      caring qualities 169, 175
      and feminism 169, 171, 174, 176-7
      power and strength 169, 173, 175, 176
    horror 168, 169, 171, 172-3, 175, 176
    romance 168, 169, 172, 175, 176, 177
  imaginative identification with 171, 173, 176, 177
  market
    adolescent 164, 168-9
    pre-adolescent 164, 168, 170
    merchandise associated with 168, 169, 171, 174
Bulger, Jamie 165
Bullen, E. 165
bullying
  of children with learning disabilities 63, 66-7
  ESLI and 83, 86
  of lesbian and gay teachers and students 48
  of minority belief children 24, 32
  and racism 190, 193, 194, 202
    see also racism
Bulmer, M. 129
Bunreacht na hÉireann *see* Irish Constitution
Burkan, W. 76
Burts, D. 235-6

Cain, A. 211, 212
Catholic Primary School Managers' Association 18
Celtic Tiger 1, 88, 183, 257
census
  2002 34
  2003 19
Charlesworth, R. 235-6
child labour 110
childhood
  perspectives on 109-13, 123, 146, 232
    developmental needs 1-2, 8, 113-14, 233, 234
    'whole child' perspective 234-5, 248
The Children's Research 89
children's rights *see* rights of children
Children's Rights Alliance 129-30
Christianity and Christian Churches
  dominant norm 7, 33, 34
  and schools 5, 6-7, 20-1, 28
    control of 3, 4, 21, 33, 247
    and ethos of schools 18, 28
    minority Christian parents and 18, 19, 23, 24, 26, 30
  and sexuality 5, 38, 39
  see also Protestantism; Roman Catholicism
Church of Ireland 19, 20
  see also Protestantism
citizenship 128, 129, 131, 141, 205, 233
  and curriculum 9, 115, 133, 245, 253
  and right to say in school lives 112-13, 128, 131, 141, 245
  and student councils 128-9, 131, 139, 141
Clarke, D.M. 20

class *see* social class
class size 61, 257
classroom assistants 64
Cleary, A. et al 17
Cohen, S. 166
Coleman, P. 87
Comenius study 213
Comer, J.P. 87
Comhairle na nÓg (2003) 128
compulsory schooling 110
computers 65
  computer games 165, 172, 174
Confirmation 18, 24, 25, 32, 80
  Travellers and 80, 93, 94, 100-1, 104
Connell, R.W. 40, 250
constitution *see* Irish Constitution
constructivist philosophy 206, 218
consumers, children as 8, 164
  see also Buffy the Vampire Slayer
critical theories 226, 227, 228
Croatia 186
The Crow (film) 172
CSPE programme 245
cultural difference 189, 190, 201, 210, 232, 256
  children's perceptions of 199, 200, 205-9, 210-17, 218, 232
  and curriculum 209, 218, 240, 248, 253
  non-recognition of 10, 245, 246*n*
  see also dominant culture; interculturalism; racism; Traveller community
cultural theorists 170, 171, 174
Curaclam na Bunscoile *see Primary School curriculum*
curriculum 6-7, 102, 136, 148, 177, 245, 252-3, 254, 256
  children's voices on 114-15, 116, 253-4
  and citizenship 9, 115, 133, 245, 253
  control over 3, 4, 114-15
  and diversity 2, 25, 206, 245, 252-3, 254-5
    cultural 209, 218, 240, 248, 253
  and Down Syndrome children 61, 64, 67, 68, 71
  history of 1-2, 113
  Primary School Curriculum (1971) 1, 2, 113-14, 235
  Primary School Curriculum (1999) 2, 9, 114-15, 136, 206, 218, 227, 252
  and student councils 132, 133, 136, 138, 140
  theories and principles underlying 2, 9, 113-15, 218, 235, 240, 245, 252-3, 255
  and Traveller children 102, 104
  in United Kingdon 131-2, 133
Curtin, C. 110

Dabrowski, K. 212, 216
Dáil Na nÓg 112*n*, 123, 128
Dalkey 31
Daugherty, A.M. 169
Davies, B. 176, 177
decision-making, children and 111, 113, 115, 121, 123-4, 128, 129-31, 240, 249-50, 251
  on learning 116-19, 133, 138-9
  no part in education partnership 4, 9, 113-15, 124
  right to 111, 129, 233
  on school rules 116, 119-21, 122
  and student councils 128, 131, 132, 141, 248
Deegan, J. 7-8, 253-4
Delpit, L. 227
democracy in education 130, 245-6, 249, 253, 255, 258
  see also citizenship; partnership in education; rights of children; student councils
demographic trends 183, 205, 233
Den TV 173
denominational schools 5, 17
  and gay and lesbian teachers 38, 41-2, 43-51, 53
  and minority belief parents 18-21, 22-34, 247
Denzin, N.K. 166

Department of Education 3
Department of Education and Science 4-5, 6*n*, 77, 78, 148, 229
and partnership in education 3, 4, 113, 247
and services to children with disabilities 58*n*, 60*n*, 63*n*
see also education policy; ESLI
Department of Health and Children 58*n*, 60*n*, 63*n*
Devine, Dympna 7-8, 227, 249
on giving children a say in school 9, 112, 113, 132, 136, 140, 251
Dewey, J. 34, 245-6
disability *see* ability/disability
dominant culture 7, 112, 144-5, 199, 230, 239, 246
assumption of homogeneity 27, 44, 246-7
Irish identity 34, 186, 198, 200
religious 7, 33, 34, 198, 199, 200
and sexuality 40-1, 43, 44-5
see also racism; Traveller community
Down Syndrome 9, 56, 62
Down Syndrome children, education of 56-7, 70-1
academic attainment 58, 68-9, 71
bullying 63, 66-7
in care units 63
and curriculum 61, 64, 67, 68, 71
hearing and language difficulties 56*n*, 59, 67
in mainstream schools 57, 59-60, 62-3, 64-5, 66, 67, 68, 69-71
parents and 56-69, 71
preschools 58-60, 62, 63, 69
school placement decisions 58, 59*n*, 60, 60*n*, 61-4, 65
school transport 60, 65-6, 67, 70
social and communication development 57, 62, 67, 69-70, 71, 227
and peers 57, 60, 62, 70, 71, 227
friendships 67-8, 69-70
in special schools 56-7, 61-4, 65-7, 70, 71
for mild learning disabilities 63, 65-6, 68
for moderate learning disabilities 56, 59*n*, 63, 65, 66, 68, 69-70
support services 58-9, 60-1, 62-3, 65, 70-1
assessments 59, 60-1
in-school supports 58, 64, 65, 70-1
speech therapy 59, 60, 62, 63, 64-5
teachers 56, 59, 61, 62, 64, 66, 71, 227
use of computers 65
Down Syndrome Ireland database 58
Drumcondra Primary Reading Test 146, 148-9
Dublin 58, 63, 96, 147, 214
Durkheim, E. 206
DVDs 171, 172, 174

Eagleton, T. 229
8-15 Early School Leaver Initiative *see* ESLI
early school leaving *see* ESLI; Traveller community
'Early Start' programme 231
Educate Together 6, 22
Education Act (1998) 2, 3, 4, 20, 58*n*, 60*n*, 114, 128, 229, 246
education policy 4, 10, 52, 70-1, 75, 81, 85, 205, 231, 236, 246-51
accountability and efficiency 151, 248
child-centred focus 1-2, 8, 113-14, 131, 235, 249
and children and diversity 225-41
and economic policy 1, 110, 113, 123, 233, 237, 257
see also curriculum; Education Act (1998); ESLI; *National Children's Strategy* (2000); primary schools

Education (Welfare) Act (2000) 4
Egan, Mercedes 227
Egan, O. 212
emigration 183, 236
employment and careers 1, 41, 50, 62, 69, 77, 80-1, 237, 257
Employment Equality Act (1998) 5, 5*n*, 9, 41, 50, 51, 52*n*
England *see* United Kingdom
enrolment in schools 20, 57
  refusal of 4-5, 26-7
epistemes 228-9, 232
Equal Status Act (2000) 4-5, 5*n*, 9, 20, 50
Equality Authority 5, 18*n*, 20*n*, 52*n*
ESLI (Early School Leaver Initiative) 10, 89, 247, 249
  activities 76, 81, 84-5
  'at risk' pupils 75, 81, 82
  Department of Education and Science and 77, 78
  district-based projects 75, 76, 77, 82
  early school leaving 75, 76, 77, 80, 83
    risk factors 76-7, 80, 81-4, 86, 87-8
  evaluation of 75, 77-9, 89
  home school community liaison co-ordinators 81, 85
  objectives 75, 76, 77-8, 78, 87
  parents and family 75, 76, 78, 79, 80, 84-6, 87, 88
  project personnel 75, 78-9, 81, 82, 85-6, 88
  schools and teachers 75-6, 79-80, 81-5, 87-9, 249
ethnic difference 52, 183, 185, 199, 206, 209, 217
  children's perceptions of 183-202, 210
    and friendships 187-9, 197, 199-201
    minority children's views 189-91, 193, 195, 197-8, 201, 228, 245, 247
  and education 1, 2, 4, 5, 6-8, 9, 202, 239, 252, 254
    and government policy 1, 225, 226, 232, 237-8, 240
    respect for difference 6, 52, 202, 205, 239
  see also asylum-seekers; racism; refugees; Traveller community
ethos of school 31, 33, 51, 246, 252
  religious 5, 18, 20, 28, 31, 41-2, 246*n*
Europe 50, 205, 208, 209
European Union 1, 113, 205, 256, 257
exclusion from schools 4-5

family 5*n*, 50, 112, 164, 227, 233, 234, 237, 238, 253
  change 8, 109, 113, 233
  see also ESLI; Traveller community
Fanning, B. et al 234, 236, 237
Feerick, A. 210
feminism 228
  and *Buffy the Vampire Slayer* 169, 171, 174, 176-7
Fendler, L. 228, 231
film 166, 172
Fine Gael 21*n*
Finglas 96
First Communion 18, 24, 25, 27, 32, 80, 94, 101
First Confession 18
FitzGerald, Garrett 20-1
focus groups 170, 171-4, 175-8
Foucault, Michel 226, 228
France and the French 166, 211, 213-14, 216
Fraser, N. 39
Freire, Paulo xii, 76
Frenkel-Brunswick, E. 210
Friday, N. 177
friendships 115, 168, 185, 235
  Down Syndrome children and 67-8, 69-70

dynamics of 187, 198-9, 201
and ethnic difference 187-9, 197, 199, 200-1
and language variation 150, 158
Fullan, M. 87

Gael Scoileanna 6
Gaeltacht 85
Gash, H. 210, 213
gay *see* sexuality
Geertz, C. 238
Gellar, Sarah Michelle 174
gender 114, 166, 167, 177
Buffy the Vampire Slayer 169, 174, 177
and discrimination 2, 52, 186, 253, 254, 255, 298*n*
and diversity 5, 6, 170*n*, 240
teachers and 254, 255, 256
and education policy 1, 232, 240
and perceptions of other cultures 213-14
and racism 185, 192*n*
research on 226, 228
and social interaction 184, 198*n*, 201
stereotyping 48, 173, 254
and views on teachers 116, 120, 121
see also feminism; sexuality
Germany 211
Giroux, H. 165
Goldstone, K. 206
Goodenough, W. 235
Gowran, Sandra 227
Greece 213
Greek Orthodox church 18, 19
Guardian-Ad-Litem 237
Gulf War 166
Gunning, M. 173
Haran, N. 253
Hargreaves, A. et al 84, 87-8
Hargreaves, D. 248
Hart, A. 128, 130-1, 133
Hart, C. 235-6
Hatcher, R. 187, 193
Health Boards 58*n*
heterosexism 37, 39-40, 44, 49, 51, 227
heterosexuality 38, 39-40, 42-3, 45, 49, 50
Hindus 18, 26
Hobbs, T. 174
'Home School Community Liaison' programme 81, 85, 231
homework 83, 87, 101, 118, 135, 137, 138
homophobia 39, 41, 46, 47-8, 50
homosexuality 5, 38, 39, 40, 43, 48-50
legal rights 50, 51
see also sexuality
hooks, bell 228, 229
horror 172
see also Buffy the Vampire Slayer
housing, segregated 5
humanist beliefs 17*n*, 18

imagination 166-7, 171, 173, 176, 177
immigration 34, 183, 205, 228, 236
in-service training for teachers 2, 104
India 186
individual attention 83, 85, 118
Inglis, T. 21
inspection of schools 3, 251
inter-denominational education 20
interculturalism 104, 205, 207-9, 235, 237, 250*n*
INTO 3, 4, 52*n*
Investment in Education (1965) 113
IQ 232
Iran 166
Irish Constitution 18*n*, 19-20, 21, 111, 233, 238
Irish language 7, 95, 117, 187
Irish National Teachers Organisation 3, 4, 52*n*
Islamic community 18, 19, 26, 100
and racism 190, 191, 192, 193, 201

Jackson, P. 119
Jewish community 17-18, 199
Junior Certificate 104

Kaveney, R. 169, 171
Kelleghan, T. et al 76, 77
Kelly, M. 194
Kenway, J. 165
Klineberg, O. 207
Kosovo 186

Labour party 21*n*
Labov, W. 145
Lambert, W.E. 207
language variation and social class 6-7, 144-5, 154-5, 159, 160-1
  children's views on 146, 147, 150-6
    prestige of the vernacular 153, 156-60
  and correction 147, 153-9
  and language of the home 146, 153, 154, 156-8, 160
  pronunciation 145, 146-7, 155
  standard language 144-5, 147, 155, 160
  and standardised testing 145, 147-51, 152
  teachers and 145, 146-7, 148-9, 150, 154-6, 157-8, 159
  and textbooks 145, 147, 151-3
Latvia 186
Leaving Certificate 80
Lee, N. 233
lesbian and gay people *see* sexuality
lesbian and gay teachers 38-9, 49-50
  in denominational schools 38, 41-2, 43-51, 53
  heterosexism and 37, 39-40, 44, 49, 51
  homophobia and 39, 41, 46, 47-8, 50
  legal rights and discrimination 40, 41-2, 49-51, 52
  'out' 42, 45-7, 49, 50, 51
  in post-primary schools 37-9, 40-4, 45-52, 53
  in primary schools 37, 38, 41-2, 44, 45, 48, 49, 50-1, 53
  silent and invisible 38, 39, 42-7, 49, 51-2, 53
Levine, M.P. 170
Libya 186
Likert-scale descriptors 210
Lindblad, S. 231, 240
linguistic diversity 7, 189, 190, 191, 211, 228
  non-English speakers 237
literacy and reading 68-9, 89, 232
  and standardised tests 145, 147-51, 152
  Travellers and 80, 83-4, 92, 94, 95, 97, 100, 101
Lithuania 186
Lodge, Anne 247, 257
Los Angeles 167
Lukes, S. 247-8
Lynch, David 168
Lynch, K. 238, 257

Maastricht Treaty 205
MacBeath, J. 83
MacDonnell, D. 228-9
McNaught, B. 44
MacRuairc, Gerry 227
Manchester 92, 93, 94, 95
Manning, Maurice 21
Marshall, T.H. 129
Martin, Micheal 63*n*, 229
masculinities 40, 48-9
Mayall, B. 170
Maynooth University 97
media 164, 165-6, 168, 178
  and cultural differences 199, 207, 209
  media texts 171, 177-8
  stereopying minority groups 39-40, 183
  see also books; computer games; DVDs; film; television; videos
Methodists 19

minority beliefs 6, 17-18, 19, 34, 201
parents and schools 4, 17-18, 19-20, 22-3, 32-4
denominational schools 18-21, 22-34, 247
multi-denominational schools 22, 23, 27, 28, 29, 30-1, 246*n*
religious instruction and rituals in schools 18-19, 20, 23-7, 28-30, 31, 32
and teachers 24, 25, 26, 27, 28, 32-3, 247
see also personal beliefs
minority groups 4, 6, 9, 104, 112, 237
non-recognition of 39-40, 52, 166, 183, 232, 235
right to voice in education 245, 246-8, 249-52, 256, 258
see also ability/disability; cultural difference; ethnic difference; gender; minority beliefs; race; sexuality; social class; voices of children
Montgomery, M. 144-5
Moore, M. 131
Mulcahy, D. 225-6
Mullingar 93, 94-5, 96
multi-denominational schools 6, 17
and minority belief parents 22-3, 27, 28, 29, 30-1, 246*n*
Mumba, Samantha 201
Murphy, E. 211, 212, 217
Muslims *see* Islamic community
name calling 66, 95, 184, 191, 192-7
racist 184, 187-8, 190-8, 200, 201
National Anti-Poverty Strategy (1997) 237
National Children's Alliance 232
National Children's Strategy (2000) 9, 112, 114, 227, 233-8, 239, 240-1
and voice for children 9, 112, 114, 128, 129-30, 233, 249-50
National Education Convention (1994) 19
National Educational Psychological Service Agency 60*n*
National Forum Proceedings on ending Disadvantage at primary level 115*n*
National Parents' Council 3-4, 249
National Schools 3, 5
see also primary schools
National Youth Council of Ireland 133-4
Nepal 186
New York 154, 166, 192
New Zealand 129
Nic Ghiolla Phádraig, M. 7-8
Nigeria 186, 187, 191, 195, 200, 216
Nightmare on Elm Street (film) 172
Noddings, N. 89, 253
non-denominational schools 38, 42, 45, 46, 49
Northern Ireland 32
Norwich 154
numeracy 68, 101, 232

O'Connor, P. 184
OECD 257
Office Franco-Allemand de la Jeunesse 211-12
O'Gorman, A. 132-3
O'Keefe, B. 184
Ombudsman for Children 112*n*, 123
Operational Programme on Local Urban and Rural Development 75-6
Orthodox churches 18, 19
O'Sullivan, D. 225-6, 228

paedophilia 49-50
Pakistan 186
Palestinians 192
parents 1, 21, 37, 118, 135, 230, 238, 249, 257
and diversity 6, 239, 240, 246, 252, 256
and initiatives for disadvantaged schools 231, 250*n*
see also ESLI

organisations 4*n*, 79, 141, 247
National Parents' Council 3-4, 249
and policy on children 230, 238, 240
relationships with children 8, 122
and rights of children 114, 129, 131, 238
rights of 4-5, 18*n*, 19-20, 21
and school management 3, 246
see also partnership in education
single parents 230, 238
see also Down Syndrome children; minority beliefs; Traveller community
Parents' Committees 79
parish 5, 18, 24, 27
Partnership 2000 (1997) 237
partnership in education 2-4, 113, 124, 247, 249, 257
children not included in 4, 9, 113-15, 124
and student councils 132, 133
see also Boards of Management
Patron bodies 18, 22
patrons of schools 3, 20, 33, 34
Pavee Point 232
PE and sport 117, 137
peer groups 8, 57, 99, 164, 234, 235, 249
and racism 184, 187, 188, 197, 200, 201, 253
student councils and 134, 139
see also Down Syndrome children; friendships
Pender, P 174
personal beliefs 17*n*, 18, 22*n*, 23, 28-9, 34
and choice of school 24, 28, 30, 33*n*
religious rituals and instruction in schools 24, 25, 26, 27, 29, 31
physiotherapy 59
Piaget 218
Plymouth 132
Pope John Paul II 39
Popkewitz, T. 226, 228, 230-1, 240
popular culture 110, 164-6, 169, 170*n*, 172
see also Buffy the Vampire Slayer; media
post-primary schools 2, 3-4, 5, 20*n*, 170*n*, 257
and disability 57, 66
ethnicity and racism 183, 185, 187*n*, 191
student councils 114, 128, 132
Travellers and 100, 101, 102-3, 104-5
see also ESLI; lesbian and gay teachers
postmodernism 168-9, 226, 227, 228
poverty 8, 77, 94, 230, 234, 237
Powis commission 3
prayers (school) 18
pre-adolescent market 164, 168, 169, 170
prejudice 7, 40, 206, 209, 210-11, 217, 239, 255
racial 206, 213
see also ability/disability; racism; sexuality; social class; Traveller community
Presbyterians 19, 20
Primary Certificate 1
Primary School Curriculum (1971) 1, 2, 113-14, 235
Primary School Curriculum (1999) 2, 9, 114-15, 136, 206, 218, 227, 252
primary schools
funding of 2, 20, 34, 257
history of 1-3, 5, 20-1, 33-4, 113-14
ownership and management of 3-5, 17, 20-1, 33-4, 50, 131, 134
see also Boards of Management; partnership in education

principals 114, 115, 134, 154
and Down Syndrome children 61, 62
and ESLI 79, 81, 88-9
and gay and lesbian teachers 51, 52
and inclusive culture 239, 251
policy on racism 195-6, 197
and minority belief parents 26, 27, 32-3
Programme for Prosperity and Fairness (2000) 237
Protestantism 5, 17, 18, 19, 21*n*, 24, 34, 201
schools 17, 18, 22-4, 25, 27, 28, 29-31, 33
psychological assessment 60-1
psychologists 60-1, 62, 76
pupil teacher ratios 257

race 52, 206, 240, 254, 256
lack of research on children and 226, 228, 231, 232, 239
see also ethnic difference; racism
racism 184, 186, 199, 206-7, 213, 253, 254
and abuse 186, 187, 190-1, 194, 197, 201, 202
name calling 184, 187-8, 190-8, 200, 201
outside classroom 184, 193
schoolyard 184, 185, 193, 200
children's understanding of 184, 186-90, 191-7, 198-202, 213
and ethnicity 183-6, 188-91, 192, 195-202
and colour 186-8, 189, 191, 192, 193-7, 198, 199-202
and cultural difference 188-90, 191, 192-3, 195-6, 198, 201, 202, 217
teachers and 190, 193, 195-7, 201-2, 217, 254, 256
see also Traveller community
reading *see* literacy and reading
Reay, D. 170
Rees, A. 129
refugees 189, 214, 228, 236, 237
religions *see* beliefs
religious ethos of schools 5, 20, 31, 41-2, 246*n*
religious instruction and rituals in schools 18-19, 20, 23-7, 28-30, 31, 32, 117
see also sacraments
religious orders 5
remedial teachers 64
Report of the Commission on Itinerancy (1963) 98, 100
Report of the National Commission on the Family (1996) 227
Report of the National Forum on Early Childhood Education (1998) 227, 232
Report of the Task Force on the Travelling Community (1995) 98
respect for children
children's views on 116, 117-18, 120, 122
right to 9, 112, 130, 133, 233, 236
rights of children 10, 110-11, 114, 129
government policy and 9, 112, 114-15, 128, 233, 235-8, 249-53
and student councils 128, 139-41
see also United Nations Convention on the Rights of the Child (1989); voices of children
Roman Catholicism 17, 19, 20-1, 38
schools 5, 17, 20-1, 23-4, 31, 32
minority children at 22-30, 33
of parents educated as Catholics 28-9, 31
religious ritual and instruction in 18-19, 23-7, 28-30, 31, 32, 117
see also sacraments
and sexuality 5, 38-9
in United Kingdom 93, 133

seen as the norm 34, 198, 199, 200
Romania 186
Ruddock, J. et al 87
rural 5, 75, 213
Russian Orthodox church 18, 19
Rutland Street Project 230
Ryan, Clare 247, 249

sacraments, Roman Catholic 23-5, 32
see also Confirmation; First Communion; First Confession
Scandinavia 129
Schneider, S.J. 170
school attendance 89, 93
School Attendance Officer (England) 93
school transport 60, 65-6, 67, 70
schoolyards 184, 185, 193, 200
Schorr, L.B. 77
Schrage, Michael 88
Scream (film) 172
secular beliefs 17*n*, 18, 19
segregation 5-6, 31*n*
segregated education 257
Travellers and 94, 101-2, 104, 105
see also Down Syndrome children
September 11th attacks in New York 166, 192
sexuality 37, 40, 169, 184
Christian Churches and 5, 38-9
and education 37-8, 42-4, 46, 47, 49-50, 51-3
lesbian and gay people 37-8, 40, 42-4, 47, 49, 51-2, 227
students 37, 44, 48, 52
and prejudice 184, 192*n*, 239, 247
sexual identity 38, 39-40, 52-3
sexual orientation 5, 6, 41, 245
see also heterosexism; heterosexuality; homophobia; lesbian and gay teachers
Sikhs 18
Sloper, P. et al 69*n*
Social, Personal and Health Education programme 115, 245, 253
social class 1, 4*n*, 6-7, 31*n*, 114, 239
and children's views on status in school 115, 116, 120, 121, 122
and educational disadvantage 6*n*, 75, 76-7, 229-30, 231, 235
prejudice and exclusion 2, 52, 210, 239, 247, 253, 254, 255
research on 185, 210, 226, 227, 228, 240
and segregation 5-6, 31*n*
and social interaction 184, 198*n*, 201, 253
teachers and 254, 255
see also ESLI; language variation and social class
social interaction 184, 198, 201, 253
see also friendships; peer groups
socialisation 144, 164, 205, 215, 217, 232
sociocultural variables 226, 228, 232, 240, 255, 256
see also minority groups
Somalia 186, 190, 200, 201
South Park 169
special needs 58, 58*n*, 61, 71, 136, 137, 210, 229
see also ability/disability
Special Olympics 69
speech therapy 59, 60, 62, 63, 64-5
SPHE programme 115, 245, 253
sport and PE 117, 137, 199, 201
status of children 113, 120-1, 129, 134, 165, 257
children's perception of 10, 115-16, 123-4
and social class 115-16, 120, 121, 122
stereotyping 169, 206, 207, 209, 210, 211, 215, 232, 255

gender 48, 173, 254
of minority groups 39-40, 166, 183
racial 199, 206, 207, 254
Strinati, D. 168
student councils 79, 114, 128-41, 248
post-primary 114, 128, 132
student voices heard 129, 130, 131, 135, 140
teachers and 131, 132-4, 135-6, 137-41, 248
voices heard, and decision making 128, 132, 141, 248
Sugrue, C. 235, 236
surveillance 118, 121*n*

teacher unions 3, 4, 49-50, 52*n*, 141, 247
teachers 2, 3, 187, 210, 212, 231, 249, 250-2, 257
and children and diversity 205, 209, 217-18, 239, 240, 246, 252-7
education of 141, 245, 248, 254-6
in-service and professional development 2, 104, 252
hiring and promotion of 3, 50, 51, 257
products of the system 28, 38-9, 43
relationship with pupils 84, 116, 122-3, 157, 159, 192*n*, 199, 249, 252
caring 87-8, 89, 116, 122-3, 233, 245, 248-9, 253-4
children's views on 116-22, 150, 154-8, 247, 249
and school management *see* partnership in education
see also Down Syndrome children; ESLI; language variation and social class; lesbian and gay teachers; minority beliefs; racism; student councils; Traveller community
television 164, 165-70, 172, 177, 178, 207
see also Buffy the Vampire Slayer
tests, standardised 145, 146-51, 152
textbooks 3, 7, 145, 147, 151-3
third level education 77, 257
Third World children 213
timetables 117, 140, 253
Tormey, R. 253
Traveller community 5*n*, 7, 9
Barnardos Traveller education project 97
in Britain 92-3, 94, 95, 96
and change 96-7, 98-9, 103-6
Confirmation 80, 93, 94, 100, 101, 104
and education 7, 80, 83, 92, 95, 97-8, 99-105
adult education and training 96, 97-8, 104
post-primary schooling 100, 101, 102-3, 104-5
and primary school 93-5, 100, 101
reading and writing 80, 83-4, 92, 94, 95, 97, 100, 101
segregated education for 94, 101-2, 104, 105
teachers and 7, 83, 95, 100, 101, 102, 103, 104
government policy and 231, 236, 237, 238
in housing 92, 93, 95, 98
identity and culture 7, 95-6, 98-9, 100, 102, 103-6, 188, 193
begging and selling 92, 93-4, 96-7
campsites and halting sites 92, 93, 95, 96, 191, 236
childminding 93-4, 95, 96
extended family 92, 93-4, 96, 98, 100, 105
marriage 97, 100, 101, 104
nomadism 7, 83, 92, 93, 96, 97, 98, 102
weddings and funerals 93, 96

parents 80, 83-4, 93, 94, 96, 97-106
prejudice and discrimination 7, 83, 94, 95, 98, 100, 101-2, 104, 183, 199, 201
racism 184, 186, 188-90, 199
racial abuse of 188-9, 191, 193, 194, 196-7
and settled community 92, 94-5, 98, 99, 100, 101, 103-4, 188-9, 199
Traveller Education Centres 97, 105
and work 92, 93-4, 96, 97, 99, 100-1, 103, 105
Trinity College, Dublin 21*n*
Troyna, B. 187, 193
Twin Peaks 168, 169

unemployment 8
United Kingdom 4*n*, 20, 57, 129, 131, 190
curriculum and student councils 131-2, 133
religion in schools 27-8, 30, 32
Travellers in 92-3, 94, 95, 96
United Nations Convention on the Rights of the Child (1989) 7, 8-9, 111, 114, 129-30, 233, 236, 237, 238
United States of America 4*n*, 27-8, 164, 192, 211, 230
urban 5-6, 31, 75, 183, 213

videos 165, 168, 171, 173, 174
voices of children 8-9, 10, 133, 146, 209, 228, 233, 239, 245-54, 258
on curriculum 114-15, 116, 253, 254
on language variation 146, 147, 150-60
minority children's 189-91, 193, 195, 197-8, 201, 228, 245, 247
on organisation of school lives 8, 111-14, 115, 121, 133, 139-40, 141
right to be heard 8-9, 111, 114, 233
on teachers 116-22, 150, 154-8, 247, 249
see also citizenship; decision-making; respect for children; status of children; student councils

Wade, B. 131
Walker, M. 177
Walkerdine, V. 164
Watt, P. 225, 226
Wehlage, G. et al 80
welfare 103, 235, 237, 238, 256
Wheedon, Joss 168, 169, 174
White Paper on Early Childhood Education (1999) 227, 229-30, 231-3, 240
White Paper on Education (1995) 52, 236
'whole child' perspective 234-5, 248
whole school approaches 237, 251-2
Whole School Evaluation Pilot Project Report (1999) 251-2
Willis, P. 159
Willow, C. 132
World Health Organisation 44
writing skills 68-9, 80, 83-4, 89
Travellers and 92, 94, 95, 97, 100, 101
Wyness, M. 131

The X-Files 168

Young, I.M. 32*n*, 247